WHO THEN IS PAUL?

CORSICA

Rom
Three Tavern
Appii Forum

Adriatic Sea

Dyrrhachium

Puteoli   Pompeii

SARDINIA

Tyrrhenian Sea

Nicopolis

Ionian Sea

SICILY

Rhegium

Carthage

Syracuse

Sea of Adria

MELITA

Mediterranean

Black Sea

Sinope

THRACE

MACEDONIA

Byzantium

BITHYNIA

CAPO PONTUS

Prusa

GALATIA

ASIA MINOR

PHRYGIA

Thasos

IMBROS

LEMNOS

Troas

Asso

MYSIA

Aegean

MYTILENE

Sea

CHIOS

Smyrna

Antioch

LYCAONIA

CILICIA

ASIA

Philadelphia

Iconium

Athens

SAMOS

Ephesus

PISIDIA

Lystra

Derbe

Tarsus

Colossae

Miletus

PAMPHYLIA

Tarsus Mts.

Cos

Attalia

Seleucia

Cnidus

Rhodes

LYCIA

Patara

Myra

RHODES

CARPATHOS

CYPRUS

Salamis

CRETE

Paphos

Fair Havens

Lasea

Sidon

Damascus

CLAUDA

Tyre

Ptolemais

Sea

Caesarea

Joppa

Jerusalem

Gaza

Alexandria

Nile Delta

WHO THEN IS PAUL?

By

HUBERT REX JOHNSON

F. SWARD

CHEVY CHASE MANUSCRIPTS : 1980
ONE CHEVY CHASE CIRCLE, WASHINGTON, D.C.

Edited by Chevy Chase Manuscripts
One Chevy Chase Circle
Washington, D.C. 20015

University Press of America, Inc.

P.O. Box 19101, Washington, D.C. 20036

ISBN: 0-8191-1365-4

ISBN: 0-8191-1364-6

Library of Congress Catalog Card Number: 80-1406

CONTENTS

ACKNOWLEDGEMENTS

Chevy Chase Manuscripts is grateful to those who have cooperated in the publication of this book, especially:

Robert R. Johnson, son of the author, for granting the publication rights of the book to Chevy Chase Manuscripts.

Howard S. Spering, legal counsel, for the preparation of three basically important documents: (1) the Declaration of Trust establishing Chevy Chase Manuscripts as a Trust Fund; (2) Agreement regarding the manuscript with the heirs of Dr. Johnson; and (3) Contract with the University Press of America; and for assistance and expert advice on many other matters.

Louis de la Haba, editorial consultant, for skillfully condensing the original manuscript to acceptable publication length, without sacrificing either its essential content or its striking beauty of style.

Dr. George Wesley Buchanan, Professor of New Testament at The Wesley Theological Seminary, Washington, D.C., for a critical review and careful editing of the manuscript. Additions and comments suggested by Dr. Buchanan appear as footnotes, identified by the initials GWB. Dr. Buchanan provided the Pauline Chronology which appears in the appendix.

Dr. George Winchester Stone, Jr., for his helpful suggestions concerning the manuscript, and for the preparation of the non-Biblical General References.

Rev. Robert Bruce Clapp, for reviewing the manuscript and urging its publication, and for offering helpful suggestions concerning it.

Frances S. Sward, for the art work in producing the many chapter heading and full page drawings, and other illustrations.

Dorothy A. Nicholson, of the Art Research Staff of the National Geographic Magazine, for adapting and drawing the maps of the areas of Paul's journeys, and providing additional illustrations.

The National Geographic Society, for granting permission to reproduce a portion of Morton Kunstler's painting of the ancient port of Seleucia, and for providing technical assistance in producing maps.

Richard J. Hoffman, teacher, typographer, printer and fine book designer, for producing the title page and cover design.

James Q. Reber, for the photography in reducing the art work drawings to publication size.

Fred C. Klein, for producing the photograph of Dr. Hubert Rex Johnson in the "About the Author" section.

Gordon W. McBride, Robert C. Horne, and Dr. Meredith F. Burrill, for their many contributions on the publication committee. Also, Robert C.

Horne for providing the photograph of the Grand Theater at Ephesus.

Charles Proffer Saylor, for the painstaking reproduction by color photography of the Hubert Rex Johnson portrait by Alexander Clayton.

The Memorial contribution honoring John Slater Sheiry, Sr., Charter Member and Elder of the Chevy Chase Presbyterian Church, by his daughter Dorothy Sheiry Hilland, and her husband, Arthur J. Hilland.

The Memorial contributions honoring Mrs. George Winchester Stone, Sr., (Mary Bradford), by her sons Bradford W. Stone and George Winchester Stone, Jr.

The many persons, some of whom knew Dr. Johnson, and many who did not, whose interest and contributions made the publication possible.

PREFACE

The purpose of this book is to lead the reader into an intimate experience of comradeship with Paul, and to enable him to know the great apostle rather than to know only about him.

Paul is the greatest interpreter and expounder of Jesus Christ; and since he lived the gospel that he preached, his life, as well as his words, exalts the Saviour of the world and becomes a powerful inducement to faith.

Paul had none of the peculiarities that indicate the absence of power, but was in such a large way a part of the world in which he lived that his whole life was filled with bold adventures, exciting events, and thrilling achievements. Fiction fades into puerility in the presence of the story of the intrepid Paul.

The plan of the book is that of continuous narrative, based upon Paul's extensive travels. Instead of discussing characteristics, learning, and theology in detached chapters, these and other subjects are woven into the narrative where they should retain their vitality. Paul is kept always within sight, and, though seen in the age and in the physical surroundings to which he belonged, his story has not been overladen with matter that strays too far from the central theme.

The mystery features of Paul's experience have been reviewed in a somewhat modern light, but the fact must always stand that they were factors in the apostle's transformation and in many of his decisions. It might be well, however, for the world to listen a while longer to the words of the scribe: "And what if a spirit hath spoken to him, or an angel?"

HUBERT REX JOHNSON

CHRONOLOGY

The events of Paul's life have not been recorded by years, but some of them may be dated approximately from their connection with Roman and Jewish secular history; and these, in turn, will yield others by computation. The most important of these synchronisms are those referring to Aretas at the beginning of his sovereignty over Damascus (Acts 9:25 with II Cor. 11:32, 33); to the reign of Herod I over Judaea (Acts 12:1-23); to the great famine in Judaea in the reign of Claudius (Acts 11:27-30; 12:25); to the procuratorship of Sergius Paulus in Cyprus (Acts 13:7-12); to the expulsion of the Jews from Rome by Claudius (Acts 18:2); to Junius Annaeus Gallio, proconsul of Achaia (Acts 18:12-17); to Felix, procurator of Judaea (Acts 23:24—24:27); and to Porcius Festus, who succeeded Felix (Acts 24:27—26:32).

Any reader of the Acts of the Apostles would readily place Paul's age near the ages of Jesus and the Twelve, and would not likely hesitate to say that he had been born about A.D. 1; a conclusion that would agree with a statement in the *Oratio Encomiastica in Principes Apostolorum Petrum et Paulum*, an ancient writing, erroneously ascribed to Chrysostom, to the effect that Paul was about sixty-eight years of age at the time of his death, and that he had served the Lord for thirty-five years.

Granting that Paul was born A.D. 1, the years of his age would always be the same as the dates of the events of his life. Thus if he was converted in A.D. 33, he was thirty-three years of age at the time; and if he attended the Council of Jerusalem A.D. 50, he was then fifty years of age.

The following dates in years are as nearly accurate as present light can make them. The place names of the three great tours, and of the voyage to Rome, are those recorded in the New Testament.

A.D.   1   Born in Tarsus.

           14   Entered the School of Interpretation under Gamaliel in
                 Jerusalem.

           32   Persecuted the Church in defense of the Law.

        33-36   Was in Damascus and Arabia—preparation for apostle-
                 ship.

           36   Went to Jerusalem to visit Peter (Gal. 1:18).

        36-45   Labored in Syria and Cilicia; certainly in Tarsus, and
                 perhaps, in Adana, Mopsuestia, Issus, Baiae, and
                 Antioch.

           45   Was called to Antioch, Syria.

46   Went to Jerusalem to explain his gospel (Gal. 2:1, 2) and to deliver alms collected in Antioch for the relief of the Church in a time of famine (Acts 11:27, 30).

47-49   His first missionary tour: Antioch, Syria—Seleucia—(Cyprus)—Salamis—Paphos—(Pamphylia)—Perga—Antioch, Pisidia—Iconium—(Lycaonia)—Lystra—Derbe—Lystra—Iconium—Antioch, Pisidia (Pisidia)—(Pamphylia)—Perga—Attalia—Antioch, Syria.

50   Attended the Council of Jerusalem.

50-53   His second missionary tour (Returned by way of Jerusalem for the Passover): Antioch, Syria—(Syria and Cilicia)—Derbe—Lystra—Iconium—(Phrygia)—(Galatia)—(Bithynia)—Troas—(Samothrace)—(Macedonia)—Neapolis—Philippi—Amphipolis—Apollonia—Thessalonica—Beroea—(Achaia)—Athens—Corinth—Cenchraea—Ephesus—Caesarea—Jerusalem—Antioch, Syria.

53-57   His third missionary tour (Returned as far as Jerusalem for Pentecost): Antioch, Syria—(Galatia)—(Phrygia)—Ephesus—(Macedonia)—(Greece)—(Macedonia)—Philippi—Troas—Assos—Mitylene—(Chios)—(Samos)—Miletus—(Cos)—(Rhodes)—Patara—Tyre—Ptolemais—Caesarea—Jerusalem.

57   Was arrested in Jerusalem.

57-59   Imprisoned at Caesarea.

59-60   He appealed to Caesar and was taken to Rome: Caesarea—Sidon—(Lycia)—Myra—(Cnidus)—(Crete)—Fair Havens—(Cauda)—(Melita)—Syracuse—Rhegium—Puteoli—Market of Appius—Three Taverns—Rome.

60-62   Imprisoned in Rome.

62   Trial and acquittal.

62-67   His last tours; but all sources are brief and subject to question.

67   Trial and execution.

(For a more extended treatment of the Chronology of Paul, see the account presented in the appendix.)

CHAPTER

1

Paul views Tarsus harbor

The Age of Impressions

"EAT, DRINK, AND PLAY; for nothing else is worth this"—[a snap of the fingers].

So is said to have run a Hittite inscription on an ancient tomb at Anchialos, near Tarsus, bearing a supposed statue of Sardanapalus, son of Anacyndaraxes, king of Assyria.[1] The statue stood with the conventionally uplifted hands, thus apparently snapping its fingers to complete the sentiment carved below in cuneiform letters. Though an ancient inscription by Paul's time, it expressed an outlook characteristic of the prosperous and voluptuous element of the thriving commercial city of Tarsus—and of all the world; a creed that soothed the purposeless existence of blinded men who saw no wisdom except in folly.

It was the oldest doctrine of surrender, held in all ages by men who lacked the necessary spiritual light and fortitude to resist the slow but relentless forces of moral death; the despairing conclusion of the Koheleth who said, "And I commend enjoyments, for a man has no good thing under the sun but to eat and drink and enjoy himself"[2]; the ground of stinging rebukes administered by both Isaiah and Jesus. It was a sentiment that was true to the dissolute and effeminate character of Sardanapalus. It had appeal, it lived, it passed down the centuries, it became a rule of life—and plagued Tarsus and the world. Aristotle thought it more suitable for the

1

grave of an ox than for the tomb of a king. Socrates, Seneca, and other wise men of the past recoiled at the infernality of the sentiment; and Paul treated it as a symbol of eternal despair.[3]

Such was the noxious taint that burdened the moral atmosphere when the world's greatest evangelist was born in Tarsus; a taint that bred all kinds of calamity, rotted the foundations of national life, and undermined the humanity of individuals.

It was when Rome was still the recognized mistress of the world, and Greek the universal tongue; when ancient religions were losing their hold on the credulity of men, and ancient philosophy lay gasping at the feet of skeptics; when serious-minded men of all nations were everywhere dreaming of a possible salvation through some mighty leader from life's intolerable burdens, and the unthinking were hopelessly seeking the same relief in a complete abandonment to the lowest demands of appetite and passion. It was, then, in a time of greatest and widest opportunity, that an approaching herald of light and hope lay laughing in the arms of an admiring Jewish mother in the Graeco-Oriental city of Tarsus.

But the laughing babe was soon to find mirrored in his own cosmopolitan city a world-wide struggle after a possible something that might make life both more endurable and more desirable. Hither came the Oriental mystic with his effective appeal to the primitive states of mind; here abode the resolute Stoic philosopher who made his hardships endurable by minimizing their importance; and here also dwelt the Jew whose consolation centered in the advent of a mighty Messiah.

But while hope could not be destroyed by lying proverbs, neither could it render its best service through the medium of any existing philosophy or religion. A new gospel was needed and the chief herald of that gospel was now in Tarsus, the Hebrew Saul, the Roman Paul; born about A. D. 1.*

Had some visiting angel[4] from the heavenly realm, one of the magi[5] from the far East, or the aged Simeon from his haunts in the temple stationed himself prophetically in the twentieth century and looked backwards he might have spoken historical truth by saying: "The world has not yet produced a more remarkable or more valuable religious teacher than Paul, the apostle of Jesus Christ to the Gentiles." After two thousand

---

*   Paul is only called "Saul" in Acts. He may really have had a Hebrew name and also a name used among Gentiles, as many Jews have done, but there are also hints in Acts that the author has intentionally written his account so that the period after Jesus (the new Joshua) would be an antitype for the typology of the period after the old Joshua. This was a period under the leadership of charismatic leaders, followed by Saul, just before the Davidic kingdom came. Like Judges, Acts presents leaders like Peter, Paul, and Stephen, who are seized by the Spirit and acted importantly. Since this is so, the author may have attributed the name "Saul" to Paul to make the pattern fit better. (GWB)

years, his great work for humanity still surges onward unabated. It was Paul who saw in Jesus a Messiah for the whole world; it was Paul who rescued the gospel, rewrote it in universal terms, and saved it from speedy oblivion; it was Paul who hurled down through the ages the mightiest transforming force the world has ever known. Millions have heard his name, but few have understood his greatness. By his enemies he has been viciously maligned; by his friends he has been sentimentally softened and morbidly sainted until the splendor of his manhood, the keenness of his mentality, and the charm of his personality have been seriously obscured, or even lost to view.

According to the Acts of the Apostles,[6] Paul was born in Tarsus, the chief city of Cilicia in Asia Minor; but according to a tradition preserved by Jerome, he was born in Gischala in northern Galilee, and was carried by his parents to Tarsus at a time when their city was scourged by the Romans. If there is anything at all in Jerome's tradition it is perhaps the possibility that Paul's earlier ancestors were natives of Gischala.

The exact date of Paul's birth is unknown but a very close approximation would be A.D. 1, which agrees with the maturity exhibited by the Apostle in his thought and work in the early stages of his ministry and with his own reference to himself, in A.D. 62, as "Paul the aged."[7] This date is supported also by an ancient tradition[8] in the work of an unknown author, perhaps in the fourth or fifth century, but ascribed to Chrysostom, to the effect that Paul "went to his rest about sixty-eight years of age." If his martyrdom occurred late in 67, his birth, according to this tradition, must have taken place in A.D. 1. Even the statement in the Acts of the Apostles,[9] representing Paul as a "young man" at the time of the stoning of Stephen, does not conflict with this date.

Paul was born where one of the great international highways between the East and the West crossed the boundary-land between the Hellenistic and Semitic worlds, and at the midpoint of one of the most enthrallingly interesting eras of all religious history—the era stretching between the invasion of the East by Alexander the Great, 334 B.C., and the nationalization of Christianity in the West by Constantine the Great, A.D. 325; the era in which the old religions of the Mediterranean Basin suffered their rapid decay, leaving a fertile field for the eastern mystery cults, which entered and swept like a submerging flood over the whole of the Graeco-Roman world; the era at the midpoint of which arose the obscure Galilean, who without pen or sword or gold founded the greatest kingdom the world has known.

Paul had no occasion in any of his letters to speak particularly about any of his kindred, though he does mention his mother in a very casual way.[10] From his letters and the book of Acts, however, it is possible to glean several facts. His father appears to have been a Jew of the tribe of

Benjamin, a Pharisee,[11] and a Roman citizen.[12]* That Paul had brothers and more than one sister would be a fairly safe guess, but without proof.

How Paul's father obtained Roman citizenship is unknown. It could have been purchased, it could have been bestowed upon him in recognition of service,[13] or it could have come through his grandfather, if that ancestor had been one of the Jews carried to Rome by Pompey in 63 B.C., and there sold into slavery, but afterward emancipated and invested with Roman citizenship.[14]

Paul's father was a man of considerable prominence and even of affluence. As a citizen of Tarsus with a voice in its councils, and a Roman citizen with the right of appeal to Caesar's tribunal, and with exemption from the disgrace of scourging and of death by crucifixion, he would command more than ordinary respect, not only from his own people but even from those who are ardent haters of the Jews. He was able to give his son the best Jewish education obtainable; and the character of his home is reflected in the tastes and culture of that son.

It is somewhat better than a guess that he was a manufacturer of military and maritime supplies, especially of tents,[15] sails, and rainproof cloth for soldiers' and sailors' uniforms, his Roman citizenship being of advantage in such a business.† The cloth used for these purposes was everywhere known as *cilicium*, being made of the hair of the long-haired goat of the Cilician Plain. Tarsus was advantageously situated for such an industry, being in easy communication with east and west by land and sea, and having near at hand an abundance of raw material.

But the father's chief distinction, so far as it concerned the son, was not in his standing with Rome, not in his importance as a citizen of Tarsus, nor in his industrial leadership, but in the consistency and rigidity of his Pharisaic life. In this mold his son's moral and religious life took form, stamped with intolerant legalism and exacting traditionalism, but at the same time preserving a clear outline of all the many merits of the Pharisaic Judaism. And so, nourished from infancy by the word of the sacred Law, Paul in later years regarded his apostleship, not as the product of a sudden

---

* Technically, only those from the tribe of Judah should be called Jews, but Benjamin stayed with Judah as a part of the Southern Kingdom when the northern ten tribes seceded. Since Benjamin was a very small tribe, people from that tribe also called themselves Jews. There are Jews still today who can trace their ancestry back to the tribe of Benjamin. (GWB)

---

† Dr. Johnson is much more likely to be correct in thinking that Paul's business was a large manufacturing plant than that Paul himself sewed tents for a living. He was a very busy man who seems to have had enough money to travel and live without outside support. This suggests that he had a business that could have been managed by someone else, with Paul receiving only periodic reports and income. (GWB)

psychological revolution but as a result of a divine call operative from the moment of his birth.[16]

According to Paul's own statement,[17] he was circumcised on the eighth day after his birth, which implies that the Jewish customs in this ceremony were followed strictly in every particular. At his circumcision Paul received the Hebrew name Shaul, "the asked, the requested." No record exists to show why this name was chosen. Being of the tribe of Benjamin, the father may have had in mind the name of the hero-king of that tribe; or the name for very ordinary reasons may have been a favorite with the family.

Paul inherited Roman citizenship and was therefore entitled to a Roman name also. This consisted of a *praenomen*, a *nomen*, and a *cognomen*, and at the proper time was submitted at Tarsus for registration and for inclusion in a Roman tribal list. Unfortunately, only the cognomen, Paulus, has been preserved, and no existing record shows why it was chosen. The name means "little;" but it was chosen long before Paul's physical maturity, and may have had no reference to his size. There were other Pauls before his day, and after; and they were perhaps no more diminutive than the Littles, Smalls, Kleins, and Petits of today.

Paul was addressed by his Hebrew name at home, at Jerusalem, and elsewhere among his Jewish friends; but the Greeks, or those who spoke their tongue, when using his Hebrew name added their own termination to the word and called him "Saulos," a rather objectionable name, since in Greek it referred to an affected, conceited way of walking.

He was not "Saul" for a part of his life, and afterwards "Paul," but was always both. Historically, he is "Paul." The book of Acts introduces him by his Hebrew name, but calls him by his Roman name after he begins his missionary tours and mingles freely with Gentiles.

If Paul's early home was one of comfortable wealth, established at an early period, it may have sheltered several families; perhaps the aged grandparents, who still presided over the home, and the families of two or more sons. Certainly Paul's ease of intercourse with his fellow men of all ranks, his natural politeness, and his exceptional powers of command indicate that he belonged to a superior family.

In accordance with Jewish custom, Saul's education would begin at home in early childhood. Before the age of five years he would be reciting short selections from the Scriptures, including the all-important Shema: "Hear, O Israel: The Lord our God is one Lord: and you shall love The Lord your God with all your heart, and with all your soul, and with all your might;"[18] and, perhaps parts of the Hallel, or "Praise."[19] He would learn the letters of the Hebrew and Greek alphabets, and perhaps become able to recognize a few words in each language.

About the age of six, he would have been sent to the local synagogue to attend school where he would have learned reading and writing, and, perhaps, some very elementary arithmetic. The only text-book would be the Scriptures, which would serve as spelling book, reader, grammar, theology, ethics, sociology, government, history, geography, and astronomy.* There, everything worth knowing could be found, and was honestly accepted as bearing the seal of divine authority. Paul's father was probably familiar with a scheme of education mentioned by a post-Talmudic writer who said of the child: "At five years old he comes to the reading of the Scripture, at ten to the Mishna, at thirteen to the practise of the commandments, at fifteen to the Talmud, at eighteen to marriage."[20]

Since no record of Paul's early years has been preserved, that part of his biography must be built up from what is known of Jewish and Hellenistic life in the first century. There are many pitfalls in such an attempt but the result should be fairly true in its general outline. There cannot be very serious error in supposing Paul to have had all the advantages of a good home: a home with its first and second stories, its roof garden open to the starry heavens and swept by refreshing breezes from the snow-capped Taurus Range, its central courts surrounded by apartments, paved with marble, and ornamented with pool and fountains and shrubs of citron, its hallways and doorways protected by hangings. All this and more could have been found in a home of moderate wealth.

From such a home through its austere doorway, Saul, clothed in his clean striped tunic, and accompanied by his father or mother, or a slave who functioned in some of the duties of a pedagogue, passed on his way to the synagogue school.

It is too much to suppose that human nature was in abeyance during those first years. The little boy if caught alone could hardly have escaped occasional encounters with street urchins, and possibly with pupils from some Gentile school. But if such did occur, Saul had too much fire in his blood always to be worsted, or even to bellow if hurt. Certainly exchanges of opprobrious names would have been frequent, for the Jews as a whole were not loved by the Gentiles. Nor were the Gentiles more than dogs to the Jews, though for business and political reasons they were endured and even honored.

For perhaps four years, Saul seated himself regularly with other boys on the floor of the schoolroom before their teacher, struggling with Aramaic and Greek and memorizing vast portions of the Jewish Law. Having no books, the boys would repeat selected passages in unison until memory fulfilled its function.

---

*   Rabbis at that time argued that everything which was in the world was in the Torah. Readers had only to search for it diligently. (GWB)

The Jews of Tarsus spoke Greek and used the Septuagint or Greek version of the Hebrew Scriptures. It is easy to show that Paul nearly always quoted from that version and repeated some of its many inaccuracies.

At the age of ten, Saul began with the simpler parts of the oral law, or Mishna.* The Mosaic law, called the Torah or Pentateuch, did not extend to every possible human contingency and had to be supplemented by other laws drawn from it by inference. The *halachoth* (rules) so derived were for many centuries transmitted orally, it being forbidden that they should be written. But the burden of oral transmission became so great that Hillel I, about the time of Paul's birth, made an attempt to systematize the halachoth and reduce them to writing. Hillel's task was never completed and no one else attempted it again for two hundred years. Thus, young Saul had to fill his memory with the contents of the Mishna from the lips of his teacher.

At the age of twelve or thirteen, Saul was taken before the elders of the synagogue, where he was declared "a son of the commandment," liable to the penalties of the law and bound to its strict observance.†

For a long while Saul had been wearing in the four corners of his shawl, inserted three thumb-lengths from the edges, the "tassel" of symbolically knotted threads, three white and one blue,[21] the latter indicating the heavenly origin of the commandments; but now as he stepped out of innocent childhood into responsible manhood he was also invested with phylacteries[22]—two of them, new, neat, coal-black, and fabricated according to minute and strict regulation. Since Saul was truly devout,[23] his father would experience great pleasure and pride in having these sacred objects ready for his son's confirmation and would take even greater pride on the following day at morning prayer to see him, upon his first attempt, go smoothly through the complicated ceremony of putting on his phylacteries. The boy's right hand had clearly caught the deftness of his father's. After placing the "hand phylactery" on the inner side of his bare left arm, he twined its long straps symbolically, and with prescribed

---

* The Mishna was edited by Rabbi Judah the Prince early in the third century, A.D. He obviously had written collections before him, but no one knows now who first put them into written form or when. Hillel and his school may have written some and Rabbi Johanan ben Zakkai and his school may have collected more after the fall of Jerusalem (A.D. 70). Collection and preparation both of Jewish and Christian canons probably became a necessary agenda after the defeat of Bar Cochba (A.D. 135). See H. Danby, *The Mishna* (Oxford: Oxford University Press, c1954), xiii-xxiii. (GWB)

---

† Paul evidently referred to his becoming a son of the commandment when he said, "When the commandment came, sin revived, and I died" (Rom 7:9). For a fuller discussion, see *The Consequences of the Covenant* (Leiden: E. J. Brill, 1970), pp. 181-184. (GWB)

prayer, around his arm until they reached the hand. He then placed the "head phylactery," with its long straps ceremoniously upon his forehead, and, after binding it there, took up the ends of the hand phylactery and wound them three times around the middle finger of his left hand. After prayer, these reminders of law observance were removed by following a reverse order. If young Saul was an extremist, he probably wore the phylacteries regularly. Otherwise he wore them only at prayer.

The neat little four-compartment, black-leather box holding bits of folded parchment on which were written certain passages of Scripture[24] stood out beneath Paul's turban in later years and proclaimed him to all Jerusalem as a Pharisee, a strict legalist, a zealous observer of the Law.[25]

REFERENCES
Chapter 1

1. See V. Langlois, *Le Denuk-Dasch, Tombeau de Sardanapalus Tarsous.* (Paris: A. Leleux, Libraine, 1853), pp. 9-11.
2. Eccl. 8:15. See also Eccl. 11:9; Isa. 12:15; Luke 12:19.
3. I Cor. 15:32.
4. Luke 2:10.
5. Matt. 2:1.
6. Acts 22:2.
7. Philem. 9.
8. See, *Oratio Encomiastica in Principes Apostolorum Petrum et Paulum, Eorumdemque Gloriosissimum Martyrium.*
9. Acts 7:58.
10. Gal. 1:15.
11. Phil. 3:5.
12. Acts 22:28.
13. Suetonius. *The Lives of the Ceasars.* II. Augustus, Sec. 47.
14. Philo. *Works.* Vol. 10, *The Embassy to Gaius.*
15. Acts 18:3.
16. Gal. 1:15.
17. Phil. 3:5.
18. Deut. 6:4, 5, or 4-9.
19. Psalms 113-118.
20. *Talmud, Sayings of the Fathers and the Ethics of the Talmud.* 5:21.
21. Num. 15:37-41; Deut. 22:12.
22. Exod. 13:9-10; Deut. 6:8; 11:18.
23. Phil. 3:6; Acts 23:1.
24. Ex. 13:1-16; Deut. 6:4-9; 11:13-21.
25. Acts 26:4, 5.

From a painting by Morton Kunstler © N.G.S.
Port at Seleucia

CHAPTER

2

The Age of Responsibility

SAUL WAS NOW THROUGH with two stages of his education, home instruction and the "house of the book." But in the meantime he had gathered from many other sources an additional store of practical and general knowledge that broadened his religious outlook and expanded his natural sympathies. His father's business perhaps gave him exceptional opportunities for learning about the active city of Tarsus with its half-million population, and about the surrounding country with its snow-capped mountains and grain-clad plain. He may be supposed to have accompanied his father on business trips among the numerous weavers' shops to purchase cloth, and to have gone far out into the narrow, fertile Plain of Cilicia, and even up to the hill country to purchase goat's hair and wool.

He would visit busy river-front wharves when shipments of cloth and tents were made to Roman military posts. And it is likely that his love for the sea was born on some short voyage on the ship-thronged Cydnus when his father went to Aulai, the port of Tarsus on the Mediterranean, to see that his goods were safely transferred from river craft to the great ships of the sea that crowded the Regma, or great artificial harbor.

Paul's manhood reveals his boyhood—intense, intelligent action, hardihood, daring, and leadership. A boy of that character could hardly remain long ignorant of his native city. He would visit the banks of the Cydnus, the beautiful little river of clear, cool, rapid, and sometimes raging waters that drained the snowy crowns of the Taurus Mountains, and on its way to the sea, cut his city in two. He would talk with his companions about the wonderful mountain gorge thirty-five miles farther up the river, the famous Cilician Gates, the great cleft in the mountains whose walls sloped dangerously and towered five times higher than the top of the Temple at Jerusalem, gates fashioned by the forces of nature as a water course but seized upon and improved by man for a highway, gates that united East and West and induced the flow of commerce through the city of Tarsus. Saul and his companions often saw long caravans of heavily laden camels and asses slowly moving towards the west, bearing grain and oils, fruits and spices, and all the products of forge and foundry, shop and loom for Ephesus and other cities of Asia, and even for cities far beyond; armed imposing merchants; wretched muleteers and cameleers; pompous Roman officials with their retinues; and Roman soldiers who patrolled the great roads—these were a few of the scenes that built themselves into the imagination of Saul the pupil to produce the intrepid Paul the traveler.

No normal boy could long remain ignorant of the gymnasium by the river, where the young men of Tarsus exercised and trained for public competitive sports and where others gathered for gossip and entertainment. Saul surely visited the place and felt his own muscles go through varied contortions as he watched the sinewy, greasy, naked bodies of men and boys who wrestled on the sand-covered floor. Did Saul wrestle? Perhaps, but hardly naked in a gymnasium. That was no place for a circumcised Jew, unless he had become hardened to ridicule. But Saul was deeply interested in sports and with his companions doubtless played all the games of his own nation, from those that belonged to childhood to those that savored of ancient military training—target practice with bow and arrows, hurling javelins, slinging stones, wrestling, boxing, and swimming.

That young Saul was familiar with the great stadium near the Cydnus, and the one in the summer city back on the foothills of the Taurus Range, can hardly be doubted; and somewhere he must have witnessed that furious crowd-maddening sport, the chariot race. He certainly knew much, too, about the circus and the amphitheater, where the prowess of trained men was pitted against the ferocity of wild beasts, and where gladiators bathed their swords in one another's blood.

It is true that some Jews, like the Zealots, condemned nearly all sports, but Paul was a Hellenist, and while he could not have approved of cruelty, yet he could see in the sports of his day certain heroic merits. Thus in his few brief letters he refers to athletic sports forty or more times, stressing training, zeal, intensity, fairness, and the glory of victory. He was not a recluse cultivating an easy negative righteousness, otherwise he would have joined the Essenes; he was a man of action, living in the open, and heeding the commandment, "Thou shalt," so obediently that its counterpart, "Thou shalt not," rarely confronted him.

At the agora, the forum or marketplace of his city, the boy Saul learned some of the most important lessons of his life. Into this great colonnaded area surrounded by public buildings and ornamented with bronze and marble statues of heroes and gods, came the most diverse varieties of the human race: the dandy Greek in his elegantly embroidered robe and spotless boots of red; the Roman in his purple bordered toga and highlaced silvered sandals; the Jew in his silk trimmed simlah and bulky turban; the tall Egyptian, the fickle Syrian, the dark Arabian, all scowling under their fillet-bound head-shawls; the gilded Persian, the wool-clad Phyrygian, and the transplanted Gaul. These and many others had poured into Tarsus over the great avenues of travel: up the Cydnus from the sea, in from the west and the north through the North Cilician Gate, and through from the east and far east by other mountain passes—the Syrian, the Amanian, and the East Cilician Gates.

Here in the great agora, Saul looked upon bejeweled and perfumed wealth, naked and rancid poverty, city magistrates in spotless robes, branded slaves in cilicium loin-cloths. Here also he saw the vile voluptuaries of his city. They were numerous: some broken and senile, some youthful and flippant. A few were Jews. When a Jew fell, he fell far. He had farthest of all men to fall. Saul more than once must have been ashamed and bitterly indignant.

But other Tarsians came to the agora—splendid men whose ideals and morals compared favorably with those of the strictest Jews. These were easily distinguishable. Saul saw them. He secretly respected them, and thus a slow erosion of his rocky Jewish prejudices set in. Though entirely unconscious of any fashioning hand, he was molded and chiseled at every step as he meandered through the agora.

At first he ventured none too near to the temples, or to the numerous and perhaps smoking altars standing here and there, or to any priest of Sandan or of Apollo or of Athena; but in time a great truth perfected itself in his consciousness: "We know that, an idol has no real existence, and that, there is no God but one." With this truth some forty years later he quieted the troubled minds of his Corinthian congregation.[1]

As he mused along under the shelter of the peristylium, he witnessed scenes and stored up impressions that were the beginning of his marvelously practical understanding of men. Here he beheld a great potpourri of the "Seventy nations of the earth:[2]" men from Parthia in the east to Spain in the west, from Pontus in the north to Ethiopia in the south, an amalgamated mass of mankind with lingering Greek characteristics and a decidedly Oriental spirit,[3] prospering as a free city under the oversight of the Roman Empire.

It is almost within the range of probability that Saul, as he approached some of the municipal buildings, had at least one glimpse of the great statesman and Stoic philosopher, Athenodorus Cananites, who had been the teacher of the emperor Augustus, and who, under that emperor's orders, revised the constitution for the Tarsian free city-state. "My father knows Athenodorus," Saul might have thought to himself— while a stone would fall from the "dividing wall of hostility"[4] between him and the Gentiles. But he surely must have seen Nestor, the Academic, who succeeded Athenodorus.[5]

On arriving at the commitium, he would feel a pardonable flush of pride because his father was one of the few holding sufficient property to entitle him to vote in the affairs of the city-state. "I too," thought Saul, "shall someday have a voice in the government of Tarsus"—and he did.[6]

Along his way, Saul saw the silent signet-makers in their cramped postures, carefully engraving rings and other devices for sealing business and official documents, and even for the use of persons who could not write their names. This scene remained with him, as may be supposed from his letters to the Romans and the Corinthians.[7] Then too, he watched the busy scribes as they sat in sheltered places with ink-horns, pens, and papyrus, writing love letters for lonely soldiers and sailors, homesick letters, bereavement letters, letters from wives to husbands, maids to men, and merchants to manufacturers. Years later, Saul employed amanuenses to write letters for him, but always adds his name in his own characteristic large hand.[8]

In the vicinity of the municipal buildings he would, perhaps, pass some of the magistrates of the city; and he doubtless knew one or more of them. Here and there he passed women so encumbered with veils that they walked with difficulty. Tarsus had the Oriental conception of woman and required the veil. Saul inherited that conception and defended it.[9] Even Dion Chrysostomus, who criticized the Tarsians rather sharply in other particulars, praised their women for the modesty of their apparel.

At the far end of the agora, Saul often heard orators practising their art from the public platform. A crowd would assemble there at any time to listen to local haranguers or to wandering teachers. Here Saul at various times, from young boyhood to manhood, may have listened to Epicurean, Platonic, and Stoic philosophers until he became fairly familiar with their doctrines and could correctly appraise his own ethics against the best that the Greeks had to offer.

But the whole city of Tarsus, as well as its agora, was busy—busy and rich. Its beloved Cydnus, on which the Athenians accused the Tarsians of getting drunk, was lined with barges, loading and unloading. Rafts of oak and pine, cypress and walnut came down from the north; galleys with passengers and merchandise came up from the south. Long streets of the city were given over to trade: wine-shops, bakeries, meat-shops, and fruit-stalls. Here also were the cloth merchants and silk importers, money changers and jewelers, cobblers and barbers. And here were the fullers, treading cloth in steaming suds, the potters treading clay in slimy mortars, and the tanners soaking hides in vats of gall-nut liquor. There were the spinners and weavers breathing the stuffy odors of goat's hair and wool. And yonder were the coppersmiths, whose hammers and mallets pounded out cups and pots and pans. Everywhere there was motion, motion and burden, burden and noise.

Among such scenes as these, Saul must have moved day after day; and always he would carry away something that entered into the fabric from which later emerged the apostle Paul. He absorbed industry, independence, understanding, and initiative and, though he did not know it, there trickled slowly into his Jewish social views a faint but permanent coloring from his constant contact with Greeks and Romans, Phrygians and Gauls. Jesus could not have found in all Palestine more suitable apostolic material for Gentile work. Such material had to be slowly evolved by an infinite interplay of delicate forces in a heterogeneous city. Tarsus was the city; Paul was the product. Without Paul the work of the Twelve would have been no more than a mark in the sand before an incoming tide.

Tarsus was old, no one knows how old. Legend gives it an Assyrian origin and makes Sennacherib the founder; but again, assigns that honor to his grandson, Sardanapalus. When the Greeks invaded the East and became masters of Tarsus, they Hellenized the old traditions slightly by making Perseus or Heracles the founder.[10] Later, Athenodorus asserted that the city originally had borne the name Parthenia; all of which invites interesting speculation, but throws little light on the origin of the city. Tarsus, however, was old, old like Damascus; and that made it a city of many gods. The Assyrians brought theirs, the Phoenicians brought theirs, the Anatolians brought theirs; and so did the Phrygians, the Egyptians, the Greeks, the Jews, and the Romans. But the gods of the nations had certain similar ranks and similarities so that a Greek might accept Baal-Tarz as his Zeus, or a Phoenician identify Zeus as his Baal. As there was no serious rivalry among the various pagan religions except, of course, for the Jews, but a strong tendency to identify equal rank and to syncretize worship, the number of divinities in Tarsus must have been considerably reduced below the total sum of national deities. Too little is known about Tarsus to say just how many gods and goddesses were worshiped there, or how many temples, street shrines, and altars Saul might have counted had he made a complete tour of the city. But temples there were, and small public and private shrines; altars there were in abundance—altars in the agora, by the river, in high places, in niches along the streets, in houses, and on housetops.

Some remnant of the ancient high Anatolian god Boghaz Keui possibly may have been known to Saul, but he knew much about the Baalim of the Phoenicians, Assyrians, and Persians, the Baalim of his Bible, and the particular Baal who became the chief god of Tarsus as Baal-Tarz, but who was abhorred by the Jews as a demon. He was still worshipped in Saul's day, and the festive occasions devoted to him were orgiastic in the extreme. Licentiousness being regarded as a religious duty took on openly its foulest and most revolting forms. The half of Tarsus reeked with the very spume of hell. Saul often saw an obelisk, or the sacred pole of Ashtoreth, or both protruding from some housetop and knew that one of Baal's altars stood by it. He recalled too with suffering shame that some of his own people had once bowed the knee to the same god, kissed his image, and burned their sons on brazen altars to him.[11]

The active god associated with Baal-Tarz, and sometimes identified with him, was the ancient hero-nature-god Sandan, who in Saul's day was identified with the Greek Heracles.[12] His worship, however, was decidedly oriental. Being regarded at Tarsus as an agricultural god, his cult was suited to the great Cilician plain on which the Tarsians depended for bread. As Nature put off her gorgeous garments and retired for the winter, and reclothed herself again in the spring, so Sandan every year had his death and resurrection. Legend said of him that, as the Roman Heracles, he had burned himself to ashes on his own pyre on Mount Oeta. His festival was celebrated with wildest joy and grossest excesses.

One feature of this festival that Saul could not have missed was the great pyre annually erected in the god's honor. A great heap of wood was surmounted by an effigy of the god that contained incense and fragrant spices. This was lighted in the presence of a great multitude, and at the moment when tongues of flame enveloped the image and released its fragrance, a trumpet blast called forth the shouts of the people: "Sandan is risen, Sandan is risen, Heracles is risen." Tarsus poured out its enthusiasm in floods. Therefore, to their shouts of victory and their hymns of praise, men, women, and children added all manner of frenzied and violent conduct, howling like jackals of the Syrian desert and leaping like hinds of the valley of Ajalon. As Sandan-Heracles had a very inferior reputation for decency, and Baal-Tarz had none, the votaries of the cults made the moral odor of Tarsus as rank as that of Syrian Antioch and almost as widely notorious as that of Corinth.

Saul doubtless looked upon these festivities as beyond his concern. He did not feel the urge of the reformer, he felt only disgust and abhorrence. These people were outside the convenant; his duty was to his own nation.

Then he would think of the festivals observed by his own people: clean, inspiring, joyful: the Feast of Tabernacles, the Feast of Pentecost, and all the rest. Even the great Day of Atonement, with its solemnity and long fasting, offered more real and lasting joy than could be found in any Gentile festival. It left men clean, hopeful, strong.

But Tarsus had other gods and goddesses; some with temples, others with altars only; some with exalting attributes, others with debasing; eastern gods with western names, and western gods with eastern names. There was the immoral Canaanitish Ashtoreth, the female counterpart of Baal. To the Greeks, she was Aphrodite; to the Phoenicians, Astarte; to the Assyrians, Ishtar. Saul knew that Solomon had worshipped her, and this knowledge was deeply galling.

The worshippers of these gods were largely the great masses of ignorant men and women who sought the material benefits over which the gods were supposed to preside, or who found in exciting worship an outlet for extreme emotion and base passion, or who sought health, success in business, power over human enemies and demons; in short, to be in favor with the gods for the sake of any advantage.

It can hardly be doubted that in Saul's day religious atrocities were frequent in Tarsus. But if not there, the Jews knew that they were committed openly elsewhere. As Baal represented the generative power of nature, and Ashtoreth the conceptive power, it was very easy for their priests to reason their way into the use of inhuman rites that revolted the Jews. At the spring festival, or Feast of Torches, in Hierapolis, the Syrians sacrificed children to these gods by throwing them from the top of the temple. "Calves, not children," exclaimed the fanatical priests. Parents brought their sons to be hacked and bled in the honor of Baal and, if especially zealous, sacrificed them as burnt offerings. At Edessa and elsewhere, the priests had a secret rite that might be called "an infernal communion." A new-born babe was put to death sacrificially. It was then boiled, mixed with meal and vegetables, made into cakes and baked. The cakes were then administered to initiates for the priesthood.

Into this reeking atmosphere that hung thick over the whole world, Saul entered every time he left the Jewish quarter of his city. He thus had every opportunity to learn the Gentile mind and heart; but the Twelve were products of Jewish soil and were hopelessly national. A successful apostle to the Gentiles had to be a product of a Gentile city. Tarsus showed Saul the heart of the Gentile world, a foul foolish heart, empty and hungry, but human—as human as his own. He did not at first know the full import of all that he was learning but he believed later that he had been divinely trained.

Saul was sufficiently Hellenized to take a reasonable degree of pride in his city. Cities in ancient times kept up sharp rivalries and either boasted by calling attention to their own merits or sneered at the merits of others. Tarsus had arisen to a position where it boasted, of its wealth, its schools, and its river; but its standing was not sufficiently high to save it from occasional ridicule. Strabo accorded the city great praise and grouped it with Athens and Alexandria as an educational center. Xenophon,[13] in the Anabasis, about four hundred years before Strabo, called Tarsus a "large and opulent city." Dio Chrysostomos[14], who lectured there about A.D. 110, or a century after Strabo's visit, had another viewpoint and, because he found the city decidedly non-Hellenic, could see nothing in it to praise, save the close veiling of the women.[15]

Whatever in fairness or unfairness strangers may have thought of Tarsus, the citizens themselves were not at serious fault in magnifying the importance of their city. Even the author of the Acts puts a bit of boasting into the mouth of the apostle Paul, making him say, "I am a Jew, from Tarsus in Cilicia, a citizen of no mean city."[16]

And truly Tarsus was no mean city. It had a long and important history, its size was commanding, and in Paul's day was an independent city-state, electing its own magistrates. It had its own coinage and enjoyed a free port, paying neither import nor export duties. It was exempt from a Roman garrison and was undisturbed in its affairs so long as it remained loyal to the superior government at Rome.

The Tarsians perhaps also felt the pride of security. According to Thuycidides, the ancients built their maritime cities at a safe distance back from the shore as a precaution against raiders from the sea. Tarsus was ten miles from the Mediterranean and stood astride a clear pure mountain river that was too small for the ascent of pirate vessels and yet large enough for small craft to ply between the city and its port.

In addition, the city was protected by a wall, double, at least in places. And then for greater security an even stronger fortress was built ten miles farther north in the Tarsus foothills, the fortress to which Xenophon says Syennesis once fled. Eventually this place became a large city with permanent inhabitants. In Saul's day it was a summer resort for wealthy families who fled the humid heat of the low Cilician plain for the cool air that descended from the snow-capped peaks of Taurus. Here Saul and his parents may have spent all their summers.

The pride of citizenship would affect a considerable number of the inhabitants directly and many others indirectly. Saul himself was not merely an inhabitant of Tarsus but a citizen. Only a citizen had a voice in the city's affairs. This privilege was acquired about 171 B.C., when Antiochus Epiphanes refounded Tarsus, making it a Greek city-state, and added to its population groups of Jews and other peoples. In the Roman period, after the reforms instituted by the noble Stoic philosopher, Athenodorus, who was sent to the city by Augustus to correct the abuses of government that followed upon the indiscretions of Mark Antony, the oligarchic constitution of Tarsus became timocratic and only those who possessed a certain amount of wealth were eligible to the privileges of citizenship.

If the archives of Tarsus could be recovered, the names of Saul and his father would doubtless be found in a list of the proud aristocratic citizens and also in the more exalted roster of specially privileged Roman citizens.

Tarsus was "no mean city" as an educational center. It was a city of schools. Its very air was surcharged with aspirations for learning. Strangers predominated in the schools of Athens and nearly as much so in those of Alexandria but Tarsus taught its own citizens, as well as strangers.

Saul of course became familiar with some of the high points in the history of his city. He doubtless knew that Cyrus the Younger, the aspirant for the Persian throne, had spent twenty days in Tarsus when on his march to the East with his ten thousand Greeks;[17] that Alexander the Great, who overthrew the Persian Empire established by Cyrus the Great, journeyed by way of Tarsus, and while suffering from incipient fever, bathed in the tempting Cydnus, and through that indiscretion nearly lost his life;[18] that Antiochus Epiphanes, the enemy of the Jewish religion and the desecrator of the temple, had refounded Tarsus and had sent a colony of Jews out of their own country to dwell there.

Then too Saul must have heard his grandfather and others speak of the great Cicero, once proconsul of Cilicia, and of Mark Antony whom Cicero denounced for his intrigues after the death of Caesar. No gossiping city could soon forget such a resident as Antony. When governor of Asia, and living in Tarsus, Antony summoned Cleopatra of Alexandria to appear before him and explain some of her political conduct with Cassius during the recent wars. Cleopatra decided to respond but took her own time about doing so. After a long delay, her royal barge appeared on the busy waters of the Cydnus. Nothing equal to it had ever been seen. Excited crowds gathered on both sides of the river and followed the craft towards the city. The high stern of the barge was finished in gleaming gold, the widely spreading sails were dyed with royal purple, the oars in two long rows were overlaid with burnished silver and kept time to the music of flutes, fifes, and harps.

Cleopatra, dressed as Venus, lay full length under a gorgeous canopy of cloth-of-gold, while young boys stood on each side to fan her; her maids were dressed as Sea Nymphs and Graces. Word flashed along the line of racing spectators that Venus had come to feast with Bacchus for the common good of Asia.

Upon Cleopatra's arrival, Antony sent her an invitation to supper; but again she toyed with his wishes and insisted that he come to her. He went. Mysteriously and suddenly, the great barge was illuminated by innumerable lights, revealing a spectacle of such bewitching splendor that Antony the judge was instantly transformed into Antony the lover. The story became one of the classics of the Cydnus; Saul must have heard it many times.

But it is impossible to enumerate all the factors that may operate in the production and development of great men. Facts, events, and circumstances that could make no impression on some lives, or would seem entirely unimportant to others, would doubtless provide an active mind like Saul's with rich material for constructive thought. Indeed, the key that unlocks genius may often be found in a circumstance of childhood or in the suggestion of an obscure companion.

A very important part of Saul's education was the trade he learned—that of tentmaker. It was incumbent upon every Jewish father to teach his son some useful occupation; a duty that was taught by Rabbi Judah, who in effect said, "Whosoever teacheth not his son an occupation is as if he taught him robbery." It may be assumed, therefore, that Saul was put to work at an early age in his father's shops where he could become fmiliar with all kinds and stages of tentmaking.

But Saul's trade cannot be taken as an index to his social standing. To the Jew, all useful trades were honorable; though indeed, some were not as desirable as others. Even the rabbis all had trades for self-support, for their services in the synagogues were rendered without charge. Shammai, that illustrious teacher who in doctrine was the very antipode of the famous Hillel and who left the world as Saul was coming into it, was a mason. Saul's trade therefore was entirely appropriate to a man of either wealth or learning. To it he could turn in case of need or misfortune.

REFERENCES

Chapter 2

1. I Cor. 8:4.
2. Cf. Acts 2:5.
3. Cf. Dio Chrysostomos. *Discourses*.
4. Eph. 2:14.
5. Strabo. *The Geography*. XIV. 5. Sec. 14.
6. Acts 21:39.
7. Rom. 4:1; I Cor. 9:2; II Cor. 1:22.
8. II Thes. 3:127; Gal. 6:11.
9. I Cor. 11:3-16.
10. Dio Chrysostomos. *Discourses*. Treatise XXXIII.
11. II Kings 17:17; Jer. 19:5.
12. Cf. Arnobius of Sicca. *The Case Against Pagans*. IV. Criticism of Various Gods. V. Jupiter, Elicius, Attis and the Mysteries.
13. Strabo. *The Geography*. XIV. v. 13.
14. Xenophon. *Anabasis* I. ii. 26.
15. Dio Chrysostomos. *Discourses*.
16. Acts 21:39.
17. Xenophon. *Anabasis* I. ii. 23.
18. See Mellink, M.J. "Tarsus," *Interpreters' Dictionary*. IV. p. 518.

Jerusalem

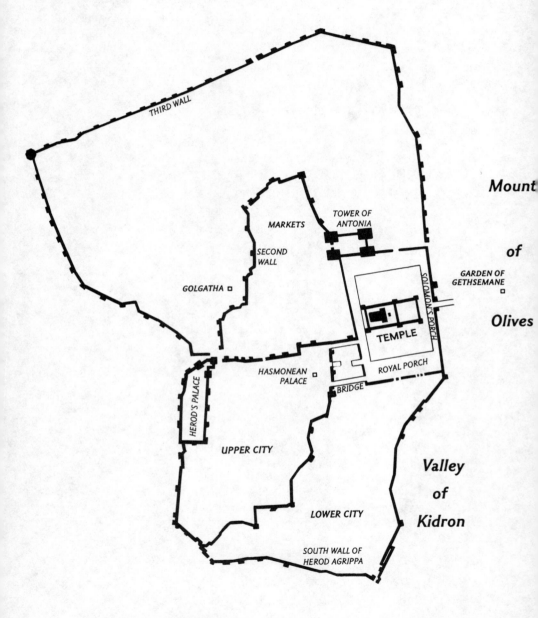

THIRD WALL

Mount

of

Olives

MARKETS

TOWER OF
ANTONIA

SECOND
WALL

GARDEN OF
GETHSEMANE

GOLGATHA

SOLOMON'S PORCH

TEMPLE

HEROD'S PALACE

HASMONEAN
PALACE

ROYAL PORCH

BRIDGE

UPPER CITY

Valley

of

Kidron

LOWER CITY

SOUTH WALL OF
HEROD AGRIPPA

Mt. Zion

Marketplace in Jerusalem

CHAPTER
3

The Holy City

AFTER SAUL HAD COMPLETED his preparatory studies, he was sent to Jerusalem to sit at the feet of the greatest Jewish teacher then living—the broad-minded Gamaliel, doctor of the Law. The boy, then about fifteen years old, had perhaps long harbored a desire to become a rabbi and had no difficulty in winning the consent of his parents.

A pleasant picture might be drawn of Saul's long cherished ambitions—the sea voyage, the overland journey, the Holy City, the Temple of Jehovah, the school. At last the day of departure arrived. Though perhaps accompanied by his father, Saul must have felt those deep heart swellings that rise at the beginning of a journey when familiar associations are suddenly severed. But he was soon out on the great wide restless sea, restless like his own surging soul. And then he began scanning the horizon for a glimpse of Cyprus, the land of copper, and searching the Syrian coast for Mt. Lebanon and towering snow-crowned Hermon. Three hundred miles of sea over which the departing sun left a canopy of scintillating stars.

When abreast with Mt. Carmel, the scene of Elijah's famous contest with the priests of Baal, Saul and his father knew that they should soon put in at Caesarea, the city of the Herodian kings. But Saul could have had no premonitions of what Caesarea would mean to him later. Here he saw the

23

Roman garrison but did not know that some of its soldiers would one day rescue him from a mob of his own people in the Holy City, here he saw the provincial prison but did not know that its doors would close later upon him for two long years.

From Caesarea to Jerusalem the journey was made on horseback, twenty-five or thirty miles along the coastal lowlands, and then a long ascent through the rugged highlands. For an intelligent youth, a journey of several days by sea and land terminating in the city that every loyal Jew wished to see at least once before he died, would create a taste for travel, release latent qualities of manhood, and fortify religious and political convictions.

At Jerusalem, Saul and his father visited the Temple, where Saul matriculated in the school of Gamaliel. Swiftly came the day of parting, a parting Jewishly affectionate. Strict Pharisee that the father was, it is hardly probable that his last words were admonitory. Already he must have seen in his son the beginnings of that powerful self-control that characterized him in later life. In his intense love of righteousness Saul was safe, safe anywhere—and his father knew it.

Jerusalem was not so large a city as Tarsus, hardly forty thousand souls, not so busy, except on feast days, and not half so kaleidoscopic. Saul could have encircled its walls and the hills on which they stood within a few hours. Tarsus was a city of the plain, with unlimited room for expansion. Jerusalem was a city of the mountain tops, hugging defensive cliffs.

Was Saul disappointed with this Jewish city, the city of his fondest dreams? Did he find Jerusalem into which he had just come inferior in extent and grandeur to the Jerusalem of his imagination, the Jerusalem of his Scriptures? There were disappointments and surprises, of course, but still it was Jerusalem, Jerusalem Holy City, the city of Jehovah's altar.* Saul certainly thought of the forty-eighth Psalm and must have taken an early opportunity to obey literally its laudatory suggestions:

"Great is the Lord, and greatly to be praised
in the city of our God.[1]
His holy mountain, beautiful in elevation,
is the joy of all the earth.
Mount Zion . . .
Walk about Zion, go around her,
number her towers. . . ."

---

* It was the author of Acts who centered Paul's activities around Jerusalem. From Paul's letters there is no indication that Paul was abnormally devoted to Jerusalem. It was only after the Judaizers had invaded Paul's territory that he decided to go back to Jerusalem to negotiate with the "so-called apostles" there, apparently to try to see if they would stay inside Palestine and leave the diaspora to him. (GWB)

Most certainly he must have crossed the valley of the Kidron and ascended the Mount of Olives, directly east of the temple, where he could behold the compact city sloping gently towards him, always in waiting for the kiss of the morning sun. There he would behold the unforgettable scene of his life. From the first soft touch of morning glow until the long uneasy shadows drew themselves up under the shelter of the western wall, Saul would watch the city, watch until the dim outline of the Temple became an entrancing blaze of glory in gold and marble.

As a healthy, normally active, and enthusiastic youth—and Saul could have been nothing else—he would soon become familiar with every place of importance within the city, and many of the famous spots beyond.

The temple was of course the first and chief attraction, already beautiful but not yet completed. Priests and their helpers were still laboring in brass and gold, carving beams of cedar, chiseling columns, and slowly erecting heavy masonry. Walls with towers and foe-defying gates enclosed the temple area; but the sanctuary or temple proper rose above the walls in imposing majesty.

The great outer court, or paved temple yard, with its enormous shelters or porticos six hundred feet long, resting against the outer walls and on rows of massive columns, was a place that would have exacted surprise and wonderment, even if no temple had been there.

Saul, of course, encircled the whole court, passing through Solomon's porch[2] on the east, through the wall cloister and the royal porch on the south, and around the Temple on the west and north.

The court was a very busy place. Here Jews from every land might be seen at any time, but on feast days the place was filled with a surging mass of such uncertain temperament that Roman soldiers had to be posted to prevent disorder. Here were individuals viewing for the first time the wonders of the temple; here were groups of men gathered around their favorite teachers, or listening to some self-appointed prophet; here were men hotly discussing their national problems, and others wrangling over whatever displeased them; here walked Pharisees and Sadducees; and little groups of those strange mystic ascetics, the Essenes.

As Saul pursued his way around the cloisters he came upon the moneychangers, those shrewd, heavily-turbaned men who sat before their little benches ever ready to enrich themselves while accommodating Jewish pilgrims who carried the coins of other lands. Here among their stuffy cages sat those who sold doves and pigeons, driving hard bargains with the poor. Here also were those who dealt in flour, measuring it out with stingy exactness. And here, too, were the men of larger business who bought and sold sheep and oxen. Everywhere there was the noise of hard bargaining, and Saul must have observed that the faces of the buyers were hard with distrust, and those of the sellers hard in their merciless advantage. That his

Pharisaic righteousness was disturbed is not unlikely but he only deplored what the fiery zeal of Jesus could not endure.[3]

Having encircled the cloisters of the temple area, and having come again to Solomon's porch, Saul now faced the awe-inspiring Sanctuary whose gate-like front, one hundred-fifty feet high and as many broad, rose above the surrounding walls of the second court. As he advanced from Solomon's porch towards the gate called "Beautiful"[4] that led to the second court, he came upon a highly ornamented wall, about breast high, surrounding the temple structures and bearing at equal intervals rectangular blocks of marble, on which was carved alternately in Greek and Latin a warning that brought every Gentile to a halt: "Let no alien enter within the balustrade and embankment surrounding the Temple. Whosoever is caught makes himself responsible for his death which will follow."[5]

But Saul did not halt, except perhaps to marvel at the splendor before him, not knowing that this very warning would lead some day to his own arrest. With the haughty exclusiveness of one belonging to a God-chosen race he saluted the temple police and mounted the steps of the sacred precincts. Onward he went through the gate Beautiful, the gate of Corinthian brass. Crossing the court of the women, he climbed another flight of steps, through the "Upper Gate," and into the court of the men of Israel. There before him in the open stood an enormous smoking altar of unhewn stone, an altar vast enough to hold a house.

Beyond the altar towered the porch of the Sanctuary—and Saul remembered that Herod had desecrated it by erecting a Roman ensign over its entrance. Deep in the doorless porch hung a great Babylonian veil, gorgeously designed in colors; white, with blue, purple, and scarlet. Saul knew that behind the veil were the sanctuary doors that led first to the Holy Place and then to the Holy of Holies. He knew that beyond these doors silence and darkness reigned, save for the lights on the great seven-branched golden lampstand and the occasional light that flared up from the thirteen kinds of fragrant spices burned every morning and evening— lights that burned steadily in the dark stillness, casting on the floor and walls multiple shadows of the attending priests.

Darker and more silent and mysterious still was the Holy of Holies, separated from the Holy Place by a great curtain.[6] Behind this veil dwelt the awful presence of Jehovah; and none dared enter save the high priest, and he but once a year, on the great Day of Atonement.

Everywhere Saul found himself face to face with overwhelming grandeur. Everywhere he saw undeniable proofs of the superiority of the religion of Jerusalem over the pagan religions of Tarsus. Here was a God perfect in holiness, a sanctuary free from defilement, a priesthood of superior men, a symbolism that spurned idolatry, and a worship that encouraged the finest virtues.

From the men's court Saul watched the priests and their helpers at their tasks around and high up on the great altar, his boyish mind wondering at the skill with which beasts were slaughtered and prepared for burning. Then his eye followed the towering column of smoke that he knew was visible to thousands of Jews far beyond the walls of the Holy City.

Everywhere there were barefooted priests, for thousands of them swarmed in and around Jerusalem. Those on duty wore their official garments—long white robes held about their bodies by ample girdles of white linen adorned with flowers—their heads covered with tight-fitting turbans. How Saul longed for a glimpse of the high priest, to see him in his gorgeous apparel just as he would appear on the Day of Atonement, censer in hand, ready to meet the awful presence in the Holy of Holies.

All these scenes entered deep into Saul's life, warmed his Jewish pride, tightened his Pharisaic strictness, justified his youthful idealism, and solidified his religious convictions. It would not be strange if his experience in the temple courts had caused him to dream of being in heaven, and there conversing with angels, or even with Jehovah himself. Certainly he dreamed.[7]

Judging from the vastness of the store of physical energy upon which Saul drew in later years, it is safe to assume that his boyhood was characterized by overflowing vitality. He was such a youth as would quickly become acquainted with every part of his new city. It is easy to think of him as surveying with somewhat conflicting emotions the Roman fortress that adjoined the northern wall of the temple court, visiting the old palace of the Hasmonaeans near the temple bridge, seeking the new palace of Herod over on the west side of the "Upper City," and looking with reverential awe at the palace of the high priest.

Jerusalem was a crowded city and its narrow streets were thronged with citizens and with visitors from many lands.* Women, too, were upon the streets but, unlike the women of Tarsus, very few wore the protective veil. Saul must have been astonished at this freedom unless he knew that the veil meant one thing in his native city and another in Jerusalem.

The sidewalks, where any existed, were extremely narrow, merely elevations for safety; and the crooked, unpaved, yardless streets were never clean.*

---

* Because the streets were narrow, bordered with tall buildings, and crowded with people, any crisis that prompted people to leave the city resulted in disaster as many people were trampled to death. Therefore the author of Matt 24:17 warned refugees not to go down into their houses if they were on the housetops. They should move from one housetop to the other, as was possible, until they were out of the city. (GWB)

The business centers of the city were known as agoras, though very different from the agora of Tarsus. Even the whole section known as the "Upper City" finally became known as the upper agora. In these sections the population milled continually.

Often in his survey of the city Saul must have differentiated Jerusalem from Tarsus. The one a Jewish city with few intruders, the other a cosmopolitan city with a Jewish quarter; the one speaking the Aramaic or Hebrew tongue, the other the Greek; the one with a transparent atmosphere, the other subject to the tremulous haze of its heated plain. Thus the youthful Saul was rapidly becoming the product of two widely diverse societies. His thoughts, though cast in Jewish molds, contained the alloy of Gentile contacts, and his attitude towards all human relations, though fundamentally Jewish, contained a Tarsian element of flexibility.

In Jerusalem there were two famous rival schools of rabbinical training, both Pharisaic, but utterly irreconcilable. One, the school of Shammai, which, while assigning a certain value to rabbinical tradition, rejected it completely when it conflicted with the writings of Moses. The other, the school of Hillel, which not only accepted the traditions, but in case of conflict, placed them above the Law.[8] Of these schools, Saul selected the latter. His teacher, Gamaliel, was then in his prime, mounting rapidly to that eminence ascribed to him in the Talmud where he is called the "beauty of the law," and where it is said in effect that "Upon the death of Rabban Gamaliel the glory of the Law ceased."[9] Though a Pharisee, Gamaliel was broad and tolerant in his views, even to the extent of recognizing a certain value in Greek learning. He became the most illustrious teacher of his day among the Jews and was one of the few men to be honored with the title of Rabban.

Somewhere within the temple precincts, Gamaliel conducted his scribal college, the highest institution of learning among the Jews. Before him or his assistants, Saul and his classmates seated themselves and endeavored to store away the knowledge that fell from the lips of their instructors.

In Saul's day the education of young lawyers was a prodigious task of memory that dragged along until they were nearly thirty years old. Judging from the statement made in one of his letters,[10] Saul must have applied himself to his task with enthusiasm.

Studies were pursued in the Aramaic tongue. The law, however, was preserved in the original Hebrew. The study of the law was pursued by the method of *midrash*, or "interpretation," which followed two lines— *halachah* and *haggadah*. Halachah means "walking" and it is a set of rules showing the way Jews should "walk." Haggadah means "narrative," and it is the collection of stories, legends, and parables used to illustrate religious beliefs.

By *haggadah*, the interpreters extracted from the scriptures the utmost meaning possible. They supposed these writings to contain a simple or literal meaning, a suggested meaning, an investigative meaning, and a mystic meaning. The last three of these, they brought out by the use of parable, allegory, and legend. But the assumptions upon which the Jewish schools proceeded led to many strange conclusions, as well as to conclusions obtained in strange ways. Judged from a modern viewpoint, the problems discussed were often extremely trivial; nevertheless the mental drill was valuable, and the moral precepts evolved were helpful.

One method of teaching was that of propounding questions for debate; the arguments for or against a proposition being drawn from Scripture. Such discussion would, of course, sharpen the wits of the disputants. That Saul was trained in this manner is evident from his style of writing.[11] That he was instructed in haggadic exposition is shown by the way he later allegorized the story of Hagar and Sarah.[12] And that he studied Hebrew literature not contained in the accepted scriptures may be supposed from the traditions he mentioned in his letters.

While Saul's studies embraced subjects of the greatest importance, they also extended to mere tricks of law. The old problem of the asses may have come up for discussion: "If three hundred asses move in line and the first stumbles and falls causing the second to fall, and the second causing the third to fall, how shall the damages be adjusted among the three owners?" But think of the possible injustice when the injuries and losses were unequal: if the first were required to pay the second and the second to pay the third. Yet such was the accepted answer. Perhaps, too, Saul may have discussed whether it was lawful to eat an egg on the Sabbath that had been laid on that day. Certainly he was familiar with this and other equally trivial questions. But to Saul and his teachers, unrighteousness, however slight, was a serious thing; and nothing was trivial that aided men in avoiding sin.

The Jews had become slaves of their own law and, in zealously pursuing a ceremonial righteousness, had missed the righteousness that is of faith. So Saul was being trained in an intolerant fanaticism that found a fertile lodgement in his natural bent.

Judging from the contents of the Mishna, the education of a Jewish scribe or lawyer included a fair range of secular knowledge. Saul therefore probably learned something of music, medicine, mathematics, astronomy, geography, and even of magic. A knowledge of music and medicine would be needed if he were to take charge of a synagogue. That he could sing, is evident from the story of his Philippian imprisonment;[13] and that he practiced medicine, is evident from the cures ascribed to him.[14] His knowledge of mathematics would consist of a little very simple arithmetic and, perhaps, some geometry. Euclid's "Elements" had been in existence for nearly three centuries, but arithmetic was still in a primitive state because of its cumbersome notation. Astronomy had some practical value for the mariner, for the traveler, and for calendric purposes. Geography was already expanding far beyond the limits of the Mediterranean Basin. Magic in all its forms was in demand everywhere. Thus the miracles reported in the New Testament met a ready demand. Indeed, the education of a rabbi in Saul's day could hardly have been complete without at least a few lectures on incantations and on the exorcism of demons. The stories of Elymas at Paphos and that of the Pythoness at Philippi would indicate that Luke regarded Paul as an accomplished magician.[15]

In addition to his Jewish education, Saul perhaps took courses in Greek learning and Roman law. It appears that Gamaliel had many students who were engaged in the study of Greek authors, and very possibly most of them were Hellenists like Saul, who felt a great need for such learning. It is true that certain Jews condemned the use of pagan literature, and were suspicious of those who knew many languages. But extreme and conflicting views on most subjects were common among the Jews. It was said of Rabbi Judah, the saint, that, being asked when a man should teach his son Greek Literature, replied: "At an hour that belongs neither to the day nor the night, for it is written: 'His delight is in the law of the Lord, and on his law he meditates day and night'."[16] However, it may be assumed from the words "great learning,"[17] which Luke puts into the mouth of Festus, that Saul had received a broad and thorough education; and Luke's humorous satire on the pedantic loafers of Athens[18] gives the same impression.

In his mature years Saul displayed the intellectual ease, confidence, and penetration that mark the scholar; but in his letters he never intentionally puts his learning on display, never makes use of current philosophy. Whatever respect he may have had for such learning in his earlier years, he afterwards found it utterly useless in the face of the final cataclysm he believed would soon occur.[19]

That Saul made a study of Roman law is almost certain. Being a Jewish lawyer and living as a Roman citizen under Roman law, he would find such a study necessary. Judging from passages to be found in his letters, he was at least well informed on the subject and, according to Luke, when on trial before a tribunal he always pleaded his own case. In writing to the Romans, he showed that he understood the very foundation upon which the whole structure of jurisprudence should be built,[20] a fundamental that Cicero in his own clear style had enunciated a century and a half earlier and that appeared again in the famous Justinian code: that there is an immutable first law written in all human hearts. And it is for this reason that, though men may plead ignorance of fact, they cannot plead ignorance of the law.[21]

In writing to the Corinthians, Paul said, "the written code kills, but the Spirit gives life,"[22] as if he were thinking of the Sabinian school of law, which placed the spirit of the law above the letter. In writing to the Thessalonians, he adopted the practise of the Augustan jurists in supplying a proof of the genuineness of his letters.[23] Among the legal analogies found in his theology is that of "adoption," and this is carried out after the manner of Roman law.[24]

There should be no inordinate desire to display Paul as a prodigy of learning, no strained effort to fill his lips with Greek philosophy, and no longing to make him a product of the Tarsian rhetorical schools. He was educated as a Hebrew, and that was quite enough to give him eminence. But if he did study in Tarsus, as the numerous rhetorical figures in his letters might be construed to indicate, yet all his Greek learning, so far as revealed in the New Testament, might have been gotten under Gamaliel or have been absorbed from the Stoic, Cynic, and other exhorters in the agora of his home city.

Although Saul's natural traits and gifts would have made him a leader irrespective of the merits and personal qualities of his teachers, yet some contact may have intensified his religious zeal. Luke intimates[25] that Gamaliel's influence should be recognized, but at the same time presents the two men in sharp contrast: Gamaliel is calm and forbearing;[26] Saul, fiery and impetuous.[27] Both, however, were ardent champions of the law, and the quiet zeal of one may have incited the fiery zeal of the other.

Then, too, from the very first hour of his contact with Jerusalem and its schools, Saul must have been profoundly impressed with the tradition of the divine call of Israel. His first years had been spent in a Gentile city, but in Jerusalem he was with his own people. Here was the one appointed altar; here was the awful and unapproachable seat of the divine Presence, the holiest spot in all the earth; and here were the expounders and guardians of the law. With convictions like these, nothing less than a catastrophe could have disillusioned the young Tarsian Pharisee.

If Paul was familiar with classical Greek, he did not use it in his letters. To have used it would have weakened his message. He wrote and spoke in the language of the people, the common colloquial Greek that had drifted far away from Attic purity. Historians, essayists, and those who affected superior learning were still clinging to the older tongue: Josephus, Plutarch, and others in Paul's day and later, followed the Attic model.

Nor should Paul's scholarship be judged adversely because of any literary imperfection found in his letters. It was his pen, together with the pens of those he inspired as New Testament writers, that erected the greatest of all monuments to the colloquial Greek of the first century. The marvel is not that a few specimens of mixed metaphor and irregular construction should be found but that a bundle of letters written under pressure, without literary aim, and with no thought of their preservation should be so nearly perfect. And besides, the Pauline letters certainly suffered accidents before they were copied for the New Testament canon; no one knows what changes were made.

The presence of Hebraic peculiarities in his letters need not be regarded as proof that he lacked command of the Greek idiom but, rather, that he was a master of both tongues. Greek was the language of his Bible and of his non-Jewish contacts. In his home, perhaps, and certainly at Jerusalem, he used Hebrew or Aramaic, a kindred language of the Hebrew. In his letters, he was presenting Hebrew thought to Greek and Hebrew minds and chose the best way of doing it.

That part of Paul's education derived from general reading must have been important. He was perhaps familiar with most of the literature of his people and found in such writings as the Book of Wisdom, Baruch, and Sirach ideas that later became fundamental to his theology. He was perhaps acquainted with the Book of Enoch, and was an early reader of the Assumption of Moses. If Origen and Epiphanius may be trusted, he quoted from the now lost Apocrypha of Elias. The Psalter of Solomon must have been well known to him and perhaps much other literature of which no knowledge exists today.

Whether Saul was more a source than a recipient of inspiration among his fellow students is a matter of conjecture. But in view of his later achievements it would seem best to regard him as a superior student.[28] His studies at Jerusalem may have extended over a period of fifteen years, with intervals of visits to his home, where he may have managed his tent-making business.

In connection with Saul's schooling there arises the question of his marriage, for that event would occur before the completion of his long rabbinical training. Did Saul marry? What a flood of light the answer to this question would throw upon his conduct and upon some of his words. But neither he nor his biographer had any occasion whatever for making explicit mention of his family—parents, wife, or children. The silence does not prove that he never married. Yet there is some evidence that he must have taken a wife at the customary age for such union—eighteen or so. The Jews always regarded marriage as a sacred obligation, basing their authority on the plain commandment of Scripture,[29] on Old Testatment examples,[30] and on haggadic inferences.[31] It was even said that "A Jew who has no wife is not a man,"[32] and that "A man without family is as a homicide, a destroyer of his posterity, whose disobedience is as if he lessened the image of God."[33]

Saul therefore as a strict Pharisee would feel it incumbent upon himself to marry promptly, delaying only, if at all, to complete his studies. There is further evidence also to be taken from his supposed membership in the Sanhedrin. If he indeed took part with that body in judicial proceedings,[34] and the rule that a Sanhedrist should be a married man and a father was in force at that time, as it was later, then he must have had a wife and at least one child.

A third argument rests on the supposition that when he wrote to the Corinthians he was a widower. In reply to questions addressed to him, he wrote about the inexpediency of marriage in view of the awful sufferings into which he believed the world was soon to be plunged: "To the unmarried and the widows I say that it is well for them to remain single as I do."[35] This passage goes far enough to prove that Paul was without a wife at that time. But was he a widower? Unfortunately for the question, the Greek word, *agamois* as used here and translated "unmarried" almost invariably took the place of the rare word *cheroi*, and may be conceived to include all unmarried persons of both sexes, or all classes of unmarried men only, or just widowers. Had Paul used *cheroi* instead of *agamois*, the question would have been answered. Nevertheless there is room for the presumption that he was a widower.

The testimony of the church fathers, whose opinions perhaps rested upon no better evidence than is available today, is clearly conflicting. Clement of Alexandria, Ignatius, and Eusebius represent Paul as married, whereas Tertullian and Jerome, whose judgment may have been governed by their opinions of celibacy, represent him as unmarried.

Some writers have suggested that Paul was addressing his wife when he exhorted someone in the Philippian church as a "true yokefellow"; and others have ventured to guess that he had entered into a union with Lydia the wealthy Thyatirian seller of purple then living in Philippi. But in the light of I Cor: 7 such speculations must be discarded.

To grant that Paul became a widower not long after his marriage, is to invite a long train of thought involving pictures that begin with nuptial joy and close with domestic tragedy: There arises before the imagination an aristocratic young Pharisee eighteen or twenty years of age. He left Jerusalem and his studies temporarily for Tarsus, where a great feast celebrated a betrothal. A year later, he went again to Tarsus, when another feast celebrated his marriage; and that just at the time when he was beginning to be known as the brilliant product of the great Gamaliel's school. Again he returned to Jerusalem, this time to complete his studies; he was accompanied by his wife.

The Talmud says: "He who loves his wife as himself, and honors her more than himself . . . is greatly blessed."[36]

"Grieve not your wife without cause, for tears come easy with her."[37]

A little family begins, love is refined, reciprocal consideration is perfected. But somewhere, at some time, a dark foreboding cloud hangs low. There is oppressive anxious silence, whispered words—weeping.

Again, the Talmud: "When his wife dies, it is to the husband as if the temple had been destroyed."[38]

Paul must have become a widower before his conversion, or at some time between his twentieth and thirty-seventh years. He makes no mention of children; but neither is there mention of Peter's children, nor those of any other apostle. Could Paul have had a daughter?

REFERENCES

Chapter 3

1. Ps. 122:3.
2. John 10:23; Acts 3:11; 5:12.
3. John 2:13-17.
4. Acts 3:2, 10.
5. One of the slabs containing this warning was found in 1871 by M. Clermont-Gannean and is now in Constantinople. For the Greek on the inscription see Josephus III edited and translated by H. St. John Thackeray. (Cambridge, Harvard University Press, 1957), p. 258, Pn. c. See also Josephus, Wars of the Jews v (194); Antiquities of the Jews XII; v (145-146). Mishnah Kelim 1:8.
6. Mark 15:38.
7. II Cor. 12:1-7.
8. Mark 7:8; Gal. 1:14.
9. Mishnah Sotah 9:15.
10. Gal. 1:14.
11. Cf. Rom. 3:1, 9; 4:1; 6:1, 15; 8:31; 9:14, 30; 11:1.
12. Gal. 4:21-31.
13. Acts 16:25.
14. Acts 20:9-12; 28:8-9.
15. Acts 13:8; 16:16-18.
16. Ps. 1:2.
17. Acts 26:24.
18. Acts 17:16-34.
19. I Cor. 1:17-21; Col. 2:8.
20. Rom. 2:14-15.
21. Rom. 1:18-20; 2:1-16.
22. II Cor. 3:6.
23. II Thes. 3:17.
24. Rom. 8:15-23.
25. Acts 22:3.
26. Acts 5:34-39.
27. Acts 22:4.
28. Acts 26:24.
29. Gen. 1:28.
30. Prov. 5:18; Mal. 2:14.
31. Gen. 5:2; Eccl. 11:6; Job 5:24, 25.
32. Talmud, Babylonian Talmud. Yebamoth. 63a.
33. Ibid. 63b.
34. Acts 8:1; 22:20; 26:10.
35. I Cor. 7:8.
36. Talmud, Babylonian Talmud. Yebamoth. 63a; Sanhedrin. 76b.
37. Talmud, Babylonian Talmud. Baba Mezia. 59a.
38. Talmud, Babylonian Talmud. Sanhedrin. 22a.

On the road to Damascus

Mediterranean
Sea

Mt. Carmel

Tyre

Caesarea Philippi

Mt. Hermon

GALILEE

Tiberias   Sea of Galilee

Nazareth

Caesarea   SAMARIA   Scythopolis

Neapolis   Shechem

Antipatris

Joppa

Lydda

Bethel   Jericho

Jerusalem

JUDAEA

Gaza

Philadelphia

Dead
Sea

A Defender of the Law

AFTER SAUL TOOK HIS PLACE at the feet of Gamaliel, no record was
made of his life until his biographer reveals him standing near the prostrate
body of the martyr Stephen. No part of this long interval could have been
spent in idleness; it would have been impossible for the impetuous Saul to
have wasted time. After completing his studies he might have become a
teacher in the synagogue of the Cilicians in Jerusalem, but it is far more
likely that he returned to his home for a time and taught in a synagogue in
Tarsus. In that case he must have taken up his trade, for rabbis were self-
supporting.

About this time John the Baptist and Jesus were attracting more than
local attention. The one quickly silenced by Herod Antipas, who beheaded
him at the request of a dancer, and the other crucified by Procurator
Pontius Pilate at the instigation of the Jews. It is not probable that Saul
ever met either of these men or that he concerned himself very much when
he first heard about the crucifixion of Jesus, for scourgings, stonings,
crucifixions, and beheadings were ordinary occurrences, and self-
appointed reformers were always numerous. But when he heard the reports
that were being circulated by the Jews about certain preposterous claims
made by the followers of Jesus and learned that these followers were
multiplying dangerously, then his indignation burst into flame: "Shall

these misguided followers of that crucified malefactor of Nazareth be permitted to speak blasphemous words against Moses and God?" he may have raged.[1] "Shall they be permitted to teach that God has discarded his ancient Law, and that our sacred traditions are no longer binding? Shall they be permitted to heap endless insult upon the Pharisees and to malign the teachers of the divine law? What," Saul probably thought, "is the high priest doing in Jerusalem? Why does the Sanhedrin do nothing more than make a few arrests, scourge a little, and issue silly warnings?[2] Has Gamaliel bewitched the rulers with his soft policies?[3] Shall a hundred misguided Galileans be permitted to loaf around the temple waiting for return of a dead man?"[4]

The more he thought about the Nazarene and his followers the more his anger burned. "Should these heretics be permitted to deceive men by proclaiming a fabled resurrection, deifying a crucified malefactor, and changing the ancient customs of the people of God? No!" And Saul's "No" would have the ring of steel.

He was still youthful and not yet hampered in purpose and action by that caution that is born of experience. "Exterminate them! Let them feel the power of the law—arrest, shackles, imprisonment, scourging, stoning, death."

That primitive innate cruelty of the human heart that breaks out now and then in hideous persecutions when a minority dares to think differently from a majority surged like billows of flame in the orthodox soul of this young Pharisee. Of course he justified himself, a persecutor always does. He believed that the Jewish code was the revealed will of the omnipotent God and, naturally, that any Jew disobeying such a law should suffer its severest penalties. In all this he was not more than a good citizen, for he was living under a theocratic government and the defense of his religion was the defense of his state.

In a short time Saul was commissioned by the Sanhedrin to suppress the new heretical sect. It was doubtless at the suggestion of Annas that Saul was appointed. Annas had been made high priest about A. D. 7 by Quirinus, governor of Syria, but was deposed about eight years later by Valerius Gratus, who put Joseph Caiaphas into his place. Annas, however, continued to exercise his power unofficially, or as coadjutor to Caiaphas, who was his son-in-law.[5] Both Annas and Caiaphas had taken part in the trial of Jesus, against whom they had entertained strong personal grievances because he had publically quoted certain words of Jeremiah as an accusation against the priests and scribes, charging them with having made the house of prayer a den of thieves.[6] Annas felt the sting of the quotation because he and his sons were enriching themselves by furnishing all manner of sacrificial supplies at good prices to visiting worshippers. They were unscrupulous, rapacious men. Even the Talmud had denounced them: "Woe to the house of Annas! Woe to their snaky hissings!" Annas was a haughty Sadducean aristocrat, who courted servility and could not brook criticism. He was soullessly vindictive and made Jesus pay with his life.

When Annas learned that the apostles were successfully proclaiming that Jesus had risen from the dead, his anger flamed forth anew. To him the announcement that Jesus had left the tomb, had ascended into heaven, and would return shortly to take over the affairs of the world was not only a declaration of nonsense but another personal insult.

After Saul's appointment to the inquisitorial office, he appears to have come into contact first with a Hellenistic Jew or Roman named Stephen, who shortly before, with six other men, had been chosen by the new sect to a kind of diaconate.[7] Stephen was a remarkable man, perhaps not unlike Saul in his positive character and vehement action. Luke represents him as a man of great faith, full of the Holy Spirit, and a worker of miracles.

The apostles had learned caution after the death of Jesus, and being native Jews were not as likely to give offense to the authorities as the Hellenists. Indeed it is unlikely that up to this time they had reasoned out the logical consequences of their faith. Stephen, however, had decided in his own mind what should happen to the whole Jewish system if Jesus were the Messiah. But when he began proclaiming his views, he fell into the hands of the inquisitors. It happened that his informers, like himself, were members of the Hellenistic synagogues in Jerusalem.[8] Jews born in foreign lands, or who had been long abroad, were either extremely conservative about their ancient customs, or extremely liberal. It was the conservatives who forced Stephen to commit himself, and among these Saul must have been a leader, since he was of Cilicia.[9]

According to Luke's account,[10] Stephen defended his position with unanswerable arguments. But his very success was his undoing. Most men hate the man who convinces them against their will—and Stephen's enemies hated him murderously.

Being defeated in debate, they garbled his statements sufficiently to make them appear criminal, and then excited a mob from which they obtained false witnesses. The mob bellowed and howled, the temple police rushed to the arrest, and the Sanhedrin hastened to meet. Stephen was charged with blasphemy, a crime punishable by death. From the moment that Stephen heard the first shout of "Blasphemy!" he knew what was to follow.

Saul was present, and perhaps chafing over his failure to best Stephen in debate. In fact he may have had a seat in the council as one of its members, or as one of the supernumerary nine who sat with the council.[11]

When the court convened the members seated themselves in a semicircle, the president and chief men occupying the middle of the arc, and the younger men the ends. Two or three scribes were present ready to record the proceedings.

Stephen was brought before the council by the temple guards, and, after certain suborned witnesses had testified that they had heard him speak blasphemous words against God, the temple, and the law of Moses, the high priest put the formal question: "Are these things so?"

All the while Stephen's face was "like the face of an angel."[12] He had alredy resigned himself to martyrdom and was at peace within his soul. He knew that a formal defense was useless, and therefore, instead of defending himself, he brought charges against the court that would have justified the stoning of every member in it. Just as John wrote an ideal last address and prayer for Jesus,[13] so Luke wrote in Jewish style an ideal reply to the question of the high priest[14] and represented Stephen as developing a bold and stinging climax that threw the whole court into disorder.

Hands grasped at robes, eyebrows lowered under heavy turbans, and pallid lips stretched wide and bare through shaggy beards—"and they ground their teeth against him." With a calm upturned face, Stephen, in an ecstasy of victory, exclaimed: "Behold, I see the heavens opened, and the Son of man standing at the right hand of God."[15] That was too much. It was bad enough to defend Jesus, but to put him at the right hand of God was vile. Court and spectators became a yelling, deaf, and murderous mob—"they cried out with a loud voice and stopped their ears and rushed together upon him."[16]

Saul was one of them: Saul the aristocratic Tarsian, Saul the brilliant young lawyer, Saul the scrupulous Pharisee. he heard the blasphemy all too clearly and shouted the louder to drown the evil words.

"Saul!" commanded the Sadducean high priest, "take charge of this traitor to Israel and see that our sentence is executed at once."

While the Sanhedrists lingered in groups to discuss the audacity of the new sect, a crowd attracted by the voice of the herald, who shouted the name of the prisoner and his crime, ran to a slight elevation beyond the walls of the city where the law of Israel was to take its course.[17] Here Saul and Stephen faced each other once more: Saul in robes of spotless white, erect, confident, masterful. Stephen in soiled and torn robes, also erect, equally confident, and disturbingly serene. They were two splendid personalities, each conscious of the other's superior worth.

"Confess your sin," commanded Saul.* Stephen's only answer was to cast him a look of pity. "Strip him," commanded Saul. At the same time the witnesses who had testified against the prisoner before the Sanhedrin removed their encumbering outer robes and laid them at Saul's feet.[18]

---

* The account in Acts (8:1) only said that Saul consented to the execution. It did not indicate that he was in charge of it. (GWB)

It was their duty to cast the first stone.[19] There was a moment of expectant silence. All eyes were turned upon Stephen. Would he confess? "Stone him," commanded Saul. While they were stoning him, Stephen prayed "Lord Jesus receive my spirit." Then he "cried with a loud voice, 'Lord, do not hold this sin against them.' "[20] He was felled upon his back, and a great stone crashed down upon his chest. Saul from ten cubits away saw the awful contortions of the once angelic face, contortions for the breath that would never return. As he moved away for safety, he heard the stones, which were now warm in the hands of the waiting mob, thud and crack upon the prostate form of Stephen.

It was his first blood and he felt a secret sickness, though he had done nothing more than to carry out the law of his people. But the deed started a reaction in his soul that was soon to change the whole course of his life. Stephen haunted him.[21] Such conviction, flawless courage, and nobility of manner, such splendor of manhood; how could these be attributes of a blasphemer? Saul doubted. Upon his return to the court he made his official report but by that time the pendulem of his feelings had swung back, and he was again the rabid Pharisee, and Stephen a common criminal.

The followers of Jesus had forsaken neither the synagogues nor the temple services, but they held meetings in one another's homes and sometimes in Solomon's Porch, a cloister in front of the temple.

Such self-segregation tended both to weaken their attachment to their former associations and to bring them under ever increasing suspicion. After Stephen's bold assertions about the temple and the law, the mild policies of the Jewish authorities became suddenly drastic. The crucifixion of Jesus had been the punishment of an individual, but the stoning of Stephen was the first blow in the crushing of a sect. The Sadducees, who controlled the temple and its wealth, and the Pharisees, who defended the law, united in a relentless campaign to eradicate the growing heresy. Saul was chosen for the task; there was none better qualified than he.[22]

Aided by his lieutenants, Saul swept Jerusalem like a mighty conflagration. More than four hundred synagogues were searched for heretics, especially for the followers of Stephen. Suspects were tracked to their homes like evil beasts to their lairs. Men and women whose only sin was that of believing that the Messiah had appeared were chained to one another and driven to prison[23] through lanes of mocking, spitting spectators. Sanhedrin and synagogue were kept busy with trials. As prisoners were brought forth from their dungeons, they were ordered to recant and to blaspheme the name of the crucified Nazarene.[24]*

---

* Not a Nazarene, but a Nazorean, a member of a Nazorean sect (Acts 24:5, 26:9; Matt 2:23). See further P. Parker *The Gospel Before Mark* (Chicago: University of Chicago Press, 1953) pp.1 45-99, 13-33. (GWB)

Some wretched souls destroyed their own self-respect by denying their Lord. Others refused to recant; and of these, some were remanded to prison, but others were sentenced to scourging. Doubtless there were many capital cases brought before the chief priests or Sanhedrin.[25] "When they were put to death, I gave my vote against them," said Saul.[26]

Scourgings were administered in the synagogues[27] to which the heretics belonged. Saul of course witnessed some of these scenes, glaring exultantly when excruciating pain drew recantation from unwilling lips, and scowling murderously when vicious blows yielded nothing but unwavering confessions of Jesus as the Messiah. Saul himself, like all other Pharisees of his time, was expecting the early appearance of the Messiah, who would make Judaism triumphant and vindicate Israel before the world, but he could not endure the profane declaration that the crucified felon of Nazareth was to fill that office. "Cursed be every one who hangs on a tree," Saul later quoted to the Galatians.[28]

Although Saul honestly believed that he was "offering service to God"[29] there was a secret uneasiness in his soul. Stephen haunted him; the cries of women dragged from their homes and children troubled him; the prayers of saints under torture saying, "Lord Jesus forgive Saul," smarted like blows of the scourges. The divine glory that shone in the faces of non-resisting victims burned into his soul like fire—it maddened him. "In raging fury against them, I persecuted them," said he.[30] Saul quickly filled Jerusalem with terror and swept it clean of heresy.

The Jews had long been subject to Rome, and the Sanhedrin was much restricted in its authority beyond the environs of Jerusalem, and even in that city itself. As soon, therefore, as the heretical Hellenists and other affected Jews became aware of their danger, those who were able to escape, fled to regions where Roman or other authority could protect tnem. Some found refuge far out in Judaea. Philip, one of Stephen's fellow deacons, and others, fled to Samaria; some went as far as Damascus. Unfortunately for Saul's plans, these refugees carried the new gospel with them, so that while he uprooted the seed in one city they planted it in a dozen others.[31] Luke seems to think that the apostles remained somewhere in Jerusalem throughout the persecution,[32] but this opinion may have grown out of his strong supernaturalism. According to Matthew and John, the apostles appear to have fled to Galilee after the crucifixion; and it is even more likely that they fled again after the stoning of Stephen.

But the persecution, however severe, did not last long, and perhaps Pilate's successor, or possibly Vitellius, the legate of Syria, may have restored order, making it safe for the less radical members of the young church to return to their homes. Those who did return quieted suspicion by living as strict Jews in all respects. They formed the Hebraistic or apostolic church of Jerusalem, over which James the brother of Jesus presided. They were Judaizers, who later sowed discord in other churches, and made endless trouble for Paul the apostle.

After his bloody whips had reached out to their limit from Jerusalem, "Saul, still breathing threats and murder against the disciples of the Lord, went to the high priest and asked him for letters to the synagogues at Damascus, so that if he found any belonging to the Way, men or women, he might bring them bound to Jerusalem."[33] Although the authority of the high priest was supposed to extend to the synagogues of all cities, however remote and in whatever land, yet letters to Joppa, Samaria, or Caesarea would have been useless. Extradition would have been opposed by the civil authorities, and Saul would have invited trouble for himself. At Damascus, however, political conditions were more favorable. Petra, the ethnarch of that city under King Aretas of Arabia, would probably not have interfered with a commission sent by the high priest to the synagogues, even if it had been given punitive powers; for the Jews were loyal to the king, who permitted them to observe their own customs without interference.

At that time, Damascus and environs had a Jewish population of perhaps more than thirty thousand—a fertile field for a new heresy. Ananias,[34] a man of unusual endowments was already at work there, and to Saul's mind he may have been a second Stephen who should be promptly silenced.

But Saul was not merely a tool of imperious masters, he was a framer of policy. The enraged Pharisees and the temple authorities were indeed glad to have his services, but Saul thought far less about helping them than about defending the faith of his fathers. Even when he requested letters to the synagogues of Damascus, he did not submit himself to orders but rather supported his own designs.

It was a long journey to Damascus. Preparations sufficient for six or eight days had to be made. Emergency food and water were necessary; also clothing, tents, and defensive weapons, for bands of robbers were not uncommon. Finally, a gruesome collection of clanking chains and manacles had to be taken for prospective prisoners.

On a mid-summer morning, Saul and his retinue, with their camels and asses, had assembled in the open space before the Damascus gate. When the heavy gates rolled inward, the company passed through into the great Damascus highway, recognized, but unquestioned, by the Roman sentries.

Having business of extreme urgency, Saul probably moved rapidly through the new country. He did not comment much on the flora and fauna of passing field and forest, pause to enjoy scenic splendors, or linger at many historic spots hallowed by the presence of famous men.

But environment, however familiar, is never a negligible factor to one who would understand the thoughts and moods of other men. A mounted officer near Bethel, a traveling prince near Neapolis, or an immaculate rabbi at Scythopolis might pass instantly from Saul's conscious mind, only to reappear as a celestial personage in some dream or vision. The shimmering light of the rising run, the long cool shadows of early morning, the strange clearness of distant rural sounds, and the skylark's welcome to the return of day, all made their imprint upon the subconsciousness of the mad emissary of the Jewish hierarchy.

The bright verdure and deep color of spring had faded away several weeks before Saul had begun his journey, and the gray rocks of the countless rounded hills stared desolately through their patchy covering of weeds and thorns. The ever-present olive groves with their misty, dull-green foliage barely relieved the scene. Beyond Bethel towards the great low plains, however, nature gradually became more lively and plumed the landscape with oak and oleander, myrtle and mulberry, palm and pomegranate, almond and apricot. On the hills of Bethel Saul's murderous haste must have suffered a reverent pause. There was the spot where Jacob had stood enthralled viewing the land of promise. In one direction was the amazing vista that faded towards the great Plain of Esdraelon, Mount Carmel, and the Mediterranean Sea; in another, across the valley of Jazrael lay the pellucid waters of the Sea of Galilee, while towards the east stretched the long green valley of the Jordan.

Saul could not pass through the vicinity of Bethel without a feeling of expectant awe. There was the place of the ladder that reached up to heaven.[35] Jacob had seen it; saw the angels of God ascending and descending on it; heard Jehovah speaking from heaven above it. Saul perhaps dreamed sometimes—dreamed of seeing angels, of hearing God speak, and even of visiting heaven. Might he not see that ladder? He lifted his eyes—so had thousands done before him.[36] But Jereboam's golden calf had desecrated the spot.[37]

Onward he pressed towards Shechem—or Sychar—in the valley of blessing and curse, the fertile valley of perennial springs, the valley of gardens and orchards, song birds and fragrant flowers. Shechem, near the site of the terebinth tree under which Abraham built his altar; Shechem, near the site of Jacob's well, the well where Jesus scandalized himself by talking with a notorious Samaritan woman;[38] Shechem, at the base of the twin mountains, Ebal and Gerezim, that stood as eternal witnesses to the solemn pledges of Israel made in loud amens across the sacred ark and a smoking altar to keep the law of Jehovah forever.[39]

As the caravan descended into the Valley of Jezrael, it entered more and more into the tropical climate that had crept far northward up through the deep valley of the Jordan, bringing with it the palm and the rush, the crane, and the stork. At Bethshan, Saul may have recalled with unpleasant emotions that his name-father's headless body had once been hanged by the Philistines against the wall of that city.[40]

It was a rugged country east of the River Jordan and up through Gaulonitis. Many rocky valleys had to be crossed during the slow ascent of nearly three thousand feet. High on a great open barren plain, Saul now moved directly towards Damascus—the phoenix of many destructions and as many resurrections, the city that had crept out of the fastnesses of the Lebanon Ranges long before man began recording history. To Isaiah, Damascus was "The Head of Syria;"[41] Jeremiah spoke of it as "The City of Praise;"[42] the Emperor Julian termed it "The Eye of the Whole East;" and the Arab poets sang of it as "The Pearl of the desert."

Variety now began to give place to monotony. The jasmine and the oleander, the oak and the mulberry were seen no more. Refreshing mountaintops and fertile valleys now gave place to a vast dreary plain through which protruded here and there masses of black basalt sheltering clumps of Syria's many cruel thorns. Here garments were readjusted and headdresses changed to meet the conditions of the sun-scorched plain. As Saul surveyed the direction of his journey, the trail faded out into nothing on a far low horizon, and this it did hour after hour on into the second day. Eastward, there was no relief from this monotony, but to the west, the faraway summit of Mount Hermon's triple crown slid slowly southward.

Though naturally hardy, Saul had not acquired the toughness of the nomad and his journey to Damascus became a punishment. The sun burned fiercely upon him and smote him as it rebounded from the heated earth. Lines of light shot before his eyes, causing his thoughts to soar in to confusion like leaves in a whirlwind. His companions were more inured than he to exposure and were less affected by weariness and heat. Moreover, Saul was a devout Pharisee. He had two days of fasting during his journey, and one of these may have fallen on the day before he reached Damascus. If so, he was a subject of heat, weariness, hunger, and intense religious emotion.

Before the fierce apostle of the Sanhedrin reached Damascus, some mysterious force seized him, nullified the orders under which he journeyed, shattered his most cherished beliefs, wrecked all his ambitious plans, and cast him to earth as an empty vessel. It all happened somewhere near Damascus, no one knows where. The old tradition says at Kaukab, ten miles or more south of the city; but the modern view places the scene in the foot-hills of Anti-Lebanon, near the gorge of the Barada at a point overlooking the unforgettable glory of the Ghutah or Damascus Plain.

Concerning the story of what happened, Saul's own account has not been preserved beyond a few allusions in his existing letters: "But when he who had set me apart before I was born, and had called me through his grace was pleased to reveal his Son to me, in order that I might preach him

among the Gentiles:[43] last of all, as to one untimely born, he appeared also
me;[44] Have I not seen Jesus our Lord?[45] For it is God who said, 'Let light
shine out of darkness, who has shone in our hearts to give the light of the
knowledge of the glory of God in the face of Christ' "[46] Of course many
other passages imply that something had happened, but they are not
descriptive. The author of First Timothy also puts a few words into Paul's
mouth: "I thank him who has given me strength for this, Christ Jesus our
Lord, because he judged me faithful by appointing me to his service,
though I formerly blasphemed and persecuted and insulted him; but I
received mercy because I had acted ignorantly in unbelief."[47]

But it is to the book of the Acts that the student must turn for the only
detailed account of Saul's unparalleled experience.* There the story is told
three times with slight variations,[48] the first account being as follows:
"Now as he journeyed he approached Damascus, and suddenly a light
from heaven flashed about him. And he fell to the ground and heard a
voice saying to him, 'Saul, Saul, why do you persecute me?' And he said,
'Who are you, Lord?' and He said, 'I am Jesus whom you are persecuting;
but rise and enter the city, and you will be told what to do.' The men who
were traveling with him stood speechless, hearing the voice, but seeing no
one. Saul arose from the ground; and when his eyes were opened, he could
see nothing; so they led him by the hand and brought him into Damascus.
And for three days he was without sight, and neither ate nor drank."

But the author of the Acts was not writing as a critical historian; he is
simply picturing a remarkable occurrence as he thinks it should have
happened. He perhaps knew only that Saul claimed to have seen Jesus,
and that the vision occurred on the Damascus road. His picture, therefore,
is a literary embellishment of these two facts; but it satisfied the writer's
own credulity, met the demands of a miracle-loving age, and provided an
adequate explanation of a marvelous transformation of religious faith.
Moreover, the picture employs the accepted language of scripture: Jesus as
the Son of God would appear as a blinding celestial light;[49] the beholder in
fear and reverence would prostrate himself upon the ground;[50] and the
blinded subject would require a leader, and finally a healer.

The variations in the three accounts are entirely unimportant. They
simply show that the author was not taking his own descriptions too
seriously. The modern reader, therefore, is free to explain the event in
accordance with the light of his own age. It is, however, not an empty

---

* Only in Acts, where there is a
concentration of events around two cities,
Jerusalem and Rome, is Paul said to have
received his revelation on the road to
Damascus from Jerusalem. Paul said after
his revelation he went into Arabia and then
returned to Damascus, implying that he
had been there in the first place. It is more
likely that Paul's revelation took place in
Damascus than "on the way" to Damascus
(Gal 1:16-17). (GWB)

event, for behind it, and in it, and through it are spiritual values that have shaken the world into a consciousness of its sin and its need of a Redeemer.

What actually happened at that undetermined spot on that undetermined Damascus road? Luke's description is imaginary and dramatic. The reader must decide for himself whether Saul's vision was truly objective, convincing the mind through the eye and ear; or whether it was mysteriously subjective, a product of the mind itself; and, if subjective, what were the contributing factors. But interesting as this problem is, it matters little what solution is proposed. The great fact will still remain that Saul was completely and overwhelmingly convinced that he had seen Jesus. So profound was this conviction that to the end of his life it was the impelling force back of all his indefatigable labor. He never doubted. "Have I not seen Jesus our Lord?"[51] said he with the emphasis of finality. Out of his belief grew his gripping theology, his elevated sociology, and his incomparable ethics. Because of it he toiled with superhuman strength and unflagging endurance, bore all kinds of scathing defamation, and suffered inhuman persecution—even unto death.

When it is remembered that Saul was a man of superior intellect, the mystery of a subjective vision clear enough to be taken by him as unquestionably objective creates no small degree of wonder. And the wonder increases boundlessly when the fact is noted that no other vision ever affected so profoundly the life of any other man, or left such beneficient results in its wake. So sure was Saul of the fact of the resurrection of Jesus that upon it he boldly, if not rashly, staked the authority of his apostleship, the truth of his message, and the hope of the Christian life.[52]

In Saul's day, visions were common occurrences; there was in fact a contagion of them, and they were taken seriously as one of the great facts of human experience. The background of current belief provided for them, and religious teachers aspired to their attainment. They originated then as they do now, falling under the same psychological and physiological laws. Many of them were simply misinterpreted sights and sounds; some were mental pictures conceived in physical fatigue or strong emotion; and others perhaps were vivid dreams.

There is a kind of dream that fits Saul's experience almost perfectly. It occurs at the moment of waking, in the light of day, and incorporates sounds that are really heard and light that is truly felt.

Let it be supposed that Saul before beginning the last stage of his journey indulged in a roadside siesta under his tent after the manner of oriental travelers. He had been thinking of Jesus, the midday sun was oppressive, his servants spoke his name; "Saul, Saul," perhaps to wake him. Thus all the elements of his vision were present and were incorporated in a momentary dream, which, as usual, seemed to cover appreciable time.

Such dreams are often overwhelmingly realistic because of their objective associations. In Saul's day they might have been taken for true visions. Thus Saul could have truly heard a voice and felt an impact of light, but his dream exaggerated both.

That the persecutor was blinded is doubtless partly true, but the vision was not necessarily the cause. Even a single day's journey over a hot plain, like that south of Damascus, will blear the eyes of one who is unaccustomed to such travel, and the effect may remain for a much longer time than three days. The author of the Acts does not falsify in his statements, he simply draws up a dramatic narrative from such facts and traditions as have reached him, and adjusts it to the prevailing ideas of supernatural events. His picture, though drawn in terms of ancient interpretation, is none too vivid since it would, indeed, be an awful shock to any man to find himself suddenly face to face with a resurrected figure garbed in the authority of heaven. Being a Hellenist, Saul must have shared in the universal belief that the disembodied spirits of men wandered about on the earth with considerable freedom, often manifesting their presence to the living; and being a Pharisee he believed also in the possibility of the resurrection of the body. He was therefore easily convinced that he had seen Jesus.

It is not necessary to suppose that Saul was more credulous than other men. He lived in an unscientific age when mysterious occurrences were supposed to have supernatural origins, and when devout pagans by silent meditation in their temples, or by induced ecstasy, trance, or frenzy were getting thrilling visions of favorite gods who imparted information and gave advice. Thus Apuleius had no difficulty in getting into communication with Isis, who visited him in dreams in the quiet of a darkened room. Ancient literature—Jewish, Pagan, and Christian— abounds with stories of the marvelous, of voices and visions, portents and miracles. It was not difficult for the Jews to believe that both Simon the just and John Hyrcanus had heard the voice of God in the temple,[53] nor for Herod Antipas to believe that John the Baptist had risen from the dead,[54] nor for an assembly of five hundred members of the early church to believe that they had been granted a vision of their risen Lord;[55] nor even for the once incredulous James[56] to believe that his crucified brother had appeared to him.[57]

While Saul regarded his vision on the Damascus road as having the same objective value as that of the Christophanies experienced by the Twelve,[58] yet in his extant letters he says but little about it, and what he does say relates to it chiefly as a subjective revelation. Nevertheless the vision marked the turning point in his religious career, and the starting point of his revolutionary theology.

According to Luke, Saul, with his head bowed to the earth, asked two questions: "Who are you Lord?"[59] and "What shall I do, Lord?"[60] It was as if a mighty engine had been thrown suddenly into reverse; the threatening persecutor had become a trembling petitioner. At the command of Jesus, Saul rose to his feet; he opened his eyes; he was blind. He could neither walk nor ride alone. His companions led him by the hand. In Damascus, he lodged with Judas, who was probably an anti-Christian Pharisee of wealth and prominence, a suitable host for an eminent guest, and who lived on or near the street called Straight. There he prayed, and refused to eat or drink. After three days,[61] Saul saw in a vision a man who put his hand upon him to restore his sight.

At the same time in another part of the city, Ananias, one of the disciples who was to have been sought out and taken back to Jerusalem in chains, was commanded in a vision to find Saul and to restore his sight. He hesitated, but on hearing in his vision that Saul was a chosen instrument of the Lord, he hastened to perform his duty. Standing over the blind man he said: "Brother Saul, the Lord Jesus who appeared to you on the road by which you came, has sent me that you may regain your sight and be filled with the Holy Spirit." And Luke adds that "immediately something like scales fell from his eyes and he regained his sight. Then he rose and was baptized, and took food and was strengthened.[62]

If Saul's eyesight was temporarily affected by the glare of the desert, a few years of tradition about it in the first century would magnify the malady and provide for it a miraculous cure. It is such a tradition that Luke has adopted, or that he has used as the basis of his accounts. That Saul and Ananias should be brought together by visions is Luke's own device for providing effective literary detail and for giving support to Saul's apostolic claims. He uses the same method again in his apology for Gentile equality when he brings Cornelius and Peter together.[63]

While Luke, who is remarkably accurate in his use of names, gives no facts about Judas, he calls Ananias "a disciple,[64] a devout man according to the law, well spoken of by all the Jews who lived there. "[65] Tradition also neglects Judas, but overreaches Luke and attempts to reconstruct history by making Ananias one of the "Seventy" disciples, bishop of Damascus, and finally a martyr. Saul himself never mentions either of them. In fact he never acknowledges any man as having contributed anything to his apostolic equipment. He claimed that his call and his instructions had come directly and solely from the risen Jesus.

According to Luke's story, Saul was baptized three days after Jesus had appeared to him, which would indicate that his conversion had taken place within that time, or rather, at the end of it. But the story must not be dismissed in so brief a form. Saul, indeed, believed that he had seen Jesus. That much of his experience was instantaneous; but to pass from hatred to love, to shake off the prejudices of a lifetime, and to reconstruct his conception of the Messiah would require a longer period than three days, even under the shock of a miracle. There must have been much previous thinking that prepared the way for his vision and the resulting conversion. And there must have been much after-thought before he became clearly conscious of his apostolic call, and before he perfected the message that has since become the world's great storehouse of theology.

Saul was familiar with the teachings and practices of the new Jesus-sect, and must have heard and seen much that later forced its way into his reasoning. It would be impossible for a man of his breadth of mind and depth of sympathy to remain unaffected by the sublime faith of his victims, by their steadfast confession, their unaffected prayers for their persecutors, and their patient nonresistance under torture even unto death.

That Saul's legal rigidity was somewhat unstabilized by the scenes connected with Stephen's death can hardly be doubted. The young persecutor had extinguished a light that was greater than his own. He felt it, he knew it; but the law sanctioned the deed, even commanded it. And it is conceivable that the forebearance and patience of the benevolent Gamaliel, his former teacher, and the conversion of his friend Joseph Barnabas were active factors in preparing his mind for a crisis.

But another, and even more important factor, that may have been operating in the persecutor's mind to produce for him a vision of a conquering Christ instead of a fleeing Jesus, was his own unsatisfactory struggle for perfect righteousness—that very righteousness which he thought should rule in the lives of men as citizens of the approaching Kingdom of God. The sacred law under which he was living was, in fact, regarded by him as good, and even spiritual,[66] but for that very reason incapable of operating in human hearts. It could reveal the fact of sin and condemn it,[67] but could not overcome man's inclination to live in it. Can the law do no more for a man than to tell him that he is a sinner? Has it no power to nullify sin and death? Is it no better than a helpless physician standing by the bedside of a patient and saying, "You have a fatal disease?"

If Saul did not struggle with this problem of righteousness before his Christ-vision, he did soon after it; for he solves it in his theology by making Jesus, whom he accepted as the Christ, to be "the end of the law."[68] Had he not solved the problem, his preaching would have been no better than the proclamation of another world ruler. Man would have been left to struggle and die in his sins. In his desperate mental conflict he shows that in the law which he had been observing the Pharasaic strictness was in itself a disappointment and required a complement in a death-conquering Messiah.[69]

Luke's narrative overlooks the fact of Saul's long struggle in order to stress a seemingly miraculous occurrence, and yet when quoting the Greek proverb, "it hurts you to kick against the goads"[70] hints that a long rebellious struggle had been waged in Saul's mind against certain powerful inner promptings, even before he met with Jesus near Damascus. Saul's Christophany, therefore, which was the culmination of many antecedent influences and much thinking, precipitated the whole messianic problem, which in turn was resolved after a time by a sudden leap of thought, a flash of intuition, that revealed Jesus to him in a new role, giving a profound meaning to his death, making him the fulfillment of the Law and the link of righteousness between God and man.

REFERENCES
Chapter 4

1. Acts 6:11-14.
2. Acts 5:40; 4:17.
3. Acts 5:38.
4. Acts 1:11-15.
5. Cf. Luke 3:2; John 18:13, 24; Acts 23:2; 24:1.
6. Cf. Jer. 7:11; Mark 11:17.
7. Acts 6:5.
8. Acts 6:9.
9. Acts 6:9.
10. Acts 6:10.
11. Acts 8:1; 26:10.
12. Acts 6:15.
13. John chaps. 14-17.
14. Acts 7:2-53.
15. Acts 7:56.
16. Acts 7:57.
17. Lev. 24:13-16.
18. Acts 7:58.
19. Deut. 17:7; cf. John 8:7.
20. Acts 7:59-60.
21. Cf. Acts 22:20.
22. Acts 26:10. See also Acts 8:3; 9:1, 13, 21; 22:4, 19; 26:10, 11; I Cor. 15:9; Gal. 1:13, 23; Phil. 3:6, I Tim. 1:13.
23. Acts 22:4.
24. Acts 26:10-11.
25. Acts 9:21.
26. Acts 26:10.
27. Matt. 10:17.
28. Gal. 3:13; Deut. 21:23.
29. John 16:2; Acts 26:9.
30. Acts 26:11.
31. Acts 8:4.
32. Acts 8:1, 14; Luke 24:49.
33. Acts 9:1-2, 14; 26:5, 10, 12.
34. Acts 9:10-18.
35. Gen. 28:12.
36. Judges 20:18, 26; 21:2; Ps. 121.
37. I Kings 12:28, 29.
38. John 4:6-11.
39. Deut. 27 and 28; Josh 8:30-35.
40. I Sam. 31:10-13.
41. Isa. 7:8.
42. Jer. 49:25.
43. Gal. 1:15-16.
44. I Cor. 15:8.
45. I Cor. 9:1.
46. I Cor. 4:6.
47. I Tim. 1:12-13.
48. Acts, chapters 9, 22, 26.
49. Cf. Ex. 24:17; 33:17-23; 34:29-35; Heb. 12:29.
50. Gen. 17:3.
51. I Cor. 9:1.
52. I Cor. 15:12-19.
53. Josephus. *Antiquities.* XIII. 10. Sec. 3, 4,6.
54. Mark 6:16.
55. I Cor. 15:6.
56. John 7:5.
57. I Cor. 15:7.
58. Acts 1:21, 22; I Cor. 9:1; 15:5-8.
59. Acts 9:5.
60. Acts 22:10.
61. Cf. Matt. 12:40.
62. Acts 9:17-19.
63. Acts 10.
64. Acts 9:10.
65. Acts 22:12.
66. Rom. 7:12-16.
67. Rom. 7:7.
68. Rom. 10:4.
69. Rom. 7.
70. Acts 26:14; Pindar. *The Odes of Pindar, Pythian Ode* II. Line 173; Oakes and O'Neill eds. *The Complete Greek Drama.* Euripides, *Bacchae.* Line 791; Aeschylus, *Agamemnon,* Line 1623.

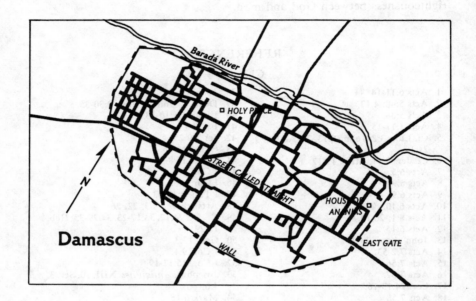

Damascus

CHAPTER

5

Gate of Damascus

Damascus and Arabia

WORD OF SAUL'S APPROACH to Damascus doubtless caused consternation among the believers, some of whom were probably refugees from the persecution in Jerusalem; but before he entered the gates of the city the story of his divine arrest had filtered through the Jewish quarter, quieting fear and exciting wonder. Saul had come as the emissary of the high priest with full authority to decide on the orthodoxy of the Damascus synagogues and with him was a company of Temple police. But Saul had dismissed them all; he had returned his apostolic commission to the high priest, sent a report of his experience to the Jewish council, and announced his adherence to the Jesus cult. Damascus rejoiced, Jerusalem raged, and Tarsus wept.

In Damascus, the followers of Jesus had gained a new adherent, but they doubted and trembled. He who had been their most powerful adversary was now to be their advocate. In Jerusalem, Judaism had lost its ablest defender, and men now spat at the name of Saul the apostate. Death awaited him, for he was now condemnable by the very arguments by which he himself had condemned others. In Tarsus, an aged father and mother had lost a son. They were prostrated with grief and disappointment because Saul had disgraced himself and dishonored them by calling a notorious sacrileger, the Messiah.

53

When Saul emerged from the house of Judas, Damascus saw a man who was in the midst of a marvelous transformation. Saul the fierce high-minded apostle of the Sanhedrin was becoming Paul the humble teacher of salvation through divine grace. A great intuitional basal thought, "Jesus the Christ, the Son of God," had taken possession of his mind, and he was eager to find a place of solitude where he could expand this thought into a consistent system of doctrine.

Perhaps he delayed long enough to visit the synagogues in company with Ananias, for Luke says, "And in the synagogues immediately he proclaimed Jesus, saying 'He is the Son of God.' "[1] But the delay could not have been long, for Saul himself does not mention it except to say in his letter to the Galatians that "I went away into Arabia."[2] He had seen the Son of God and now held a commission from Him. Only the mystic cloud of the golden sunset over the Anti-Lebanon, and the whispering stars of solemn night harmonized in any way with his new thought—"And the dead in Christ will rise first; then we who are alive, who are left, shall be caught up together with them in the clouds to meet the Lord in the air;"[3] "for star differs from star in glory, So also is it with the resurrection of the dead."[4]

To have tarried in Damascus, or to have returned to Jerusalem, would have been fatal. Saul knew that within three weeks orders for his arrest would reach Damascus and that he should be taken back to Jerusalem in chains. Within a few hours thereafter he would die as Stephen had. He was no longer the pursuer but the pursued. He fled to Arabia, not as a coward but as a weaponless man who would save his life for fiercer combat.

Arabia? Where was Arabia, and in what part of it was refuge to be found? In history the name covers different areas, even including Damascus. In a general way it occupied the greater part of the region lying between the Euphrates river and the Red Sea.[5] But the exact place of Saul's seclusion is unknown, although his own words, "went away into Arabia" seem to imply that it was not far from Damascus. Had he been a man of romantic tastes, he might have gone to Mount Sinai where Moses spent forty days with God,[6] or to some other holy spot, but it is more likely that he trusted himself to the austere hospitality[7] of some ascetic Essene community a few days' journey from Damascus.

Notwithstanding that Luke was not writing a biography, it is remarkable that he makes no reference to this sojourn; for here it must have been that Saul received the first of his many revelations. Here he entered a unique theological seminary—he the first and only pupil, Jesus the first and only teacher. In his vision by the Damascus road he had been convinced that a resurrection from the dead had occurred and this in its turn proved that Jesus was the Messiah, the Son of God. And it did more, for it required that the terms "Messiah" and "Son of God" should coalesce in the character of Jesus and take on higher meanings than they bore in the Old Testament and in the apocryphal writings, where the Messiah was only vaguely more than a natural scion of David's line, and where "son of God" normally referred to the King,[8] who enjoyed the special favor of God.

In his Arabian retreat Saul wrestled with the perplexing problem that arose from his acceptance of Jesus. Fasting and excluding the world from his thoughts until he felt himself mystically alone, he sought the presence of the risen Jesus. Praying as Jesus had done in Gethsemane, he attained such states of religious ecstasy that he seemed to have passed into a divine atmosphere where peace took possession of his soul. It was then that his thoughts seemed inspired by the presence of Jesus, and he could say, as he did later, "For I would have you know, brethren, that the gospel which was preached by me is not man's gospel. For I did not receive it from man, nor was I taught it, but it came through a revelation of Jesus Christ."[9]

Saul was entirely honest in his claim that his gospel had come directly from his Lord, for among both Jews and Gentiles the psychology of the day recognized the ecstatic state as a medium of revelation. The depth of his conviction is revealed in his letter to the Galatians, where he ventured to anathematize any one, himself included, who might dare to preach any other gospel than that committed to him.[10] So sure was he about the authoritative character and completeness of his revelation that he felt no need of instruction from the other apostles. In fact he must have regarded the gospel message of the Twelve as incomplete. Theirs was only a national, not a world message; only a vague expectation, not a philosophic system.

But what a marvelous gospel Saul brought forth from the lonely rocky wilderness of Arabia! A great universal redemptive plan that brought man and God together without violence to human nature, or impairment of divine justice. It was not a cold passionless philosophy, nor a wearisome religion of magic rituals. It was instead a gospel overflowing with love, hope, joy, peace, enthusiasm, victory, and glory; a gospel that made life beautiful and desirable, and robbed tribulation and death of their power and terror; a gospel that lifted religion to new and vastly grander heights.

But his theological structure was of necessity built upon the fixed opinions of his time, and was fashioned from existing material. Thus he accepted the cosmogony and pneumatology of his day, and though he drew chiefly upon Jewish material, his letters show traces of Gnostic, Stoic, and perhaps other foreign elements. Then, too, his revelation left many details to be worked out later, some of them long after, as exigencies of his missionary labors.

The only clue to the length of time spent by Saul in seclusion is found in his letter to the Galatians,[11] where he says, "nor did I go up to Jerusalem to those who were apostles before me; but I went away into Arabia; and again I returned to Damascus. Then after three years I went up to

Jerusalem to visit Cephas." From these words it may be assumed that the greater part of three years was spent in Arabia, and a year or more in labor in Damascus. Certainly the animosity of Jerusalem could not have subsided greatly in less time, and many months would have been required to bring a mass of new theological ideas into such consistent interrelationship that they could be defended before both Jews and Gentiles.

But whatever the length of time, Saul came forth a new man,[12] as one born anew,[13] as one raised from the dead,[14] as one newly created.[15] He had dwelt in the mystical presence of the Son of God until he could say, "it is no longer I who live, but Christ who lives in me."[16]

Having discovered what he believed was the purpose of God in permitting the Messiah to suffer death, Saul felt an immediate apostolic urge to proclaim to the world the new way of righteousness and salvation—the way of the Cross. He was at all times remarkably swift in his decisions and his transitions from faith to action were instantaneous. His mind had no room for motionless creeds, to believe was to act. He may have proclaimed his gospel first to the white-robed Essenes who had given him shelter; but these being few in number, he chose Damascus as his first important field of labor: "I went away into Arabia, and again I returned unto Damascus." He dared not labor in Jerusalem and, besides, that field was the headquarters of the other apostles.

When Saul returned to Damascus he was perhaps thirty-five years of age, in the very prime and vigor of manhood. He was buoyant, eager, confident. He now believed himself to be an apostle of the Messiah, a claim that was soon to be challenged and to require constant defense but which was the only claim great enough to satisfy his prodigious energy. He now had a great, definite, urgent mission, and was fully conscious of his responsibility. "Woe unto me if I preach not the gospel," he said later.

Damascus was a city of small area, scarcely that of a good farm and less than three miles in perimeter, but within its massive walls with their five score and more towers it fairly bulged with population. Seven or eight gates led into the various sections of the city. Saul perhaps entered by the one in the eastern wall. This was the triple gate that led directly into Straight Street, the one great avenue of the city. This street was divided lengthwise into three lanes by four colonnades of Corinthian columns, the side lanes for vehicular and animal traffic, and the covered middle one for pedestrians. A Roman arch spanned the street about midway between the ends.

Somewhere the returning apostle entered a narrow street that led to the Jewish quarter. He was seeking the home of Ananias. There, Saul would hear the news of what had happened during his absence, what steps the authorities at Jerusalem had taken for his apprehension, and how the local council, or lesser sanhedrin, had regarded his conversion. Ananias, on his part, would hear the story of his guest's revelation and get a full outline of his theology. It may well be imagined that, while Ananias respected Saul's learning and accepted the account of his Christophany, he nevertheless found it difficult to agree with the implications of his revelation: that, if Christ was the fulfillment of the Mosaic Law, then the observance of that law should cease with the advent of Christ. "Can it be possible," Ananias might have exclaimed, "that the holy altar at Jerusalem is to be forsaken and our ancient sacred rites of the sanctuary are to be abandoned!" "Yes," Saul would have replied, "their purpose has been accomplished. They simply anticipated a great final sacrifice that would be holy enough to atone for all sin for all time. Christ is that sacrifice." "But what shall we do with our holy books?" Ananias would continue. To which Saul would reply, "They are sacred history; their moral and religious precepts remain in force forever, and it will be in the nature of the 'new man in Christ Jesus' to obey them with delight."

Saul now girded himself for his Herculean task. He was the recipient of a special message, broader and fuller than that preached by the Twelve. "My gospel," he called it;[17] "the good news of God;" "the good news of Christ;" "The good news of our Lord Jesus;" "the good news of the glory of Christ;" "the good news of the grace of God." He held also an apostolic commission that he regarded as being fully equal in authority to that of the Twelve:[18] "Called to be an apostle, set apart for the gospel of God;"[19] "called by the will of God to be an apostle of Christ Jesus;"[20] "an apostle of Christ Jesus by the will of God;"[21] "an apostle . . . through Jesus Christ and God the Father."[22] He knew that the validity of both his gospel and his commission would be called in question, for visions and revelations were easy to doubt but difficult to prove. And he knew, too, that his message was full of violent explosives that might at any moment wreck his whole career.

Saul's apostolic consciousness doubtless began to develop very soon after his vision of Jesus and matured in Arabia. That he should extend his mission to the Gentiles was a thought that must have developed immediately out of his apostolic consciousness. The Lukan stories carry it back to his conversion, just as the Galatian letter sees a pre-natal preparation for his whole career.[23] The story of his trance in the Temple,[24] at the time of his first visit there after his conversion, contains a charge supposed to have been uttered by Jesus: "Depart: for I will send you far away to the Gentiles," which perhaps points to the moment when the inclusion of the Gentiles in the full benefits of the gospel clarified itself beyond a doubt in his mind. The question was precipitated at that time by the bitter and unalterable antagonism of the Jews to Saul himself, who was regarded as nothing better than a presumptuous imposter. Later, when the church at Antioch appealed to him for assistance,[25] he discovered his full mission as an apostle but he never permitted anyone to forget that he held his commission, not from man, not even from the Twelve, as Matthias did,[26] but from Jesus Christ alone. The fruit of his labors was his proof; "for you are the seal of my apostleship in the Lord," he once wrote to the Corinthians.[27]

When Saul went forth from the house of Ananias, he had for his hail the cry of the messenger: "Besorah," "Euaggelion," "Good Tidings."[28] He did not know that the word would reverberate through the world for two thousand years. To him its limit would come within his own lifetime. John the Baptist and Jesus had used the more somber word, "Repent,"[29] and drove directly at the heart and will of sinners. But Saul, full of the joy and light of the mystical indwelling of the Christ, proclaimed the infinite saving grace of God.

The disciples in Damascus were still faithful to the synagogue, but as in other cities, held daily meetings of their own in their homes. At these meetings a communal meal was served, known as the "agape", or "Love,"[30] a feast that included a memorial of the Last Supper. These were watch meetings in which the "brethren" engaged in exhortations and in prayers for the speedy return of Jesus to the earth to establish his kingdom. Some of these brethren may have been among those who many months before watched at the temple for the sudden appearance of the Messiah,[31] and in fact, several may have carried on their bodies the blue checkered welts of scourgings that had been administered under Saul's own lowering glare.

Saul's first appearance at an agape must have provoked curiosity and wonder, and the story of his conversion and his subsequent revelations must have been received eagerly. In the synagogue, however, his appearance would be regarded with suspicion, and the story of his conversion would create a variety of reactions, all of which he could read in the eyes of his audience. For perhaps eighteen months he proclaimed his gospel. Believing that the end of the age was drawing near, he strove to have men prepare for that event by acknowledging the spiritual Jesus as their Lord. He had no plan for a church whose history would extend through thousands of years. Time was short, the last trumpet[32] was almost due, and temporal things were soon to pass away.*

---

* The last trumpet referred to the jubilee trumpet (Lev 25:10-17) which should announce that all Jews who were indebted to other Jews would have their debts cancelled and their land that was mortgaged returned. This logic was transferred to the national eschatology, understanding that on the jubilee year diaspora Jews ("captives") would return to the promised land, which would then be free from foreign rule. That which would pass away would be the Roman rule. (GWB)

In one short sentence Luke sums up the work of Saul in Damascus: "But Saul increased all the more in strength, and confounded the Jews who lived in Damascus by proving that Jesus was the Christ."[33] These words show that the apostle labored successfully, and with his accustomed vehemence.

History is silent about much that must have happened to the apostle during his ministry in this ancient city, but the very success of the gospel must have brought him unceasing trouble. His powerful defense of the Messiahship of Jesus made enemies for him among those who would not believe, yet could not refute his arguments; and the drift of the Gentiles of the synagogues towards the new faith certainly enraged those Jews who would "encompass sea and land to make one proselyte." Josephus says that most of the Gentile women were "addicted to the Jewish religion," and it is known that from the beginning the Gentiles of the synagogues were those most easily won over to the new faith.

And then when Saul began adding to his proclamation of the Messiah such theological deductions as that the law of work was abrogated by the law of faith, it was certain that the local council would condemn his doctrine as heresy. But most serious of all would be the lingering antagonism in Jerusalem which would find its way to Damascus, transforming opposition into persecution.

It is almost certain that the local council or lesser sanhedrin eventually ordered Saul's arrest, found him guilty of its charges, and condemned him to be scourged. "Five times I have received at the hands of the Jews the forty lashes less one,"[34] wrote the apostle some years later. Of these scourgings, one may well have occurred in Damascus. And when it would be found that scourging failed to silence the intrepid and incorrigible advocate of heresy, then the decree of death[35] would be passed upon him.

Upon his arrest, excitement in the Jewish quarter would become intense. The Jews, always demonstrative in both word and gesture, would soon collect into an ominous mob. Witnesses could easily be found among them, who would testify that Saul had been teaching doctrines subversive of the law; and his condemnation would quickly follow. Four men would execute the sentence of scourging, which, judging from the details given in the Mishna[36] would, in brief, be conducted somewhat as follows.

First, Saul would be examined for his power of resistance. If found to be below normal and likely to die under thirty-nine lashes, the number would be diminished. The judges, however, decided that he was of full strength. Meanwhile, the *chazzan* stood by toying with a scourge, a vicious instrument, having a short handle to which were attached two straps—one of ox-hide,[37] slit into four thongs, and one of ass-hide slit into two thongs, all bearing cruel knots at intervals. Saul knew how they would feel, he had seen the writhing agony of other men. The upper part of his body being bared, he was thrown supine, and his hands made fast to a low stake. The *chazzan* moved to his position.

"If you are not careful to do all the words of this Law,"[38] began the chief judge as he read from the Scriptures. At the same moment the second judge called out, "Strike him." Instantly the *chazzan* struck with all his force, and the third judge began to count. The flesh of Saul's breast quivered; it rose up in welts. Saul prayed, not because he lacked courage, for he rejoiced to suffer. It was like an atoning penance for his own cruel deeds.

At the thirteenth stroke the *chazzan* paused. Saul's breast was like a flame of fire and his breathing was laborious. His position was then changed, and the *chazzan* delivered thirteen stripes diagonally across Saul's back over the right shoulder. Again the *chazzan* changed his position, this time to strike over the left shoulder. The welts then crossed one another, cutting bloody diamonds upon the sufferer's back and multiplying his agony. Thirty-seven, thirty-eight, thirty-nine; Saul counted, but uttered no groan, betrayed no moral weakness. When his bruised hands were loosed from the stake, he arose pale and halting. There was no sullen scowl upon his countenance, he had suffered for his Lord, he had felt his Lord's sustaining presence.

The apostle's agony was not yet over. His garments now tortured his broken swollen flesh and for many days his cot offered him no position of rest. But Ananias ministered to him and prayed over him.

Saul was not the kind of man to be easily frightened, not one to be dissuaded from a line of duty. He believed in his apostleship and in his message, both of which excluded all consideration of ease and safety, except for life itself. He therefore continued to proclaim openly the less disturbing facts of his gospel and to give instructions privately in the intricacies of his theology to those who were willing to learn. But most of the Jews were obdurate. Not believing in the Messiahship of Jesus they, of course, could not be persuaded that the Mosaic institutions had been nullified by fulfillment. The council therefore decided that Saul had brought upon himself the penalty of death, and accordingly proceeded to seize him. The Jews in foreign cities were permitted, within certain limits, to govern themselves according to their own laws, but where the Romans exercised direct authority, a death sentence could not be executed without permission.

At this time, however, the government of Damascus was administered by a governor or ethnarch[39] under the king of Arabia, Aretas IV, whose capital and stronghold was the rock-bound city of Petra. The Jews therefore appealed to him for aid in their plans to apprehend Saul. It also happened that Herod Antipas, tetrarch of Galilee, had married a daughter of Aretas, but in A.D. 29 divorced her in order to marry Herodias, who had been the wife of his half brother Philip—the marriage of which John the Baptist and other strict Jews in general had disapproved.[40] Naturally Aretas took offense and a bitter quarrel ensued, ending in war. It is possible, therefore, that the ethnarch, without any personal ill will towards Saul, granted the request of the Jews in order to hold their friendship for his king in a time of war. He accordingly not only sanctioned a legal death, or assassination of Saul, but provided a garrison to patrol the city and to watch the gates for his capture, the Jews having furnished Saul's description to the sentries.

Saul was promptly notified by his friends. He would not flee from a scourging, but it was his duty to preserve his life. Day and night the gates of the city were watched and suspects closely questioned. Saul's work in Damascus was now at an end. To escape was his only hope.

Secretly he found his way to a friend whose house adjoined the city wall. There in the darkness and silence of night, the disciples, after a prayerful parting, lowered him through a window over the wall in a great rope hamper or basket. Saul called it a *sargane*, referring to its material or construction;[41] but Luke called it a *spuris*,[42] referring to its use as a container for grain and other provisions. Of course everyone recalled the scene, so engagingly pictured[43] of the two spies sliding down a rope through Rahab's window, and of the more serious scene[44] of David descending on a rope from his own window.

It is not difficult to picture Saul's uneasiness as he reached the ground. Like a hunted thing, he instinctively distorted his posture and disguised his walk. At any moment he might be seen and recognized. His greatest safety lay in reaching the western mountains. Onward through the night he fled, sometimes pausing for sounds of pursuers, always watchful of dangers ahead. When the gray dawn of morning began to illumine the snowy peaks of Hermon, he was mounting the welcome slopes of the Anti-Lebanon.

The hunted apostle now decided to go to Jerusalem for a conference with Peter. He had found in Damascus that the believers trained under the apostles were reluctant to free themselves from the bondage of the Mosaic Law and he suspected that the apostles themselves were unfriendly to his gospel. The Twelve were men of average intelligence, content to proclaim the Messiahship of Jesus without theological speculation, but Saul was a gifted man, and philosophically inclined. It was impossible for him to keep his gospel within the limits of the prevailing apocalyptic ideas. He had to know how the Kingdom of God would operate, how its laws could be justified, and what effect its coming would have on existing institutions.

Saul refers only incidentally to his conference with Peter: "Then after three years I went up to Jerusalem to visit Cephas, and remained with him fifteen days. But I saw none of the other apostles except James the Lord's brother." To this he adds: "Then I went into the regions of Syria and

Cilicia. And I was still not known by sight to the churches of Christ in Judaea; which were in Christ: they only heard it said, 'He who once persecuted us is now preaching the faith he once tried to destroy.' And they glorified God because of me."[45] Luke tells the story thus: "And when he had come to Jerusalem he attempted to join the disciples; and they were all afraid of him, for they did not believe that he was a disciple. But Barnabas took him, and brought him to the apostles, and declared to them how on the road he had seen the Lord, who spoke to him, and how at Damascus he had preached boldly in the name of Jesus. So he went in and out among them at Jerusalem, preaching boldly in the name of the Lord. And he spoke and disputed against the Hellenists; but they were seeking to kill him. And when the brethren knew it, they brought him down to Caesarea, and sent him off to Tarsus."[46]

Perhaps the same visit was in Luke's mind when he wrote the speech that Saul was supposed to have delivered at the time of his last arrest. "When I had returned to Jerusalem and was praying in the Temple, I fell into a trance, and saw him saying to me, 'Make haste and get quickly out of Jerusalem, because they will not accept your testimony about me' . . . And he said to me, 'Depart: for I will send you far away to the Gentiles,' "[47] And again, Luke has him say before Agrippa, "Wherefore, O king Agrippa, I was not disobedient to the heavenly vision, but declared first to those at Damascus, then at Jerusalem and throughout all the country of Judaea, and also to the Gentiles, that they should repent and turn to God . . . ."[48]

Luke in elaborating the limited data at his command a half century after the event, evidently uses tradition that may have belonged to some other date or that contained error such as naturally creeps into oral tradition. He was writing a conciliatory document and wished to present a true picture of Saul's spirit and daring, but fell into error about the apostle's movements. Thus Saul says that he saw only Cephas (Peter), and James the Lord's brother; but Luke seems to say that he had met the Twelve, or most of them. Saul says that he went from Jerusalem to Syria and Cilicia and was unknown by face to the churches of Judaea; but Luke says in one account that he had preached in Jerusalem, and, in another, that he had preached in both Jerusalem and Judaea.

Saul's very brief statements were made in defense of his doctrine, and he had no occasion to give details of his stay in Jerusalem. He may indeed have visited the synagogue of the Hellenists where Stephen had preached three years before and he may have seen Joseph Barnabas, who seems to have been an old friend and possibly a schoolmate in Jerusalem, or even in Tarsus. But Jerusalem was a dangerous place for Saul. The Sanhedrin was likely at any moment to order his arrest, mobs were ready to seize him on sight, and the Grecian Jews, most of all, were eager for his blood, for Saul himself was a Hellenist, and had been their leader at the time of Stephen's arrest.

Perhaps one of the most important conferences in the history of the early church was this fifteen-day session between Saul and Peter. It resulted in the recognition by the Jerusalem church of Saul as an evangelist. Although an enthusiastic understanding was not achieved, it enabled Saul to claim the advantage of unison with the Twelve in the work of spreading the gospel. Cooperation was difficult, however, as is clearly seen from the book of Acts, where Luke constantly and delicately strives to exhibit and preserve a relation of harmony between the apostolic and Pauline branches of the church.

Saul and Peter may have seen each other three or four years previously, and each may have recognized the other instantly at this meeting—Peter the fisherman, the "unlettered and provincial" man,[49] and Saul the tent maker, the man of "great learning."[50]

What did they talk about, the man who had denied his Lord,[51] and the man who had persecuted Him?[52] Both were already convinced that Jesus, the carpenter, was the "Son of Man," the Messiah; and both regarded themselves as his apostles. Certainly they discussed plans of cooperation, and then doubtless held long conversations about the death, resurrection, and manifestations of Jesus;[53] about his person, his work, and his imminent return. They would have much to say about the Messianic passages in the Hebrew canonical Scriptures, the testimony of the *Sibylline Oracles,* the *Book of Enoch,* the *Psalms of Solomon,* and other apocalyptic literature, and about the opinions of eminent rabbis. Saul would learn much about the earthly life of Jesus; and Peter, much about Saul's gospel.[54]

But the visit was short, for Saul's life was in danger. Luke said in one place[55] that the "brethren" saved his life by sending him away to Tarsus, and in another that Saul had received warning from his Lord in a trance as he prayed in the Temple and was told to leave Jersalem because the Jews would not receive testimony from him.[56] Saul was now a prophet without honor.[57] His former associates regarded him as an apostate, the church hesitated about receiving him as a disciple, no one called him an apostle, and no one endorsed his bold deductions from the accepted messianic beliefs. In fact the Twelve never took him into their circle and never gave him more than a reluctant recognition. Even Luke, his biographer, never calls him an apostle except in an ordinary sense along with Barnabas.[58] Nevertheless, Saul made a few friends in Jerusalem, who learning of the hatred seething against him, aided him to escape and sent him to Tarsus by way of Caesarea and the sea. Tarsus was then one of the cities of the region known as Syria and Cilicia.

REFERENCES
Chapter 5

1. Acts 9:20.
2. Gal. 1:17.
3. I Thess. 4:16-17.
4. I Cor. 15:41, 42.
5. Cf. Xenophon. *Anabasis* I. 5. Par. 1; Herodotus. *History of the Greeks*. II. 8; III. 5-9; Josephus. *Antiquities*. XIV. 1. Sec. 4.
6. Ex. 34:28.
7. Josephus. *Wars*. II. 8. Sec. 4, 6.
8. Ps. 2 and 110. See Louis F. Hartman, "Son of God," *Encyclopedic Dictionary of the Bible*, 2264-2270.
9. Gal. 1:11-12; cf. Eph. 3:3.
10. Gal. 1:8-9.
11. Gal. 1:17, 18.
12. Cf. Eph. 4:24.
13. Cf. John 3:3.
14. Cf. Eph. 5:14; Rom. 6:13.
15. Cf. II Cor. 5:17.
16. Gal. 2:20.
17. Rom. 2:16; 16:25.
18. Gal. 2:7-9.
19. Rom. 1:1.
20. I Cor. 1:1.
21. II Cor. 1:1; Eph. 1:1; Col. 1:1.
22. Gal. 1:1.
23. Gal. 1:15.
24. Acts 22:17-21.
25. Acts 11:25.
26. Acts 1:26.
27. I Cor. 9:2.
28. II Sam. 18:31.
29. Matt. 3:2; Luke 5:32.
30. Jude 12.
31. Mal. 3:1.
32. I Cor. 15:52.
33. Acts 9:22.
34. II Cor. 11:24.
35. Acts 9:23.
36. Mishnah *Makkoth* 3:10-14.
37. Isa. 1:3.
38. Deut. 28:58, 59.
39. II Cor. 11:32; Acts 9:23-25.
40. Mark 6:14-29.
41. II Cor. 11:33.
42. Acts 9:25.
43. Josh. 2:15.
44. I Sam. 19:12.
45. Gal. 1:18-19; 21-24.
46. Acts 9:26-30.
47. Acts 22:17-21.
48. Acts 26:19, 20.
49. Acts 4:13.
50. 26:24.
51. Mark 14:66-72.
52. Acts 9:5.
53. Gal. 1:18.
54. Rom. 2:16.
55. Acts 9:30.
56. Cf. Mark 6:4.
57. Cf. Mark 6:4.
58. Acts 14:14.

Cilician Gates

CHAPTER

6

Syria and Cilicia

WITHOUT ANOTHER WORD LUKE now leaves Saul in Tarsus, and permits ten years of history to elapse before bringing him again into his narrative. Saul, however, reports enough in his letters to show that during this period his labors in the Gospel were arduous and highly successful: "Then I went into the regions of Syria and Cilicia;"[1] "He who once persecuted us is now preaching the faith he once tried to destroy;"[2] "for he who worked through Peter for the mission to the circumcised worked through me also for the Gentiles."[3] Then, also, the letter sent out by the Council of Jerusalem was addressed to the Gentile converts in this very region where Saul had labored—"Antioch, and Syria and Cilicia."[4] And, again, on his second missionary tour he "went through Syria and Cilicia, strengthening the churches."[5]

It was perhaps in this period that Saul suffered most of his terrible scourgings, "forty lashes less one" of which he wrote.[6] And here, too, he may have suffered a number of other hardships enumerated in the same letter; a list long and terrible, narrated reluctantly as a rebuke to his critics: "with far greater labors, far more imprisonments, with countless beatings, and often near death. Five times I have received at the hands of the Jews the forty lashes less one. Three times I have been beaten with rods; once was I stoned. Three times I have been shipwrecked; a night and a day have I

67

been adrift at sea; on frequent journeys, in danger from rivers, danger from robbers, danger from my own people, danger from Gentiles, danger in the city, danger in the wilderness, danger at sea, danger from false brethren; in toil and hardship, through many a sleepless night, in hunger and thirst, often without food, in cold and exposure."[7] Saul was not boasting. The story of his sufferings was forced from him.[8] It was his reaction to a case of that deplorable tendency of men to spurn their liberators.

Antioch and Tarsus were the chief cities of Syria and Cilicia, and perhaps were the chief scenes of Saul's labors for the silent period after he left Damascus. Scourged in Antioch, he fled to Tarsus—"when they persecute you in one town, flee to the next,"[9] said the Master. In his own city of Tarsus Saul was adjudged an enemy of the sacred Law, deserving even to death. The Council, however, was aware of his Roman citizenship and dared not carry out the death penalty. They ordered him to be scourged. Once more the *chazzan* heaped purple welts across the Apostle's scar-marked body. But such heroes are unconquerable, and their work is indestructible; to persecute them is to imbue them with additional will and power.[10]

About this time, perhaps when recuperating from his scourging, Saul had two remarkable visions in which he thought that he had been "caught up to the third heaven," and "into Paradise," and had "heard things that cannot be told, which man may not utter."[11] If his Corinthian letter that tells of the experience was written about A.D. 56, then the visions occurred fourteen years earlier,[12] when he was about forty-two years old. The impression of these visions was profound. It confirmed all his former experiences, revealed to him the Kingdom of God as an attainable reality, and swept his soul with flaming zeal. To him the Paradise of his vision was as real as the city of Tarsus itself. But it left him mystified about his body; he could not decide whether it had been left behind, or had shared with his spirit in the heavenly honor. Ezekiel, in his prophetic vision, knew that his spirit had remained with his body when he was transported from the banks of the Chebar to Jerusalem, because he represents himself as having been lifted by a "lock of my head;"[13] but Saul was not conscious of either the presence or the absence of his flesh.

There was an ancient widespread belief that specially favored men might appear in either of two forms; or, at the same instant might be seen by some observers in one form, and by others in another. Related to this belief was another: that the spirit could leave the body temporarily on errands of its own without disturbing the life of the flesh. Or, as the Mithraists represented it, the mystic, spiritual, or "perfect body" might leave its outer, living, material body and ascend to the highest heaven. Saul's bewilderment, therefore, was simply a reflection of popular beliefs. Also his conception of three heavens was in harmony with the thinking of the time and may have been colored somewhat by the Mazdean belief that Paradise was reached by three stages. Lucien, a Greek satirist, sends one of his heroes to Jupiter's paradise by three stages: the moon being the first stop and the sun, the second.

The Chaldean idea of a succession of seven heavens, which was long popular in the early Church and among the Gnostics, was doubtless well known to Saul from the *Book of Enoch* and other sources but it did not chance to picture itself in his visions. Of course such visions have no value today, except that they reveal religious or superstitious tendencies; but in Saul's day, as well as long before and long after, they were accepted as good evidence of a man's claims to superior righteousness and divine favor.

Among the eminent Jews of the first and second centuries who boasted of their ecstatic visions in which they had visited Paradise were Elisha Ben Abuyah, Simeon ben Azzai, Simeon ben Zoma, and the famous R. Akiba ben Joseph. The philosopher Plotinus claimed to have experienced three such visions; and Posidonius, one of Cicero's teachers, who taught a system of astral mysticism, claimed to have been lifted by ecstasy into the sacred chorus of the stars. Saul's experience, therefore, creates no surprise and invites no disparagement of his physical or mental soundness. However, his great vision, like some logical and convincingly realistic dreams, must have contained a mass of the usual absurdities. He left no record of what he had seen and heard, although a writer in the second century, taking advantage of this fact, related a highly imaginative religious fiction entitled the *Revelation of Paul*. The story, however, does not conform to Paul's own paradoxical statement about his adventures.

It appears that the apostle was familiar by experience with most or all of the forms of rapturous or ecstatic phenomena, or at least recognized their place in religious practice. He heard voices,[14] received communications,[15] beheld heavenly visions,[16] visited Paradise,[17] and spoke with tongues.[18] But he never uses the word "trance" (*ekstasis*) in any of his letters, although Luke in one instance makes him say, "When . . . I was praying in the temple I fell into a trance."[19] Undoubtedly by predisposition, or by cultivation, or by both, Saul, like many other men, became psychically supersensitive. Certain statements in the Old Testament enriched by later speculation, together with the observed practices of the Gentiles and of certain Jewish sects, provided the atmosphere of credulity in which visions and other psychic phenomena could thrive and even become epidemic.

The Jews believed that in the last days there would be a great outpouring of the Spirit of God accompanied by unmistakable signs, for the prophet Joel had said, "Your sons and your daughters shall prophesy, your old men shall dream dreams, and your young men shall see visions."[20] When Saul joined the infant Church, its members were already claiming the fulfillment of this prophesy, and were demonstrating their possession of the Spirit by speaking with tongues.[21] As a Pharisee, Saul had no difficulty in accepting the religious phenomena of his day. He regarded the ecstatic vision as desirable and practiced the usual means by which it was induced, such as protracted fasting, intensive prayer, or extreme and prolonged concentration of thought. Peter experienced his vision in the quiet of a housetop.[22] Saul on one occasion appears to have sought the seclusion of the Temple.[23]

Ecstatic experience neither began nor ended with Saul; it has always been characteristic of certain types of intense lives. Plotinus, Francis Assisi, Thomas Aquinas, Joannes Scotus, Savonarola, George Fox, and Swedenborg are well-known examples. But ecstasy varies in degree, and may manifest itself differently in different persons. Philo and Josephus enjoyed a kind of inspirational ecstasy while writing, and even Tennyson experienced a mild form of it. Numerous examples of extreme and morbid degrees can be cited; such as, the experiences of Saint Theresa of Spain, whose mystic visions brought her great celebrity. Then, too, ecstatic experiences may become epidemic, as they evidently did in the infant Church, when visions, glossolalia, and other phenomena were common. But epidemic states usually manifest themselves in a single form with a tendency towards primitive behavior. Thus in the Middle Ages an ecstatic "dancing" spread over Germany and Italy. Later, in France, the Jansenists, hoping for miraculous healing, threw themselves into convulsions at the tomb of a holy man in the cemetery of St. Medard near Paris. In the United States, in the religious revival of 1800, the "falling exercise" became common, and recurred sporadically for many years; and, about 1830, in Scotland, an epidemic of speaking with tongues spread over the country.

With the view held of the Holy Spirit by the early Church, it was perfectly logical to believe that the coming of so mighty a presence into the lives of men should be accompanied by a demonstration of ecstatic and miraculous phenomena. Even the pagan world reasoned in the same manner about its theophanies. Every Christian was supposed to possess the Holy Spirit in some measure, from just enough to say that "Jesus is Lord,"[24] up to a fullness[25] that was manifested in special gifts and fruits. The apostle recognized some of these gifts of the Spirit,[26] but he rose above the paganism and even above the Pharisaism of his day. To him, the Holy Spirit, being the Spirit of God and the Spirit of Jesus Christ, could never be the source of any wrong or foolish thing. By the Spirit were such gifts as wisdom, knowledge, faith, truth, and power to heal, the power to work miracles, and the ability to detect the character of spirits. The apostles believed, as others did, in the existence of hordes of evil spirits[27] as well as hosts of good ones. John once said, "Test the spirits to see whether they are of God."[28]

There is no record of the length of Saul's ministry in Tarsus, but it must have extended over several years. His contacts, for a time at least, were made through the synagogues, where he reached both Jews and proselytes, and, perhaps, also even in the agora. That his work was successful is evident from the fact that in the year A.D. 50, when he began his second missionary tour, he and Silas "went through Syria and Cilicia strengthening the churches."[29] This was the region of Antioch and Tarsus where he had been laboring. By the time of the Council of Nicea, Tarsus had an episcopal see; and shortly before the year 600, the Byzantine emperor, Maurice, built a church and named it for Paul. It probably took the place of one erected at a much earlier date. A great church outside the city was named for Peter. It was destroyed by the Moslems in 885.

In Tarsus, though a fugitive from Damascus and Jerusalem, Saul did not act as one who had been crushed by defeat—defeat was impossible to a man of his spirit. Besides, his heavenly commission called for constant exposure to danger and suffering, that being the only means by which the Gospel could be made successful in its conflict with Jewish prejudice and pagan darkness. Tarsus could not be a place of refuge even for its own son, it was but another outpost of conquest. In due time Saul would forge his way westward. Always his step was firm, and his eye, level and steady—he believed in his apostleship. Opposition in Tarsus, like expulsion from Damascus and rejection at Jerusalem, were to him the sure proof of duty well performed. Among the Jews he was a master of their own Law, among the Gentiles he believed in the superiority in his own philosophy; therefore, he was attuned to his surroundings: the lively waters of the Cydnus still sang their accustomed delight, the billows of cool perfumed air still rolled down from the snowy peaks of Taurus, and the canopy of night still glowed with countless "stars of light."

Saul was now a greatly changed man and, therefore, was better understood by those who had once feared and doubted him. Ten years of toil earned for him the praise of even the Judaean part of the Church: "They glorified God because of me,"[30] he declared to the Galatians. By this time he must have discarded most of his Pharisaic practices as being inconsistent with his new faith. Also his thinking had become more mature[31] and his views of the world had broadened and gained in charity—he had now become a composite of Jew, Greek, and Roman,[32] and his former Pharisaic aloofness from his pagan neighbors had broken down.

A part of Saul's Syro-Cilician work was prosecuted during the reign of Gaius Caesar, that profligate young emperor of Rome who had been nicknamed "Caligula" (boots), who had brazenly elevated his horse, "Ineitatus," to the priesthood and the consulship, and who enraged the Jews by proposing to have his statue erected in the Temple at Jerusalem as an object of worship.[33] While the latter act must have seemed to Saul the very nadir of insult and sacrilege, yet he possibly recognized in it a portent of the end of the age and a sign that the Temple and the Law had fulfilled their purpose in preparing the world for the Messiah's reign.

While Saul was still in Tarsus, Herod Agrippa, grandson of Herod the Great, started a persecution of the fourteen-year-old Church by killing one of the apostles.[34] Luke, without attempting to be exact about the chronological arrangement of what he writes, says that Herod about that time "killed James the brother of John with the sword." James and John had been named the "sons of thunder" by Jesus,[35] and it is very likely that James, like John the Baptist, had been too outspoken for the comfort of royal sinners. So far, it had been the Roman law that had sheltered James from the fate of Stephen, but now it was the law in the hands of Herod that put him to the sword. This deed pleased the Jews, who had not dared to stone the apostles; and Herod, hoping to ingratiate himself still further with them, next arrested Peter and attempted to hold him in prison for a few days, "intending after the Passover to bring him out to the people," who, of course, would have been permitted to stone him.* But Peter escaped,[36] and Herod soon after perished miserably,[37] bringing to a sudden end the second persecution of the infant Church. Within less than a week, the news of this attack upon the apostles could have reached Saul, who would know that if Herod should permit the stoning of Peter, the whole Judaean church would be in danger of extinction and his own life would be less secure. But "the blood of the martyrs is the seed of the Church"[38]—and Luke reports triumphantly that "the word of God grew and multiplied."[39]

It was about this time that events were shaping themselves to enlarge and modify Saul's field of endeavor and to enlist his mighty energy for a definite task. While Saul taught a universal gospel, he nevertheless felt that the Jew should hear it first; and so far, he had appealed to those Gentiles only who attended the synagogues. But ten years of test and training had now fitted him for his special lifework. Fitness and opportunity had met, and Saul became the "apostle to the Gentiles."

Luke, who tells the story, has written a cautious narrative in which he first justifies Gentile evangelization and links it with the activities of Peter by allegorizing a tradition about a certain Roman military officer named Cornelius,[40] who had been admitted by Peter to baptism. He then adds that certain Hellenistic Jews, men of the island of Cyprus and of Cyrene in

---

*   Reports of Jews' and Christians' enemies suffering miserable deaths should be understood *con grano salis*, when Jews or Christians make the report. It was customary for these groups to attribute monstrous deaths to their enemies (Josephus, *The Wars at The Jews I* [655-71], Eusebius, *Ecclesiastical History* I, viii. 4-16; M.R. James, The *Apocryphal New Testament* [Oxford: Clareodon Press, 1953] pp. 153-159). (GWB)

Africa, products of the first Christian dispersion,[41] had offered the gospel to the Greeks in Antioch. He thus finds divine authority for offering salvation to the Gentiles, represents Peter as sanctioning such work, and gives the Hellenists credit for making the first direct appeals to him in the gospel. In this manner he defends Saul from the charge of having started an innovation, but withholds from him the honor due in his Syrian work.

When the Church in Jerusalem heard that many Gentiles in Antioch were turning to the new faith,[42] Joseph Barnabas was sent to Antioch to investigate the report and, perhaps, to learn whether any irregularities of Jewish practice had been permitted. Barnabas was so well satisfied with the new movement that, after exhorting the converts "to remain faithful to the Lord with steadfast purpose," he hastened over to Tarsus to seek his friend Saul as the one man most competent to direct Gentile work.

Saul was well known in Antioch. He had made converts there, and the church would urge Barnabas to find them. The conference between the two men in Tarsus involved far more than a simple request for assistance. It must have included certain problems that were sure to arise if the gospel were freely offered to the Gentiles: Should circumcision be required? Should separate tables be maintained? Should there be a separate Gentile church? Saul saw clearly that the Church should be one, and that all differences of opinion should yield to that central fact, even if the necessary concessions should be extremely difficult for the Jews to grant; unless, indeed, they could be convinced that the old dispensation had passed away.

Saul was eager to accompany Barnabas. He regarded the awakening of the Gentiles as a sure sign of the early return of the Messiah and he now saw the opportunity to preach his gospel in all its fullness. The two men probably traveled to Antioch by sea. It was in early spring, perhaps in the year A.D. 45. The long silence of winter has passed, and noisy trade had opened on the Cydnus. High in the air with black wings outspread to a man's length, there passed now and then long columns of red-legged storks on their way from the heat of Africa to cooler haunts in Asia and Europe. It was one of the familiar and inspiring sights of spring.

At Seleucia, the busy port of Antioch, the vessel entered a great artificial harbor after passing between two long stone jetties that many years later were named "Paul and Barnabas." The city, clustered around the base of Mt. Pieria like chicks under a hen, was preparing for the trade that would soon pour in from the east for distribution in the south and west. Vessels lying in the harbor were undergoing repairs or taking on shipping. Dirty half-clad slaves drove their overburdened, ropegalled, steadily paced donkeys through the streets and out upon the quays. Everywhere was the same confusion of race, raiment, and color so familiar to Saul in Tarsus.

An overland journey of seventeen miles brought the two men to Antioch on the Orontes River, the city that was almost a second Rome—"Antioch the Golden." It was the third in population among the Roman cities, a city of wealth, palatial homes, and public luxuries. But it had a hybrid population of fickle, pleasure-loving, turbulent people who were notorious for their arrogance, scurrility, and immorality. The city had won the praise of Cicero for its art and literature, but Juvenal was less complimentary when he complained about the presence of Antiochians in Rome and about the demoralizing customs and befouling vices that flowed in with them.

It was perhaps near the time of the spring festival, or Feast of Fertility, when Saul began proclaiming to the Gentiles of Antioch the coming of the Jewish Messiah. The foul orgies accompanying this and other festivals had become notorious everywhere. In the Grove of Daphne, a few miles beyond the western gate of the city, the temple prostitutes of Apollo inflamed the passions of dissolute spectators by sporting nude as nereids and naiads in the perfumed waters of the Hymphean Lake. But while such dissipation drew multitudes to the resort, it also created revulsion in the minds of serious men and women, some of whom turned to the Jewish synagogues for a purer atmosphere—and there encountered the ministry of Saul.

It is not likely that Saul ever visited the Grove of Daphne, nor did he ever think that a Christian church would some day occupy its site, but he certainly was familiar with its story. It was there that Apollo spied the beautiful nymph, Daphne, and pursued her as she ran from him. The nymph prayed for protection and was changed suddenly into a leafy shrub of fragrant laurel. The spot of concealment was in a beautiful level tract of land thrust out from between two rugged mountains against the south bank of the Orontes and had a circuit of nearly ten miles. Nature had bestowed upon it some of her finest handiwork in the form of rocky shade, banks of ferns and moss, cool springs, rippling streams, lacy cascades, noble trees, and fragrant air. Here was the village of Daphne with its princely homes, and here the gilded many-colonnaded temple of Apollo standing in a grove of towering cypresses, and sheltering a colossal statue of the god. Everywhere marble statues peered out from clumps of sacred laurel upon visitors and votaries. Nearby also was the great stadium, maintained by the city of Antioch, where the Olympic Games were celebrated and where harlots plied their trade.

Ancient writers lauded Daphne as the most beautiful spot in all the earth, even Milton sang of it as the "sweet grove of Daphne."[43] Apollonius of Tyanna, however, withheld his praise because the "half-barbarous" priests of Apollo in that place refused to hear his proffered advice. In his vexation he exclaimed: "O Apollo, change these dumb dogs into trees so that at least as cypresses they may become vocal."[44] So enervating and destructive of health and morale were the dissipations of Daphne that it was off limits to Roman soldiers, though Antioch itself was no purer than her suburb.

The arrival of Saul and Barnabas in the Syrian metropolis attracted no attention beyond the humble circle of Nazarenes. Unlike his contemporary, Apollonius of Tyana, the theurgist, Saul did not seek audiences with poets, philosophers, and temple priests. He had a message that, if true, or even half true, was superior to all the wisdom of the schools—a message that in his own life had supplanted all his other learning.[45] Apollonius was rejected, but Saul was welcomed. He aided in a work that made Antioch a city of churches, gave it a cathedral, brought to it ten church councils, and honored it with the presence of many eminent men.

Saul's first public appearance could have been no ordinary scene. Surrounded by an expectant assemblage of friends, recent converts, and inquiring Gentiles, he spoke with the authority of the apostle of Jesus the Christ. A new door of opportunity stood wide open before him, and the full realization of his mission must have throbbed in his consciousness. With his first address, the shackles of Judaism fell from the limbs of the church, and that which otherwise might have perished as a Jewish sect was now saved by the timely infusion of Gentile blood. Perhaps no other city offered better conditions than were found in Antioch for the initial approach to the Gentiles, for there the Jews who had enjoyed many favors from the time of Alexander the Great through the Seleucid period and into the Roman occupation, were particularly friendly towards the Greeks, and made many proselytes among them.[46] From these proselytes and the new recruits that were won over came the Gentile membership of the church.

It is possible that Saul often spoke to promiscuous crowds in public places, especially near the forum or marketplace, that being the common practice of orators and itinerant teachers. In fact, John of Antioch preserved a tradition that Saul preached in Singon Street, just near the market, pantheon, theater, and amphitheater; also under the eye of Charon's head, an enormous bust carved in the rock of the mountain side.

Several languages were spoken in Antioch, but Greek was generally understood. When the Hebrew or Aramaic tongue was used, Jesus was called "Messiah," "the annointed;" but when Saul began preaching in Greek, he may at first have Hellenized the word, as others had done, into "Messias;" but later he preferred a translation, and so, called him the "Christos," or Christ. Very soon, someone, mistaking the title for a personal name, called the followers of Jesus "Christiani" or Christians. No Jew would have used such a name in this way at that time, nor would the followers of Jesus have suggested it, since they called themselves "disciples" and "brethren"; and certainly Saul did not invent it, for he never uses it in his letters. It could have been coined by a Greek after existing analogy; but judging from the Latin termination, -ianos, -iani, it was more likely coined by some Roman, perhaps a member of the official class, or some irreverent nomenclator among the soldiers. Luke's brief statement about the name, that it was first used in Antioch,[47] seems to indicate that it was spoken insolently in the Antiochian manner. It is possible that the name began to circulate soon after Saul took charge of the evangelistic work of the city. Gradually it spread throughout the Roman world taking on more and more reproach[48] until it brought suspicion, torture, and death upon those who were designated by it. To be a Christian was to give one's blood to the Roman sword, to offer one's body for a flaming torch, or to dedicate one's flesh to the fangs of hungry beasts. Finally, when the name was purged and glorified by the blood of many martyrs, it was accepted and used by the church itself as no longer conveying reproach, but as conferring the highest honor.

The presence of Saul among the disciples at Antioch greatly quickened their enthusiasm for Gentile evangelization by giving apostolic endorsement to what had been a casual venture. The Jews had lost or distorted the great world vision of their prophets[49] and thought only of making individual proselytes. It was in this manner that the men of Cyprus and Cyrene approached the Hellenes preaching Jesus.[50] But the supposed near advent of the Messiah added a new and powerful argument to that of Judaism and won adherents for the church in surprising numbers.

It was Saul who caught again the old vision of the prophets, though from a new viewpoint, and saw a kingdom that was to be won from all nations and in which national differences would disappear.[51] Citizenship in that kingdom would begin immediately upon repentance and the acceptance of Jesus as Messiah and Lord. But in such a kingdom the Jew, if consistent, would have to fraternize with Gentiles, even before the return of the Messiah to earth. This was not so difficult for the liberal Jews of Antioch as it would have been for the stricter Jews in Jerusalem. Antioch, therefore, became the cradle of Gentile Christianity and the birthplace of Christian missions.

There was a group of five principal workers in the church at Antioch called prophets and teachers:[52] Joseph Barnabas, Symeon Niger, Lucius of Cyrene, Manaen who had been brought up with the foxy[53] tetrarch Herod Antipas, and Saul. Of these, Saul, though named last, was the prophet of authority. In addition to his knowledge of the Scriptures and their traditional interpretation, together with certain highly valued semi-sacred writings, he possessed further knowledge that seemed to him to have come supernaturally as revelation. With this equipment he was a teacher of teachers as well as an evangelist.

Through one whole year[54] Saul assisted in the work at Antioch, meeting with the various groups of believers that were praying for the speedy return of their Lord, singing hymns, holding love feasts, and celebrating the Lord's Supper, "till He come." At times of great emotional stress, some of the brethren would speak with tongues, and new converts would demonstrate their right to a place in the brotherhood by speaking "as the Spirit gave them utterance."[55]

When Saul and his associates were busy among the Gentiles of Antioch, Peter and others were busy among the Jews of Judaea, Galilee, Samaria, where also an occasional proselyte to Judaism was won over to the new faith. But judging from Luke's story of Peter and Cornelius,[56] not one of the apostles had ever thought of proclaiming salvation to any others than Jews and proselytes,[57] and certainly they had never thought of entering a Gentile's house to eat bread with him,[58] or of celebrating the agape at the same table with him, or even of speaking to him. Luke, however, attempts to show that a growing liberalism had begun, at least on the part of Philip the deacon, and Peter the apostle[59] but he credits the change to divine intervention, and accordingly adorns his stories with miracles. But Peter's Gentile sympathy was doubtless awakened at the time of Saul's fifteen days' visit with him,[60] though he lacked the moral courage to act freely and openly on his conviction.[61] To the end of his life he remained an apostle to the circumcision.*

The remarkable work at Antioch soon attracted wide attention and the searching eyes of Jerusalem rested upon it menacingly, questioningly, or half-approvingly according to the attitude of those who took notice of it. Gladly would the Pharisees have gone down to seize Saul had their jurisdiction extended that far. Peter, however, made the long journey to behold the new wonder of salvation; the prophets went down to foretell the approach of a grievous famine that would bring great suffering to the mother church in the holy city; and the newly fledged Judaizers went down to interfere with the ritualistic liberty of the church of Antioch.

As Peter descended Herod's gay street of columns, he gripped his robe uneasily, feeling that he was about to compromise himself with the church at Jerusalem: Shall I eat the love feast and celebrate the Last Supper with

---

*The apostle to the uncircumcision went to the Jews in the diaspora. Rabbis said that people who lived in Palestine were called "circumcised," circumcised or not, whereas those in the diaspora were called "uncircumcised," circumcised or not (Mishna Nedarim 3:11). Paul could not have evangelized the entire area of Asia Minor if he had spoken only to Gentiles, who were not familiar with Jewish hopes and beliefs. He probably had only to tell Jews in the diaspora that the Messiah whom they had expected was Jesus. See further "The Samaritan Origin of the Gospel of John," *Religions in Antiquity*, ed. J. Neusner (Leiden: E.J. Brill, 1968), pp. 149-75. (GWB)

these uncircumcised Gentiles—men gathered into the church out of a city notorious for its unmentionable immoralities? Peter's intentions were good enough but his weakness was soon to precipitate the most surprising scene in all church history—one apostle suddenly rebuking another.[62] Peter was a welcome visitor and, as one of the twelve, his exhortations must have commanded intense interest. He was the hero of the hour. He and Saul had not met since their visit together in Jerusalem nearly eleven years before. At that time they discussed the messiahship of Jesus, at this time it was the vexing problem of the barrier of the Mosaic law between Jew and Gentile. Peter admitted that if salvation were all of grace through faith, then circumcision, the ancient seal of the Israelitish covenant, had no value for that purpose and should not be required of the Gentiles. He also admitted that the Jew should be at liberty to eat with the Gentile. Suppressing whatever scruples he may have had, Peter did in Antioch as the Antiochians did—he ate with the Gentiles. But James, who, because he was the elder brother of Jesus, had inherited or assumed that presidency of the church, sent observers[63] to Antioch thinking perhaps that Peter might be carried away with the new movement as Barnabas had been. These emissaries must have been an important body of men, for Peter became afraid and withdrew from the Gentiles. Then all the Jewish Christians separated themselves, and even Barnabas, who had so often proved himself to be Saul's loyal and helpful friend "was carried away by their insincerity."[64] For a moment Saul's great hope of a unified humanity under one Savior faded. Jews and Gentiles had parted. Like Elijah,[65] he stood alone. The greatest crisis of the early church confronted him. Had Saul been a weaker man this deflection would have wrecked the church for all time; only a perishing sect of Jews would have remained. Sickening anguish must have wrenched the apostle's soul, but righteous anger sped to his relief. Turning to Peter as with superior apostolic authority, he said in the presence of them all, "Cephas!"[66]—not his Greek name, "Peter," but the smooth Aramaic name by which Jesus had characterized him[67]—and then followed a rebuke such as Peter had not heard since his Lord had called him an adversary.[68] Very few of Saul's words have been preserved, but his speech was sufficiently impassioned, eloquent, and convincing to reunite the severed church and silence the meddlers from Jerusalem. Behind the controversy of eating with the Gentiles was, of course, the ever-present question of the ceremonial law, which, in turn, centered itself in the question of circumcision.

Since Luke and Saul wrote very briefly and for different purposes, the chronological sequence of the events to which they referred cannot always be determined. This is true especially of the events at Antioch. A maintainable order that can do no serious violence to history, however, would place the visit of the prophets next after that of Peter's. Luke said

"In those days Prophets came down from Jerusalem," and that one of them named Agabus "foretold by the Spirit that there would be a great famine over all the world."[69] Agabus, having the reputation of a seer, was soon made by tradition to foretell a famine that had already entered upon its first stages. The literary tastes of the age led all other men, as well as Luke, to imbue their writings with mystery. Most likely the prophets came down to solicit alms for that little communistic group of saints in Jerusalem and Judaea who were anxiously awaiting the return of the Messiah[70] and who had already shared their possessions with the poor of their own brotherhood, believing that the time was near at hand when earthly goods would not be needed.

The famine came in the reign of Claudius Caesar, some time between A.D. 41 and 54. But according to Suetonius and Tacitus, frequent famines occurred in the Roman Empire in that period. Josephus, however,[71] speaks of a severe famine that occurred in Judaea in the procuratorship of Cuspus Fadus and his successor Tiberius Alexander, or between A.D. 44 and 48. Judaea was a densely crowded region and its inhabitants were little more than able to produce sufficient food for themselves, even in good seasons. A drought lasting two or three years, as in this case, would result in much suffering and many deaths. Agabus may have made his appeal as early as A.D. 45 but more likely in 46.

Antioch was on a great commercial highway and would suffer less than the inland city of Jerusalem. Also the members of the church there were not living communistically or, if so, had not exhausted their property. There was a prompt and willing response to the appeal of the prophets for aid and Saul and Barnabas were selected to bear the contribution of the elders of the church in Jerusalem,[72] who though unwilling to eat with Gentiles did not disdain their gifts.

Before the contributions of the church were ready, Saul received what he believed to be a revelation, directing him to go up to Jerusalem and explain his gospel to the apostles and elders. It is altogether unlikely that Saul would have consented to carry gifts to Jerusalem merely as a gesture of good will, but since his commission from the church and his revelation coincided, the two missions could be performed together with advantage. It was a courageous move on the part of the apostle to venture back to Jerusalem again, for the Jews had not forgiven him and never would. Even many Christian Jews were his bitter enemies. But, though courageous, Saul was not rash; he did not invite unnecessary trouble nor did he attempt to win his way by exhibiting any signs of subserviency. To show that he stood firmly on his own gospel, he took with him Titus, an uncircumcised Gentile convert, as a visible challenge to any who might insist on the observance of the Mosaic ritual. Unfortunately, Luke has nothing to say about this conference; and not only is Saul's account of it[73] brief, but his manuscript evidently suffered damage before it was collected for preservation, requiring editorial corrections. These, however, were badly done; but enough is clear to show that Saul and Barnabas held a private conference with James, Peter, and John, and later appeared before the whole church.

The private conference was a master-stroke by which the much quoted "pillars" of the church were won to the desired position before the Judaizing members could confuse the issues.

In communicating his gospel to the "pillars" of the church, Saul sat and taught as a theologian having authority. He did not go up to Jerusalem to learn and says plainly that he learned nothing. Indeed his language seems almost ironic when he says of Peter, James, and John, "those who were reputed to be something (what they were it makes no difference to me: God shows no partiality). . . ."[74] However, his irony was directed towards certain Jews who were continually quoting these men as their highest authority on the contents of the gospel. To Saul, the gospel was a revelation and the opinions of the apostles, himself included, had nothing to do with it.

But it should not be supposed from the passage in Galatians that Saul displayed any rudeness or sharpness towards his fellow apostles, the very object of his visit had been to win them over to cordial relations—lest he "should be running or had run in vain."[75] Evidently he had succeeded in securing at least a promise of immunity in his work, for he says that the "pillars" gave him and Barnabas "the right hand of fellowship, that we should go to the Gentiles, and they to the circumcised; only they would have us remember the poor, which very thing I was eager to do."[76]

Having won the "pillars," Saul went before the whole church to explain his gospel, allaying suspicion against himself, and checking interference with his Gentile work. But there were spies present who, claiming to be of the brotherhood, demanded that Titus be circumcised. Paul and Barnabas met the issue with such a storm of eloquence and argument that the church did not accede to the demands of the Judaic spies or to those of its own Judaizers. While this victory committed the Jerusalem church to a recognition, if not a defense of Saul's gospel, it also embittered certain radical elements within the membership and increased the enmity of those without.

While in Jerusalem, Saul and Barnabas perhaps stayed with Mary, an early disciple whose comfortable home had evidently been opened freely to the use of the church. On leaving they took with them Mary's son, John Mark, cousin of Barnabas, a young man who was probably eager to accompany them on their missionary tours. At Antioch, Saul reported the success of his mission in winning the recognition of the Jerusalem authorities to the rights of the Gentiles in the gospel. The news created a scene of joy and enthusiasm in which the church decided immediately to put missionaries into the field even in a time of famine.

REFERENCES
Chapter 6

1. Gal. 1:21.
2. Gal. 1:23.
3. Gal. 2:8.
4. Acts 15:23.
5. Acts 15:41.
6. II Cor. 11:24.
7. II Cor. 11:23-27.
8. II Cor. 12:11.
9. Matt. 10:23.
10. II Cor. 12:10.
11. II Cor. 12:2-4.
12. II Cor. 12:2.
13. Ezek. 8:3.
14. Acts 9:4.
15. Acts 16:9; 18:9; 27:23.
16. II Cor. 12:1; II Cor. 12:2.
17. II Cor. 12:4.
18. I Cor. 14:18.
19. Acts 22:17.
20. Joel 2:28; Acts 2.
21. Acts 2:4.
22. Acts 10:9.
23. Acts 22:17.
24. I Cor. 12:3.
25. Eph. 5:18.
26. I Cor. 12:8-10.
27. Eph. 6:12.
28. I John 4:1-2.
29. Acts 15:41.
30. Gal. 1:24.
31. I Cor. 13:11.
32. I Cor. 9:22.
33. Josephus. *Antiquities*. XVIII. 8.
34. Acts 12.
35. Mark 3:17.
36. Acts 12.
37. Acts 12:23.
38. Jerome.
39. Acts 12:24; 8:4.
40. Acts 10.
41. Acts 11:19, 20.
42. Acts 11:21.
43. Milton. *Paradise Lost*. IV. Line 272.
44. *Apollonius of Tyana*. I. xvi.
45. I Cor. 2:2.
46. Josephus. *Wars*. VII. 3. 3; *Antiquities*. 3, 1.
47. Acts 11:26.
48. I Pet. 4:14, 16.
49. Isa. 56:6-8.
50. Acts 11:20.
51. Rom. 10:12.
52. Acts 13:1; Eph. 4:11.
53. Luke 13:32.
54. Acts 11:26.
55. Acts 2:4.
56. Acts 10.
57. Acts 11:18.
58. Acts 11:3.
59. Acts 15:7.
60. Gal. 1:18.
61. Gal. 2:12.
62. Gal. 2:11-21.
63. Gal. 2:12.
64. Gal. 2:12-13.
65. I Kings 19:10.
66. Gal. 2:14-21.
67. Cf. John 1:42.
68. Mark 8:33.
69. Acts 11:27-30.
70. Mal. 3:1; Acts 1 and 2.
71. Josephus. *Antiquities*. XX. 5. Sec. 2.
72. Acts 11:29-30; 12:25.
73. Gal. 2:1-10.
74. Gal. 2:6.
75. Gal. 2:2.
76. Gal. 2:9-10.

First Missionary Tour:
Antioch, Syria — Antioch, Pisidia

AT LAST THE GEOGRAPHY of the world lay open before Saul. No
longer could Syria and Cilicia confine his vision or satisfy his expanding
ambition. Wherever the golden eagle of Rome should soar, there he would
go. Now had come the first clear view of his destiny, now was set before
him the definite task for which long years had been preparing him, and
now he was in truth the ambassador of the Christ to the nations.

Having gained the good will of the church in Jerusalem, Saul and
Barnabas next established official relations with the mixed church at
Antioch, constituting that church the headquarters of Gentile evangelism.
Luke tells the story thus: "Now in the church at Antioch there were
prophets and teachers, Barnabas, Symeon who was called Niger, Lucius of
Cyrene, Manaen a member of the court of Herod the tetrarch, and Saul.
While they were worshiping the Lord and fasting, the Holy Spirit said,
'Set apart for me Barnabas and Saul for the work to which I have called
them.' Then after fasting and praying they laid their hands on them and
sent them off."[1] In order to emphasize the work of the Holy Spirit, Luke
here ignores all initiative on the part of Saul and Barnabas: the Spirit calls
them, the Spirit orders them to be commissioned, and they are sent away.

But the ceremony of separation, if Luke has not anticipated later ecclesiastical procedure, could not have been taken by Saul as conferring spiritual gifts or any authority that he did not already possess, for, in his letter to the Galatians,[2] he vehemently disclaims all dependence upon man for either his office or his gospel. From Jerusalem, Saul and Barnabas had been dismissed with a rather flaccid right hand of fellowship coupled with a request for alms, but from Antioch they were to go forth bearing upon their heads the official benediction of an enthusiastic church.

It was spring. The east winds had brought maritime safety, and great ships were moving out from Seleucia. Saul, Joseph Barnabas, and John Mark, their attendant, were growing impatient to be upon their way. It was perhaps partly through deference to the wishes of Barnabas, and partly from a desire to visit one of the sources of the Gentile movement,[3] that Saul agreed to make Cyprus the beginning of their tour.

Save for a little band of brethren, Antioch did not concern itself about the departure of the three Jews. If any deigned to notice them at all, it was solely for the amusement of shouting opprobrious names: Christianoi! Christianoi!

After crossing the Orontes, the three men rode westward down towards Seleucia. It was a busy highway rich in variety of scenery. To their left stood Mt. Silpius like a faithful sentinel over the city; in the southwest rose the imposing cone of Mt. Casius piercing the very blue of heaven; and in the northwest, Mt. Pieria, fading away towards the Syrian Gates. Then came views of the deep-hued Mediterranean, with now and then a glimpse of some full-rigged ship that had ventured out from its winter haven. Even Cyprus could be discerned as a faint line of mountaintops far away on the horizon.

At Seleucia, Saul and his companions embarked for Salamis, on the island of Cyprus. It was to be a sail of about one hundred and forty miles, with the mountaintops of either Syria or Cyprus always in view. Cyprus was a busy island. It contained two important cities, Salamis and Paphos, and numerous towns. Its forests had long furnished the choicest timber for the great grain ships of Egypt and its superior copper was familiar in Corinthian and Roman bronze. It had been a source of wealth to Herod the Great,[4] that perpetrator of inhuman crimes, who also was the builder of the last temple and the adorner of the city of Antioch.

Greeks and Jews were numerous in the island and to these Saul and Barnabas were to make their first appeals, beginning in the synagogues of Salamis where they hoped to reach proselytes and God-fearers as well as Jews. News of the arrival of the missionaries circulated rapidly, and men came, eager to hear Barnabas of whom they knew much already and to see Saul whose strange history had long before filtered into their city.

As Saul, Barnabas, and John Mark entered the synagogue, each covered his head with a yarmulka and his shoulders with a prayer shawl and took his seat with the other worshipers. The room was severely plain but contained the usual latticed partition, benches, reading desk, candlestands, and lamps. The ark, or chest, containing the sacred rolls, stood as always behind a veil on the side nearest to Jerusalem. The very plainness of the place made it inspirational. After the prayers and the readings were over, the archisynagogus invited the strangers to give a word of exhortation, precedence being given to Barnabas, who told the story of what happened during the past year in Antioch and perhaps named a member of their own synagogue who had been the first to offer the Gospel to the Greeks of that city. Saul in his turn, after proving from scripture and his own visions of revelations that the Messiah had appeared, then appealed to his hearers to prepare themselves for the Kingdom of God which would be inaugurated upon the imminent return of Jesus. It had been said of the Lord that he had spoken "as one who had authority"[5] but Saul spoke as having authority from the Lord. With a faith that knew no doubt, Saul urged his hearers to turn to Jesus by whom alone they could be saved in the approaching cataclysmic ending of the age.

As usual, there was belief, doubt, and unbelief; but there may have been additions to the Christian brotherhood, for Luke says that "they had also John as their attendant,"[6] from which it may be supposed that John Mark had been baptizing converts.

According to Luke, Saul and Barnabas went "through the whole island," evidently meaning that they had preached at points along the way to Paphos. The journey, more than a hundred miles, would require several stops, and it is certain that Saul would seize every opportunity to proclaim his gospel. Luke brings him into Paphos suddenly, and there credits him with only a single experience, and that largely an embellished tradition.

Sergius Paulus, the proconsul at Paphos, had under his patronage a Jewish Magus named Bar-Jesus. Luke calls him a false prophet, drops his sacred-sounding patronymic, and calls him Elymas, the Arabic equivalent of Magus. The title "Magus" might have meant anything from "wise man,"[7] "counselor," "philosopher," or "prophet" (interpreter of portents and dreams) down to "enchanter," "astrologer," "magician," "sorcerer," "fortune-teller," or "trickster;" or it might have included all of these together.[8] Everywhere the Magi, by whatever name they were known—whether Magi, Chaldaeans, friends, or sorcerers—were numerous and influential. They were regularly consulted by people of all ranks.

When the proconsul heard of Saul and Barnabas, he sent for them wishing to hear their new and startling message. He, of course, assembled his friends, among them being his magus, who was expected to express his opinion on the new theology. It is possible that Saul and Barnabas had met Bar-Jesus in some synagogue or elsewhere about the city before they encountered him in the proconsul's audience chamber.

The hearing was conducted with formality, Sergius Paulus being "a man of intelligence,"[9] and Saul and Barnabas being men of exceptional talents. Apparently Saul was the principal speaker. He told of the ancient promise that had been made to his fathers of a Messiah who would save the people from their sins[10] and who in the "last days" would establish a heavenly kingdom of righteousness into which the nations of the earth should flow.[11] He declared that the promised Messiah had appeared in the person of Jesus of Nazareth who had been crucified for the sins of the world, but who according to many proofs had risen again from the dead, had ascended into heaven, and soon would reappear in the clouds to terminate the present age and inaugurate his everlasting kingdom.

When Saul declared that he had been commissioned to bear the gospel of salvation to Greeks and Romans as well as to Jews, and when his words were being well received, Bar-Jesus arose and attempted to dissuade the court from acknowledging the crucified Nazarene as the Messiah. He perhaps mocked the apparent contradiction in the the thought of a crucified Savior, defended the judgment of the Sanhedrin, praised Pilate, and disputed the evidence of the resurrection.

But it was all to his own undoing. Saul was a master in debate, to him the magic arts were powerless folly, and ridicule had long before ceased to have any effect upon him, but blasphemy against the Son of God, and that by a Jew, was beyond endurance. He arose in his towering spiritual strength and exclaimed: "You son of the devil, you enemy of righteousness, full of all deceit and villainy, will you not stop making crooked the straight paths of the Lord?"[12]

Of course this terrible arraignment is Luke's conception of what Saul might have said, but it is true to the impetuous and fearless character of the man. Then also, his use of the word "devil" did not at that time betray coarseness as it might do now, for demonology was a very serious subject in the first century. Luke also embellishes and adds a tradition such as was required in his day to give a tragic touch to a great encounter. At Saul's command, a mist and darkness came over the Magus' evil eyes, "and he went about seeking people to lead him by the hand." And then follows the triumphal note: "Then the proconsul believed, when he saw what had occurred, for he was astonished at the the teaching of the Lord."

Up to this point Luke has discreetly honored Barnabas by giving precedence to his name, but after the contest with Bar-Jesus the order was changed and Paul thereafter is named first. Cyprus had once been the home of Barnabas and later became his field of labor. Luke and Paul therefore paid tribute to his name throughout the tour of the island. At Paphos also, where the tour ended, Luke begins to speak of Paul by his Roman name, never again using the Hebrew name Saul except when

and therefore a contradiction of his claims; he could not wear an air of superior privilege, for the Jews would connect his afflictions with some hidden sin.[28]

Thus every attack of fever was a reminder that not he, but God, was to be glorified in the dispensation of the gospel. Every prick of the thorn reminded him that he was still an imperfect mortal, and every rap from the messenger of Satan proved that he was only an earthen vessel.

On a Sabbath after Paul had recovered sufficiently, he and Barnabas visited the synagogue at Antioch in Pisidia and after covering their heads with veils selected seats. After the services had proceeded from the call to worship through the reading of selections from the law and the prophets, the rulers of the synagogue sent the clerk to Paul and Barnabas inviting them to speak, if they had "a word of exhortation for the people." It was Paul who arose and, beckoning with his hand after the manner of the Greeks to secure attention, he preached one of the most epoch-making sermons of all time; the sermon that led to the separation of the Christian church from the Jewish synagogue and that led perhaps to the first purely Gentile Christian organization.

Luke understood the great significance of this sermon and attempted to reproduce it in epitome.[29] His effort is a good example of early Christian reasoning and of the method of introducing the gospel story to a Jewish audience, but it is hardly vigorous enough to be strictly Pauline, especially on the subject of justification.[30] He traced the history of the people of Israel as they lived under the guiding hand of their God up to the time of David their king, through whom had been promised a Savior. He then showed that Jesus, whose death and resurrection had been predicted, was the fulfilment of this promise and that "by him every one that believes is freed from everything from which you could not be freed by the Law of Moses."[31]

This sermon was almost certainly based upon the first chapters of Deuteronomy and Isaiah: two chapters, the one from the law and the other from the prophets, that came together in the Jewish lectionary for the same Sabbath and which had been read just before Paul was invited to speak. The clue to this remarkable fact is found not only in the use made of the historical matter in Deuteronomy and the allusion made to the remission of sins proclaimed by Isaiah, but also in the use of two Greek words that point definitely to these two chapters, where they are found in the Greek version used by Paul and Luke.

The first word,[32] which is unusual in form and strange in meaning, has been translated variously in such phrases as, "suffered he their manners," "bore them as a nourisher," and "bore with them in the wilderness." The second word,[33] which is used metaphorically, has been translated "made the people great." There can be no reasonable doubt therefore, that sermon ascribed by Luke to Paul was founded on Deuteronomy 1 in connection with Isaiah 1. From them Paul skillfully proved the inadequacy of the Mosaic law for justification, and then proclaimed free salvation by grace through faith in Jesus, whom he proclaimed to be the Messiah.

The sermon reached hungry hearts that in turn inspired Paul with persuasive eloquence. Since the law, laden with tedious traditions, had become a burden to the Jews and a barrier to the Gentiles, many of the hearers turned gladly to the gospel. At the close of the service, these gathered around Paul urging him to repeat his message on the next Sabbath and many followed him about to hear what else he might have to say. So startling had been the message of salvation and of the near advent of the Messiah, that "almost the whole city." according to Luke's hyperbole, came together a week later. If ever Paul needed his "thorn in the flesh," it was then. He perhaps had never before been received with such enthusiasm, not even in Syrian Antioch.

But the Jews too, needed a thorn, for at the sight of the crowding Gentiles they were filled with jealousy. They had "compassed heaven and earth" to make their proselytes, but Paul by a single sermon seemed about to win the whole city. Immediately they began to contradict the self-constituted apostle and to blaspheme his proposed Messiah.

Paul and Barnabas had been inspired at first by the the curiosity and spiritual hunger of the crowd, but now they felt the fiery inspiration of self-defense. Boldly they replied; and when they saw that the instincts of the mob were about to prevail, they even more boldly hurled back as a parting word, one of the most caustic rebukes recorded in the New Testament: "It was necessary that the word of God should be spoken first to you. Seeing you thrust it from you, and judge yourselves unworthy of eternal life, behold, we turn to the Gentiles. For so the Lord has commanded us saying: 'I have set you to be a light for the Gentiles, That you may bring salvation to the uttermost parts of the earth.' "[34]

By this bold stroke Paul and Barnabas severed the believing Gentiles from the synagogues of Antioch and forthwith ushered a new epoch into religious history by establishing a gentile Christian church.

But while they were busy gathering new converts, indoctrinating them, and training them for self-government, the Jews also were busy, but with schemes of obstruction and an ultimate desire to bring the two intruders to Jewish justice. Antioch, however, being a Roman colony and a garrison city would not permit mob action, nor would it interfere with the religion of the people unless the order of the city required it. The Jews therefore resorted to intrigue and approached certain women of the Roman aristocracy who worshiped at the synagogue. These were urged to use their influence with the "leading men of the city" for the punishment of Paul and Barnabas as disturbers of the peace. Many weeks must have elapsed before anything was accomplished, for the colonial magistrates had to obtain the sanction of the procurator of Galatia.

In the meantime the apostles followed up their advantage with incessant labor until their gospel message had spread throughout the region. At last, however, the complaints of the Jews prevailed, and Paul, the doctor of the law, and Barnabas the Levite, were ignominiously cast out of the city. It is possible that they were roughly handled and perhaps even beaten with rods after the Roman fashion. Paul was told to get himself back to Tarsus where he belonged, and they chased him in that direction.

As the angry Jews paid their last infamous tribute, the two men shook off the dust of their feet against them, as much as to say, "The guilt is yours, you have adjudged yourselves unworthy of the gift of eternal life."

The Jews were defending what they believed to be right, and Paul was contending for what he believed to be true; but one resorted to force, while the other employed argument.

REFERENCES
Chapter 7

1. Acts 13:1-3.
2. Gal. 1:11-12.
3. See Acts 11:20.
4. Josephus. *Antiquities.* XVI. 4. Sec. 5.
5. Matt. 7:29.
6. Acts 13:5; I Cor. 1:13-17; John 4:2.
7. Matt. 2:1.
8. Acts 8:9-24.
9. Acts 13:7.
10. Matt. 1:21.
11. Isa. 2:2; Micah 4:1-2.
12. Acts 13:10.
13. II Cor. 11:23-28.
14. Gal. 4:13.
15. Acts 14:27.
16. Gal. 4:14.
17. Acts 16:6.
18. Acts 16:7.
19. II Cor. 1:8-10.
20. Cf. Jer. 32:14; Herodotus. *History of the Greeks.* III. Sec. 96.
21. II Cor. 4:4.
22. II Cor. 4:6.
23. II Cor. 4:7-11.
24. Phil. 3:13-14.
25. II Cor. 12:7-10.
26. II Cor. 12:2.
27. II Cor. 12:4.
28. Luke 13:1-5; John 9:2.
29. Acts 13:16-41.
30. Cf. Gal. 3:1-14.
31. Acts 13:39.
32. Acts 13:18 with Deut. 1:31.
33. Acts 13:17 with Isa. 1:2.
34. Acts 13:46-47.

CHAPTER

8

First Missionary Tour:
Antioch, Pisidia — Antioch, Syria

THE SULTAN DAGH FROWNED down through a hazy atmosphere upon the two outcasts as they drew up their robes and tightened their girdles for travel. The summer heat had burned down the vegetation of the plains, leaving only fringes of fading verdure among the hills and along the streams. With their faces set towards Iconium, the two men began a footsore journey of eighty miles. Along the way, they perhaps found Jewish brethren in the villages and thus avoided the promiscuous inns of the idolatrous Phrygians.

As they pierced the last ridge of mountains, the walled city of Iconium with its surrounding population came into view and, with it, a great plain that faded eastward into the far horizon. Iconium was old, like Damascus and Tarsus, and like them it drank from a snow-born mountain stream and fed from the adjacent fertile plain. It still had much of its ancient Phrygian blood notwithstanding the influx of Greeks, Gauls, Jews, and other races; and it still worshiped the Mother-goddess, Cybele, or the Zizimmene Mother, as she was known from her mountain home, Zizima, in the mining region a few miles north of the city.

Evidently Paul and Barnabas were familiar with the political boundaries of the region in which they were preaching, for by fleeing to Iconium they passed beyond the jurisdiction of Antioch. There was no waste time in the apostles' movements, for "the king's business required haste,"[1] and the return of their Lord would not be long delayed. Promptly on their arrival in Iconium they visited the synagogue and again gave the Jews the first opportunity of hearing the Gospel, with the result that "a great company believed, both of Jews and of Greeks."[2] But there were conservative Jews in the synagogue who refused to be convinced that Jesus was the Messiah and who objected to Paul's views about the law and to his un-Jewish offers to the Gentiles. These doubtless knew what had happened at Antioch and, like their brethren there, tried to defeat the apostle in argument and to discourage him by ridicule. But they did not know the equipment and the mettle of the man. Their arguments were answered out of their own law and their threats and ridicule fell like shafts broken against armor.

Emboldened by opposition and encouraged by success, Paul and Barnabas toiled through the fall and winter, preaching in the homes of both Jews and Gentiles until opposition became open persecution. The author of Second Timothy believed that Paul's sufferings here, and also at Antioch and Lystra, were both numerous and inhuman. The Jews, failing in their first attempts to intimidate the two missionaries, resorted to inciting the unbelieving Gentiles of the lower superstitious classes against the "brethren," or converts to the new faith. This move divided the city; one part, the illiterate mob, aligning itself with the unbelievers among the Jews, and the other with the apostles. Luke's narrative gives the impression that the city magistrates had agreed that the apostles should be subjected to some humiliating punishment, and that the rulers of the Jews in secret session had decided that the two men were guilty of blasphemy and should be stoned to death. In either case, action would be swift. But Paul and Barnabas, being warned, escaped.

During their short stay, the missionaries had planted widely and deeply and, to their minds, their ministry had been justified by approved "signs and wonders"[3] among the believers, such as the outpouring of the Spirit, the gift of tongues, and the attainment of ecstatic prophecy. The two men believed that many of their hearers had been won over securely for the Messiah's kingdom.

There is a famous old story known as the "Acts of Paul and Thecla" that attaches itself to Paul's work in Iconium and that professes to give an icon or description of the apostle as he appeared when between forty-five and fifty years of age. If the reference in Tertullian[4] to this story is authentic, the perpetrator of it was a presbyter of Asia, who for his act was degraded from office, notwithstanding his assertions that he composed the fiction "from love of Paul." Although glimpses of ancient customs may be obtained from the story and though much use of it was made by the early church, its various episodes are nevertheless so incredible that they seem to be without any possible basis of fact for their origin.

The description it gives of Paul is characteristic of that morbid asceticism that associates holiness with eccentricity, harmless ugliness, and vacuous beauty. It, of course, presupposes a Jewish type, and may have been built up from an erroneous interpretation of one of Paul's statements[5] together with the supposed effects of great suffering; from the meaning of his name; from the fact of his connection with the tribe of Benjamin, which was characterized as a "ravenous Wolf;"[6] and from the statements of Luke that he was once taken for the god Mercury, and later for an Egyptian.[7] The description without its later additions is as follows: "A man small in size, baldheaded, bandy-legged, well-built Greek, with eyebrows meeting, rather long-nosed, full of grace. For sometimes he seemed like a man, and sometimes he had the countenance of an angel."[8]

The description varies somewhat in the different versions of the story. Thus the Syriac version says that he had large eyes; and the Armenian, that his eyes were blue and his hair curly. The apocryphal story known as the *Acts of the Holy Apostles Peter and Paul* mentions his baldness, and Lucian refers to him as "the baldheaded Galilean with eagle nose, walking through the air to the third heaven.[9] The so-called "*Passion of Paul*," in describing his arrest, says: "he was easily recognizable, having a crooked body, a black beard and a bald head."[10] The pseudo-Chrysostom speaks of him as "the three cubit man."[11] John of Antioch says he had round shoulders, an aquiline nose, and meeting eyebrows.[12]

Later writers, of course, quote from the earlier, and painters and sculptors have almost always turned to these apocryphal sources for their inspiration and have thus failed to reveal the true Paul of either the Acts or the Epistles. From the possibly ancient bronze medallion in the Vatican Library to the greatest masterpieces of ancient and modern art, there may be detected a tendency on the part of most or all artists to think of something unattractive in the apostle's appearance, or uncongenial in his temperament. This tendency is unquestionable in Durer and easily discernible in Rembrandt.

Since the descriptions of Paul are evidently built up from misconceptions of Scripture rather than from official *menusi*, or even from tradition, it is not likely that they contain much, if any, truth. The passage in the Corinthian letter, which Paul quotes from his calumniators, is dynamic with erroneous suggestion if wrongly interpreted: "His letters are weighty and strong, but his bodily presence is weak, and his speech of no account."[13] But there is no intentional reference in these charges to Paul's physical condition or to his habits of speech. His detractors, like troublemakers in general, had mistaken his kindliness, when he was in

Corinth, for softness, and on his departure had attempted to run the new church in their own way. When Paul warned them by letter, they said among themselves: "his letters are very threatening, but if he were present he could neither speak nor act as boldly as he writes."

Another wrong deduction is made that the phrase "least of the apostles"[14] refers to Paul's stature; and incautious reasoning has found a proof of diminuitiveness in the statement of Luke, that the Lycaonians mistook Barnabas for Zeus and Paul for Hermes.[15] But Luke says expressly that Paul was taken for Hermes "because he was the chief speaker."

Because Paul was of the tribe of Benjamin, it was easy to ascribe to him certain qualities of the wolf, which was the symbol of the tribe. Tertullian[16] carried out the analogy to some extent, but extremists, as if desiring to be literal, have given the Apostle a dwarfed body, crooked legs, and shaggy meeting eyebrows.

If Paul had been as unattractive as invention has made him to be, the evidence of the fact would most likely have appeared in many records in unambiguous language. It is better, therefore, to think of him as meeting the requirements of a successful candidate for the Sanhedrin, as set forth in the Babylonian talmud: a man of stature, possessed of wisdom, master of magical arts, able to use Greek. He could not be a eunuch, a childless man or an old man.[17]

It was early summer when Paul and Barnabas fled from the Iconian mob. They decided to go southward to Lystra, a journey of eighteen miles. Lystra was another Roman colony that had been established by Augustus a few years before Paul was born, perhaps on the site of an older town. The city sat conspiciously on a mound in a beautiful narrow vale on the north side of a mountain stream that loitered eastward until its last weary ripple was sucked in by the hot salty plain. There were a few Jews in the city but history has left no record of a synagogue. The population was largely Lycaonian, some of whom understood Greek, while others used only their native tongue. The governing class was Roman and spoke Latin.

Paul and Barnabas inquired at the gate for the ghetto and after threading ill-smelling streets, so narrow that the two walls could be touched at once, they found accommodations with their own people. It was not long until they made the purpose of their visit known, first to individuals and then to the devout Jews who gathered at their praying place. Among the converts in these meetings was a young half-Jew named Timothy. With him perhaps were his mother and his grandmother, and possibly even his Greek father. Though a resident of a barbarous city, Timothy was soon to become one of Paul's most useful traveling assistants.

After proclaiming to the Jews the approach of the Messiah's kingdom the two missionaries turned to the Gentiles with the same message of salvation, preaching in the city marketplace, by the roadside beyond the city walls, and in the houses of converts. Incident to this part of their ministry, Luke relates a tradition that Paul had healed a cripple in a very dramatic manner and, in consequence, was mistaken for a god. It appears that on one occasion when he was preaching before the city gates, or near the enclosure of the temple of Zeus, that he saw seated near him a man so crippled in his feet from his mother's womb that he had never walked. Seeing in the man's expression the clear evidence of faith, Paul commanded in a loud voice, "Stand upright on your feet." Instantly the man sprang up and walked.

This part of the tradition offsets a similar miracle accredited to Peter, but which was less skillfully performed, just as the story of Paul and Elymas offsets that of Peter and Simon Magus. There was an evident effort on the part of Luke to keep the supernatural gifts of Peter and Paul fairly well balanced, and he doubtless found many stories about the deeds of each from which to make his selections.

But the story of the crippled man introduces a subsequent incident that in the main may have a basis of fact. Luke's account of it runs thus: "And when the crowds saw what Paul had done, they lifted up their voices, saying in Lycaonian, 'The gods have come down to us in the likeness of men!' Barnabas, they called Zeus, and Paul, because he was the chief speaker, they called Hermes. And the priest of Zeus whose temple was in front of the city, brought oxen and garlands to the gates and wanted to offer sacrifice with the people."[18]

The occurrence is not surprising since Zeus was regarded as the patron of that region and an old Greek legend about a theophany of these same gods was still told and believed by the superstitious Lycaonians.

The story of this theophany was beautifully versified in Latin by Ovid near the time of Paul's birth and the Romans in Lystra had probably read or heard it often. It appears that Zeus and Hermes, in the guise of men, visited Lycaonia to investigate complaints about the cruelty of the people. In a certain village they were roughly turned away from every door except that of an old Phrygian couple named Philemon and Baucis, who lived apart from the others. Here the gods found a cordial welcome; and to reward their hosts for their hospitality, Jupiter changed their humble home miraculously into a temple to himself and made Philemon and Baucis priest and priestess in charge. The village and its inhabitants he submerged in a miraculous lake.

Of course, the superstitious Lycaonians were on their guard and were eager to propitiate any visiting god. Paul and Barnabas, having the manners of men accustomed to comfortable city life and having a message that surpassed all others in hope, must, in fact, have appeared godlike to the uncultured shepherd people. When someone started a cry in the

Lycaonian tongue that "The gods have come down to us in the likeness of men!" a great wave of excitement swept the crowd.

Apparently the apostles did not know the meaning of the excitement until they heard the flute-players and saw the priest and his acolytes in their regalia approaching with the white bulls to the outer gates of the temple. Then, through an interpreter, they learned the shocking fact that they had been taken for the very gods from whom they were trying to lead their hearers. An instantaneous impulsive horror caused both men to tear their garments, cloak and tunic, and spring into the crowd with cries of warning. If they were amazed at what was happening, the Lycaonians were equally amazed at the spectacle of the two gods trying to undeify themselves. Luke has left an outline of an appropriate address.[19] by which Paul quieted the people, and prevented the sacrifice.

Barely had the apostles avoided one disaster when they were overtaken by another. The Jews of Antioch in Pisidia, becoming more and more enraged as they witnessed the steadfastness of the new church, sent emissaries in pursuit of Paul and Barnabas. At Iconium, these were joined by other Jews and, when they came to Lystra, they denounced Paul and declared that according to divine law and the decisions of the Jewish courts at Antioch and Iconium he should be stoned to death. Since a dead Jew at Lystra would not create serious excitement, the officials of the city permitted the executioners to carry out their own law, and the idlers who once shouted, "The gods are come down to us!" now stood by indifferently as if about to witness some new sport.

Whether Paul was seized in his lodgings or was attacked while preaching in some public place is unknown, but certainly the stoning took place in the city and was the act of a Jewish mob. Paul would be defiant in attitude but submissive to what he believed to be the will of God. He would hurl into the teeth of his tormentors the charge that they had crucified and denied their own Messiah and had adjudged themselves unworthy of eternal life. But every word would only add accuracy and viciousness to the stones that came thudding into his body. Bruised, lacerated, and bleeding, Paul must have turned his eyes heavenward to ask forgiveness for his enemies, but when another stone found a vital mark, he fell motionless and unconscious. They turned him over, pronounced him dead, and dragged his body out of the city to be eaten by dogs.

But after his disciples had gathered around him, Timothy and Barnabas perhaps among the number, he showed signs of life, revived, and returned into the city. It was such sublime defiance of suffering and death that inspired heroism and martyrdom in the early church and saved Christianity from extinction.

Concealed in the home of some disciple, Paul prepared himself for a new adventure. After sympathetic hands had bathed, medicated, and bound up his wounds, he and Barnabas rested through the night until the opening of the gates, when they left for Derbe. Painfully Paul rode out from Lystra, forded the nearby river, and set his face toward the northern slopes of Kara Dagh. By the time that the two men were skirting the foothills of the frowning mountain, the Jews were on their way back to Iconium and Antioch eager to report that Paul had been executed.

On the evening of the second day the missionaries were at the gates of Derbe. The city was a frontier customs station through which traders and travelers were constantly passing. It stood in the drains of the Taurus Mountains and looked northward over a vast salt desert. Its landmark was a great conical peak, a mile and a half high, and its contribution to trade was beautiful white marble, much used by sculptors.

The record concerning the work in this city is very brief, but Luke says that Paul and Barnabas "made many disciples" and that they extended their work to the region round about Lystra and Derbe. The work at Derbe must have been carried to completion; that is, the church there was fully organized, having at least elders, who were charged with the duty of teaching and administration and who were provided with an orderly but unwritten ritual. It is even possible that Gaius[20] became a disciple at this time and that he served as one of the elders.

After their success in Derbe, the missionaries decided to return to the cities from which they had been violently ejected and there complete the organization of the churches they had started. It was a daring but necessary adventure, a deliberate self-exposure to imprisonment, to the scourge and the rod, and to death by stoning. Back to Lystra, back to Iconium, back to Antioch; would they find that the disciples had kept their new faith? Paul knew that to return would soon incite violence against the churches and therefore as he visited each he rehearsed the proofs of his gospel and exhorted the disciples to continue in the faith, saying to them that "through many tribulations we must enter the kingdom of God."[21] He knew that some would be cast out of their homes; that husbands and wives would disagree; that men would discriminate against the disciples in business; that false witnesses would testify against them; that some would be fined, imprisoned, and scourged; and that others would go to the arena to be slaughtered by wild beasts for amusement. With the kingdom of God just in sight, Paul, glowing with the majesty of the Messiah's Apostle, and himself devoted to martyrdom, appealed for a martyr church—and reached the mightiest emotions of the human heart.

Assembling their disciples, Paul and Barnabas organized them for mutual comfort and assistance; for orderly instruction, worship, and self-government; and for the extension of the Gospel to other cities. They had no thought of establishing fixed arbitrary forms of government to which future generations should turn for models. They simply adopted the practices of their day, making such modifications as experience required. Luke groups briefly and informally all the church officers under the single name "elders" who in various capacities were to act as "overseers," or bishops, some or all of these being teachers, exhorters, or even acting as deacons. The church was simply a very temporary organization or "assembly" of disciples who expected within their lifetime to behold the Messiah coming to receive those who should believe in him. It was the very definiteness of this expectation that made Paul's gospel irresistible.

Perga now had its chance to hear the gospel. Paul could not have lingered in the hot plain of Pamphylia on his former visit but now the cool air of the uplands was gliding down the valley of the Cestrus, sweeping out the summer malaria. Pamphylia was a kind of everyman's land, though governed by a propraetor nominated by the emperor of Rome. Several of its seaports were trading posts for pirates, where some of Paul's early acquaintances may have purchased ill-gotten goods; for Strabo[22] says that the Cilicians traded there. Evidently the evangelists did not regard Perga as one of the strategic points of their itinerary but rather as merely incidental. The great diversity of races and tongues would have made evangelistic work in that city slow and difficult. Paul and Barnabas could not have afforded to lose time. They had to find vital centers from which the gospel would afterwards filter down to the lesser places. Although there is no record of what was accomplished in Perga, yet a few converts may have been made. Certainly Christianity had a foothold there later.

From Perga the apostles rode down through the fragrant spice lands between the Cestrus and the Catarrhactes rivers and after a few hours came into Attalia, the home of traders, pirates, and brigands; the pirate seaport from which they intended to sail for Syria. Here, they must have found Jews and Greeks among the mixed population and doubtless used every moment in proclaiming the good news of salvation and the coming of the kingdom of Heaven, for they certainly were not timewasters. Here, as in Perga, Christianity took root, if not from the work of the apostles, certainly from the work of other evangelists.

The great sea was now growing restless and its deep blue was everywhere flecked with white. Migratory birds were warning mariners to hasten to their winter ports, and the Pleiades and Hyades heralded the approach of autumnal storms.

After Paul and Barnabas had exhorted their converts to remain in the faith, they were soon looking back to the city that sat like a crescent at the head of its beautiful harbor. Their course lay between Cyprus and the mainland and covered a distance of three hundred miles. Before them lay Seleucia, the port of Syrian Antioch, and as they approached, both men felt the joy of homecoming and the thrill of having fully accomplished their mission.

Paul and Barnabas made speed and were soon sitting with Symeon, Lucius, and Manaen, assuring them that the greatest era in human history had now begun, for God had "opened a door of faith to the Gentiles." Promptly, the church of Antioch was assembled to receive the reports of its missionaries.

After an absence of perhaps two and one half years, from the spring of A.D. 47 to the fall of 49, Paul and Barnabas planned to remain in Syrian Antioch through the winter, since travel by land and sea always ceased for the winter months.

The report of their return soon spread, awakening the antagonism among some Hebrew Christians. Some of these went down to Antioch and began persuading the Gentile converts that they could not be saved unless they obeyed the law of Moses and submitted to circumcision. Paul remembered a former delegation that had been sent down by James, the acting head of the church in Jerusalem, to protest against Jews who ate the love feast with Gentile Christians[23] and he doubtless believed that James was again "spying" on him. Barnabas, too, uncomfortably remembered the former occasion, for at that time he and Peter had weakened and then had been publicly reprimanded by Paul. On this occasion, however, Barnabas was firm and stood with Paul through a long period of heated debate and "no small dissension," as Luke's Greek implies.

As the Judaizers refused to be convinced, both sides agreed that the question should be laid before the apostles and elders at Jerusalem. The Judaizers must have had good grounds for thinking that the Jerusalem Church would sustain their views.

It was, of course, impossible for Paul, even in a conference with the apostles, to agree to any compromise on any essential point of doctrine without conceding error in his professed revelations, and he could not have taken orders from them without exposing his own apostolic call to doubt. But his faith in himself never wavered and he was prepared to pursue his own work in his own way, even at the risk of an open break with James and the Twelve.

The dispute in Antioch was not confined to a few individuals, for the church took the matter up officially, chose Paul and Barnabas and certain others, and sent them up to Jerusalem to complain, defend the liberty of the Gentiles, and to prevent, if possible, any further interference with the work at Antioch or elsewhere.

It was a long journey, more than three hundred miles of tiresome riding, but the delegation made good use of its time and opportunity by spreading along the way the joyful news that the Gentiles were turning to the Messiah. The journey must have required nearly two weeks; and it was made over a Roman highway that followed the coast through Phoenicia and Samaria, affording many entrancing views of the Mediterranean Sea.

At Ptolemais, they turned inland, following the great plain of Esdraelon, still in its seasonal slumber, and reached Jerusalem by the Damascus road.

At Jerusalem the delegation was received by the whole church, which assembled to hear what Barnabas and Saul had to tell about the turning of the Gentiles and about the "door of faith" through which they were permitted to enter the Kingdom of Heaven along with the Jews. It is not likely that the two men made much reference to their hardships and persecutions but they described the scenes of repentance and conversion and the miraculous proofs of faith.

But there were certain Pharisees present, perhaps the very men who had interfered with the work at Antioch a few weeks earlier. While they believed Jesus to be the Messiah, they believed also that the ceremonial law of Moses was still in force. They arose therefore, with cooling effect on the enthusiasm of the assembly, and while admitting the conversion of the Gentiles declared that "It is necessary to circumcise them, and to charge them to keep the law of Moses."[24] These men were extremists and would have been so regarded even among non-Christian Jews, for it had long been a debatable question whether circumcision should be exacted of proselytes to Judaism.[25]

The question of circumcision now being raised, the apostles and elders went aside to determine what action should be taken. It was a critical moment not only for the Church but also for the apostles themselves. If they were to decide in favor of the Judaizers, then Antioch and all the churches of Syria and Cilicia as far as Tarsus would go with Paul. At the same time they would offend the liberal-minded members of the Jerusalem Church and be untrue to their own secret leaning. If they were to decide unqualifiedly in favor of the delegation from Antioch, then the Judaizers would make trouble and the whole Jerusalem Church would be exposed to possible persecution.

After much discussion the apostles and elders agreed on a mild compromise that was supposed to quiet the disturbed churches and to satisfy the liberal Jews. The church was called together for a second meeting and was given a voice in the final action. Luke does not say how many apostles were in Jerusalem at the time, although he mentions Peter and James. Nor does he speak of delegates from any of the Judaean churches. The congregation, therefore, was only the Mother Church in Jerusalem, not an ecumenical council or a synod. In his report of the proceedings, Luke used the few general facts that he had learned. From his imagination, he supplied appropriate speeches and other details, but in a skillful manner that makes a truthful and beautiful picture.

Peter was the first speaker.[26] He reminded the brethren that God had chosen him to bring the first Gentiles into the church—referring of course to the Roman centurion, Cornelius, and his household,[27] and implying that his act had been approved by the church.[28] "Now" he said, "why do you make a trial of God by putting a yoke upon the neck of the disciples which neither our fathers nor we have been able to bear?" His address, as Luke has imagined it, was decidedly Pauline in its theology—salvation by grace through faith[29]—and almost too courageous for Peter, except in his impulsive moments. The audience sat silent in intense expectation, not even a Judaizer offering his protest.

After Peter had completed his testimoney, Barnabas and Paul "related what signs and wonders God had done through them among the Gentiles." Thus it was shown that salvation was independent of the ceremonial law.

James then arose, and after referring to Peter's testimoney and quoting a passage from Amos[30] in its support, said: "Therefore my judgement is that we should not trouble those of the Gentiles who turn to God, but should write to them to abstain from the pollutions of idols and from unchastity and from what is strangled and from blood."[31] These prohibitions came from the so-called "Noachian Laws" that Phariseeism had drawn by rabbinic interpretation from God's covenant with Noah.[32] They constituted part or all of the pledge that was required of "proselytes of the gate" who would not consent to observe the whole Mosaic Law but still desired to have connection with the synagogue. The proposal, therefore, was equivalent to saying: Let the Gentiles upon conversion be received into the church on the same terms that they would be admitted into Judaism as proselytes of the gate. The church then gave its approval to the compromise, ordered the proposed formal letter to be written, and selected Judas Barsabbas and Silas, "leading men among the brethren," to go to Antioch along with the delegation from that city to vouch for the authenticity of the epistle.

The letter was addressed to "the brethren who are of the Gentiles in Antioch and Syria and Cilicia." Besides the conditions to be imposed upon the churches, it contained the assurance that the brethren who had troubled them had not done so under orders from the mother church.

At Antioch, after the multitude had assembled to hear the report from their delegates, Barnabas broke the seal of the epistle and read the decision of the council. Judas and Silas then affirmed its authenticity, and the assembly responded enthusiastically.

Judas and Silas then were formally dismissed to report back to Jerusalem. Thus the conference resulted in a victory for Antioch and in a vindication of Paul's doctrine of grace. It imposed nothing on the Gentiles as a condition of salvation and asked only for the observance of certain moral and humanitarian restraints that involved no theological compromise. Although defeated at the conference, the Judaizers did not cease to demand the full observance of the Mosaic law and a little later gave Paul one of the most anxious periods of his life, and that, apparently, without any interference from the authorities at Jerusalem.

Paul would find great satisfaction in the fact that his work was now definitely linked with that of the other apostles or, rather, theirs with his, for he knew that the Gospel as he proclaimed it was richer, broader, and more daring than the primitive form.

In his report of this first recorded apostolic council, Luke recognized James as the presiding officer of the church. Since the duty of the apostles required them to travel, such an officer was necessary for the good order and unity of the numerous groups of Christian worshipers. Paul also recognized him as the head of the Judaic church but not as an authoritative interpreter of the gospel. Luke always wrote ironically and in this instance he made Peter and James willing defenders of the liberal movement that began in Antioch, but he protected Paul from unreasonable charges of aggression by keeping him sufficiently in the background. He even gave Barnabas precedence at the council by naming him first.

REFERENCES
Chapter 8

1. I Sam. 21:8.
2. Acts 14:1.
3. John 4:48.
4. Tertullian. *De Baptismo Liber* (Homily on Baptism). Chap. 17.
5. II Cor. 10:10.
6. Gen. 49:27.
7. Acts 21:38.
8. *The Acts of Paul and Thecla* 1:3.
9. Lucian. *Dialogues*. Vol. 8. "The Patriot." 12.
10. Acts of Paul in Hennecke, New Testament Apocryphia, Vol. 2:354. Philadelphia. Westminster Press. 1965.
11. Principes Apostolorum, etc., Migne, PG, 59, col. 493.
12. John Malalas. *Phronographia*, X, in Migne, PG, 97, col. 389.
13. II Cor. 10:10.
14. I Cor. 15:9.
15. Acts 14:12.
16. Marc. V. 1.
17. Talmud, *Sanhedrin*. 17a. 366.
18. Acts 14:11-13.
19. Acts 14:14-17.
20. Acts 20:4.
21. Acts 14:22.
22. Strabo. *The Geography*. XIV. Chap. 5
23. Gal. 2:11-13.
24. Acts 15:5.
25. *Talmud, Babylonian Talmud. Yebamoth* 466-476; 1376; *Kehltoth* 9a; *Abodah Zarah* 57a; *Shabbath* 135a.
26. Acts 15:7-11.
27. Acts 10.
28. Acts 11:18.
29. Acts 15:9-11.
30. Amos 9:11-12.
31. Acts 15:19-20.
32. Gen. 9:4; Book of Jubilees (Aprocrypha) 7:20.

Second Missionary Tour:
Antioch, Syria — Philippi

DURING THE EARLY MONTHS of A.D. 50 Antioch was the scene of great religious activity. Paul and Barnabas with many others proclaimed the Kingdom of God to all who would hear, and groups of believers met every day for instruction and worship and for fellowship in the eucharist and love-feast. But as spring began to improve the highways, Paul became eager to continue his work in other cities. In discussing his plans with Barnabas, he brought up the question of an attendant. Barnabas insisted in sending for John Mark, but Paul would not accept him, because he had abandoned them on their former tour. Soon the contention became sharp. A precious friendship of many years yielded to the strain and the men "separated from each other." Barnabas sent to Jerusalem for John Mark and the two "sailed away to Cyprus." Luke never mentioned them again.

The break must have greatly saddened the two co-workers. Paul's heart was indeed tender, offsetting his characteristic but sterner virtue of quick, direct, and positive decision. But Luke seems almost to lay the blame on Barnabas, and certainly the church at Antioch did not seem to think the less of Paul.

As his assistant, Paul now selected Silas, one of the Jerusalem prophets, who, like himself, was a Roman citizen, intending later to make the youthful Timothy of Lystra their attendant to take the place of John Mark.

The church assembled to honor the evangelists, who then "departed being commended by the brethren to the grace of the Lord." Antioch was then preparing for its spring festival, the "Feast of Fertility," a feast that had lost its simple beauty and had become one of open licentious revelry. Gorgeous parades were soon to make the great colonnaded streets vibrant with the music of trumpets, cymbals, and flutes, colorful with festoons and garlands of flowers, redolent with Arabian myrrh, Indian nard, and smoking spices, but strident with wild shouting and Bacchanalian with strong wine and animal passion. Paul and Silas were glad to escape it.

Northward over the Orontes they followed a familiar road to Tarsus. City by city, they visited the churches that Paul had founded during the first period of his ministry: almost surely Pagrae, Alexandria, Baiae, Issus, Mopsuestia, and even Adana, the city of pirates. With every church he left a copy of the Jerusalem epistle for defense against the arguments of the Judaizers.

In Tarsus, Paul was at home. There, perhaps, still dwelt many of his kindred and the companions of his youth. There, still faithful, was the church he had founded before Barnabas called him away to Antioch. It would be a pleasant picture to see him seated with his aged parents and his brothers and sisters, all now in the brotherhood, telling of his recent work and present plans. But such a picture, however simply or extravagantly drawn, would be purest conjecture, for neither Luke nor Paul, with a single exception[1] ever had the slightest occasion to refer to the Tarsian family.

At Tarsus the evangelists must have lingered until the high mountain passes were free of snow and safe from floods. It was probably some time in May when they would join a west-bound caravan to make the slow ascent of the Taurus Mountains and reach the great plain nearly four thousand feet above Tarsus, where lay the cities of Derbe, Lystra, Iconium, and Pisidian Antioch.

After about four days, Paul and Silas reached Derbe and may have gone to the home of Gaius, who was a man of importance in the church, or certainly was at a later date. Very soon the church was called together for a joyful celebration of the agape and eucharist. Then for several days the two heralds of the Messiah instructed the brethren of the church. Luke thought that the Jerusalem decrees were delivered here and also to the other Galatian churches,[2] but if they were, the Judaizers ignored them later.

From Derbe, the apostles went to Lystra and doubtless to Iconium and Pisidian Antioch, though Luke left this fact to be inferred from the general statement that "the churches were strengthened in the faith, and they increased in numbers daily."[3]

At Lystra, it seems that Paul and Silas were entertained in the home of a Greek who had married a Jewish woman who had a son named Timothy.[4] The unknown author of the second letter to Timothy says that the name of the young man's mother was Eunice; that of his grandmother, Lois; that both were women of faith; and that Timothy had been trained in a godly life.[5] During Paul's absence of a year from Lystra, this young man made a good reputation as a religious worker, not only there, but also in the neighboring city of Iconium. When Paul learned of his work and saw that he possessed superior gifts, he decided at once to make him his attendant.

But Timothy, though trained in the Hebrew faith, had never been circumcised, and since his duties would require him to visit many a synagogue, and would bring him into contact with strict Jews, it was necessary that he should bear the seal of the Jew. As a prudential act, therefore, Paul circumcised him. There was danger of course that his enemies would regard the act as a sign of weakness or see in it a departure from his own position on the ceremonial law. But the very fact of such danger was a proof of Paul's independence and courage. He was not obliged to take Timothy with him and there was no betrayal of his own principles, since to him neither circumcision nor uncircumcision had any place in the Kingdom of Grace.[6] Then, too, his moral courage was well known, for he had previously taken Titus, an uncircumcised Greek, with him to Jerusalem for the very purpose of facing such an issue and of defending his position before the apostles.

After Paul, Silas, and Timothy left the gates of Lystra, they evidently visited Iconium and Antioch[7] and then went to Troas, three hundred miles northwestward from Antioch. Their course was not direct, but there is no record of the cities through which they passed. Luke told the whole story in fifty-four words:[8] "And they went through the region of Phrygia and Galatia, having been forbidden by the Holy Spirit to speak the word in Asia. And when they had come opposite Mysia, they attempted to go into Bithynia, but the Spirit of Jesus did not allow them; so, passing by Mysia, they went down to Troas." Apparently this description left time and room for an excursion eastward into north Galatia through Pessinus, Ancyra, and even Tavium, but Luke did not mention these cities by name at any time.

Pessinus and its neighbors doubtless received the gospel from the south Galatian churches while Paul and Barnabas were laboring there, or very soon afterwards. Certainly they became important Christian communities later. It was Paul's policy to keep his gospel moving towards the ends of the earth while he himself labored in strategic centers. But in Luke's narrative the words "Phrygia" and "Galatia" were intended to be taken adjectively. Accordingly Paul and his companions went through the Galatic Phrygian region but not through the Asian Phrygian region. Such a course would indicate that they had not planned to visit north Galatia but rather to continue westward visiting such cities as Colosse, Laodicaea, and Ephesus.

In some manner Paul or Silas received what Luke believed to be a communication from the Holy Spirit, forbidding them to speak the Word in the Province of Asia. Political conditions, the presence of other trustworthy workers, the state of the Jewish mind, Paul's own inner urge to reach Europe, or even some realistic dream may have brought about a subjective state that was to them equivalent to a command from the Holy Spirit. They changed their course, therefore, crossed the mountain ridge north of Antioch to Philomelium, followed the highway to Synnada, and then turned northward towards Bithynia, perhaps intending to visit Nacaea and Nicomedia, where Jews were probably numerous. But again, when approaching their destination, perhaps near Borylaeu, or Cotyaeum, the Spirit—or the "Spirit of Jesus"—interposed and changed their course.

At the border of Bithynia, they turned westward through Mysia, the northern part of the Province of Asia. They perhaps followed the valley of the Rhyndacus until it turned northward, when they followed the uplands toward Troas. As they undertook no work in that region they must have intended crossing the Aegean Sea into Europe.

At Troas Paul dreamed, not of the beautiful goddesses in Homer's epic who came to the foot of Mount Ida to solicit the aid of Paris, but of a serious, earnest man who stood by the side of his couch "beseeching him and saying, 'Come over into Macedonia, and help us.' " Here, Paul appears to have met with Luke, who, doubtless, was a former acquaintance and already a Christian and who was soon to be known as the "beloved physician."[9] His conversation with this man was perhaps the cause of the vision that determined his next move.

For two or more weeks, Paul and his companions had traveled by faith. Like Abraham, they went out under sealed orders, "not knowing where,"[10] except as new orders at successive stages closed or opened the doors. At the entrance to Asia, the Holy Spirit said, "It is not this way;" at the borders of Bithynia, the Spirit of Jesus said, "It is not this way;" but at Troas the vision said, "It is this way." Accepting the apparition as proof that God had called them to preach in Macedonia, Paul, Silas, and Timothy, and now Luke—hurried to obey.

Troas was a Roman colony, enjoying the Roman administration. It was one of the largest cities in the northwestern part of Asia and was the port of communication between Asia and Macedonia. Its walls formed a rectangle about five miles in perimeter, and its harbor consisted of a walled basin four hundred feet long and two hundred feet wide. The city must have had a vigorous social life, since it maintained a theater, odeum, stadium, and gymnasium. On account of its importance as a port, and because of the legendary history of the surrounding region, Julius Caesar once thought seriously of making it the center of government for his empire. Paul must have looked upon the city as an inviting field in which to preach his gospel, but it lay in the prohibited area, and he had to pass through in silence.

When the four travelers went down to the harbor, they learned that the wind was favorable to a speedy journey. After the ship was loosed from its moorings, it was maneuvered slowly out of the harbor and then submitted full-sail to the propelling winds. It was a "direct voyage" before the wind to Samothrace, not a zigzag course of laborious tacking. The favorable wind even eased the current of inland waters that bore out upon them from the narrow Hellespont. Every hour swept them over waters, past coasts, and near islands rich in historic and legendary lore—first, the coast of Asia with its islands, and then the shores of Europe.

Beyond the island of Tenedos, the ship came into line with the islands of Imbros and Samothrace and farther north cut squarely across the current from the Hellespont, not far from the scene of the famous story of Hero and Leander. Then, rounding the island of Imbros, it brought into full view the great mound of Samotrace protruding boldly from the sea to the height of nearly a mile.[11]

In the evening, under the northern shelter of Samothrace in a quiet sea, the crew cast anchor for the night. Perhaps the "master" or the owners of the ship had been initiated on that very island into the secret mysteries of the Kabeiri, and felt secure under their benevolent care. Paul, Silas, Timothy, and Luke, however, were trusting, not in a group of planetary deities, but in the very Maker of heaven and earth Himself.

As the darkness lifted on the following morning, they weighed anchor and sailed for Neapolis, the seaport of Philippi. The whole voyage from Troas to Philippi took only two days, whereas a later voyage in the opposite direction required five.[12] Here for the first time Paul's feet rested upon the shores of Europe. No one awaited his arrival. Nor did anyone fear his coming, or care that he came, or suspect that he bore a message that would release a new force in the making of history, rock the thrones of kings, and put paganism to flight.

On the day after their arrival in Neapolis, the four men were on their way to Philippi, nine or ten miles inland from its port, after the manner of ancient cities. It was an inspiring ride. Immediately beyond the city, the road ascended a high ridge, from one side of which there burst into view an overpowering sight of the Aegean Sea and its islands, and from the other a great fertile plain, the Plain of Philippi, that thrust itself far back against the marble slopes of lofty mountains. Towards the southeast lay the island of Thasos, and far beyond rose the gray peaks of Samothrace, the Samos of Thrace, for there was a famous Samos of Ionia two hundred miles south. And surely there was a pause when the eyes of the group came into line with flaming Mount Athos that towered like a mighty beacon at the end of a long narrow peninsula.

On the low ground near the marshes, Paul must have looked with admiration upon the profusion of indigenous roses that for centuries had been characteristic of the region. Theophrastus, a botanist, wrote of them four hundred years before Paul visited Macedonia; and Pliny, another naturalist, wrote of them again in Paul's own time.

Beyond the great plain, on the slope of a ridge, stood Philippi, proclaiming the name of Philip of Macedonia. It was a strongly fortified little city, with two concentric walls and numerous towers. The wall of the lower city formed a rectangle, and that of the upper city, or acropolis, a triangle. Paul and his company entered below. It was a border city and a Roman colony, therefore soldiers were numerous. It was a mining town, for gold was found in the nearby hills, and therefore many slaves and men of wealth thronged its narrow streets. It was a highway city, for it stood upon the great Via Egnatia that connected Rome with the far East, and therefore was a city of taverns and travelers—an ideal place from which to broadcast the gospel.

Luke led the way through the crowded lower city, perhaps to his own home, or to the home of a friend. Very soon the four men looked for a place to begin their work, and perhaps, like other traveling teachers, selected the agora. The details of their labors were not recorded, though to some extent they may be conjectured from certain incidents related by Luke and from Paul's own letter to the Philippians.

It was Paul's rule to visit the synagogues, where any existed, before he offered his gospel to the Gentiles, but evidently there was no synagogue in Philippi. On the first Sabbath Luke led the party beyond the gates towards a place by the Gangites River where he supposed the Jews, if any, and their proselytes would assemble for prayer. The Jews who had formerly dwelt in Philippi had obtained a plot of ground where the waters of the Gangites were suitable for ceremonial ablutions and where the oak and mulberry spread out their leafy boughs to form a temple dome.[13] There, the evangelists found a group of praying women.

It is possible that the edict of Claudius expelling the Jews from Rome[14] may have extended to Philippi also and, if so, the oratory at the time of Paul's visit was still in the possession of proselytes, most or all of whom were women. In Macedonia, the woman was the head of the family and enjoyed the privilege of holding property and conducting business in her own name. Then, too, those women who had been attracted to the high standards of Judaism were equally ready to turn to the promised Messiah when they learned that He was the Savior of the Gentile as well as of the Jew. These conditions gave Paul and his aides a powerful leverage in Philippi.

The place of worship was perhaps only an open shady place, possibly it was a walled roofless enclosure, it may even have been a house. But on that first Sabbath, it became a Christian church, the first in all Europe, and there for "many days" Paul, Silas, Timothy, and possibly Luke, proclaimed the gospel of salvation and baptized those who believed.

Among the first converts, and that, perhaps, at the first meeting, was a woman named Lydia, a native of Thyatira in the old kingdom of Lydia in Asia Minor. She was a "seller of purple," the costly cloth and robes of that color, or of the dye itself, or of both. She probably maintained connection with the guild of dyers in her native city or even with those of Tyre and Miletus.[15] Evidently she was a woman of wealth and influence.

At the first meeting in the "place of prayer," the speakers sat and gave their message informally. While Lydia was listening to Paul, her heart was stirred with emotion[16] and she believed the thrilling story of the risen Christ and of his power to save. After she was baptized along with her household, she urged Paul and his assistants to accept the hospitality of her home. She persisted until they yielded and then opened her house for the observance of love feasts and the celebration of the commemorative Supper. Christianity then was an intense faith. It involved a perfect brotherhood of love, the complete subjugation of self in the service of the Lord, and the hourly expectation of the Lord's return.

The supposition sometimes set forth that Lydia was a widow, is wholly unnecessary. In Philippi, she was the head of her household and it would have been discourteous to her to have spoken of her husband as host. Luke is brief and had no occasion to mention explicitly a husband, sons, or daughters. Lydia was acting within her own prerogative, even if her husband was living and was at home. But to carry the supposition farther, and to suggest a love affair between the apostle and his hostess, is as unpardonable as the act of the presbyter who wrote the ancient fiction about Paul and Thecla.

The Greek and Roman gods had their votaries in Philippi but with one or two exceptions were less corrupted than in the other cities where Paul had labored. Minerva and Diana, Hercules and Mercury had their shrines, and even the Syrian Men or moon-god. Queer old Silvanus had been honored by the Romans with a temple and, like most gods, he had suffered from confusion with others of similar domains and occupations.

But the old cult of the region, which was still vigorous at the time of Paul's visit, was the worship of Dionysus, or Bacchus, the god of wine. He was served by priestesses who at his festivals led wild orgiastic dances, whirling violently with disheveled hair and distorted faces and shrieking like maniacs.[17] Also there were certain men in the city who played upon the credulity of the people by the practice of divination; and among these were two or more men who owned a remarkable slave girl, who was reputed to be a Pythoness.[18] In mythology, the Python was a reptilian monster that guarded the famous oracle of Delphi. It was slain by Apollo, who succeeded to its prophetic power and even to its name.

Because the girl was supposed to possess a spirit of Python, many people consulted her owners for advice. The young woman had learned of Paul, and for many days followed him and his helpers, shouting: "These men are servants of the Most High God who proclaim to you the way of salvation." Only guesses can be made about her meaning or motives. Perhaps her owners sent her out hoping to confuse Paul's work with their own and thus draw trade. Certainly her wild utterance was a familiar one in paganism and one that the Philippians would readily apply to Apollo.

Paul was annoyed and perhaps knew the danger of interfering with the girl but he finally turned upon her, rebuked the evil spirit that he supposed had possession of her saying, "I charge you in the name of Jesus Christ to come out of her." Luke records the incident from the point of view taken in his own day, when he and Paul and everyone else believed in demoniacal and other spirit possessions. Within the hour, the evil spirit departed.

The girl's owners were enraged, for "their hope of gain was gone." They seized Paul and Silas and dragged them into the agora before the city judges, followed by an ever-increasing mob, hungry for violence. The case was quickly passed to the magistrates, and the crowd followed. All knew the fame of the Pythoness. Soothsayers everywhere commanded a certain kind of respect and their complaints were likely to receive prompt attention.

Paul and Silas had been roughly handled, but naturally hoped for an opportunity to defend themselves before the court. The magistrates sat upon their tribunal. The soothsayers brought two charges. Both were serious, or rather, could be made to appear so: "These men are Jews," and, "They teach an unlicensed religion;" or, as Luke quotes them, "These men are Jews and they are disturbing our city. They advocate customs which it is not lawful for us Romans to accept or practice."

The magistrates were in full sympathy with the mob and believed that the prisoners had committed a crime by exorcising the spirit of the Pythoness. They flew into a religious frenzy and, if Luke's words may be taken literally, ignored the law that required a fair trial and without giving the usual formal charge, "Go, lictors, strip them," sprang from their bench and with their own hands tore the garments off Paul and Silas and then commanded the lictors to beat them with rods. These quickly put aside their robes for freedom of action and "inflicted many blows upon them."[19]

Paul and Silas then were turned over to the jailer, placed in the inner prison, and had their feet locked in stocks.

At this point Luke's taste for the miraculous enters, and his statements become a bit improbable though not intentionally erroneous. He believed in divine interventions and told his story as he thought things should have happened. It runs as follows: "But about midnight Paul and Silas were praying and singing hymns to God, and the prisoners were listening to them; and suddenly there was a great earthquake, so that the foundations of the prison were shaken; and immediately all the doors were opened and everyone's fetters were unfastened. When the jailer woke and saw that the prison doors were open, he drew his sword and was about to kill himself, supposing that the prisoners had escaped. But Paul cried with a loud voice, 'Do not harm yourself, for we are all here.' "[20]

The coincidence between Paul's imprisonment and the occurrence of an earthquake need not be regarded as miraculous; life is full of coincidences. Besides, seismic disturbances were numerous over a wide region along the northern and eastern Mediterranean for the whole period of Paul's life up to the destruction of Pompeii by the eruption of Vesuvius in A.D. 79. Tacitus, Seneca, and Josephus mention one or more of the following places:[21] Rome, Apamea, Phrygia, Sardis, Laodicea, Campania, Crete, Achaia, Syria, Macedonia, and proconsular Asia.

Neither should there be amazement at Luke's descriptions in which factual statements are made rhetorically in order to produce desired effects. "Everyone's fetters were unfastened" means, perhaps, that the rings to which the prisoners were chained had been shaken loose by the shifting of the stones in the prison walls.

Luke now proceeds briefly and dramatically with an account of the jailer's conversion as he had heard of it and as he remembered it after many years. He knew that the jailer had never been given charge of two such offenders as Paul and Silas. They were impressive personalities with almost dangerous self-possession, a strange combination of tenderness and strength, the very embodiment of moral power.

The hardened master of desperate criminals called for torches, rushed into the dungeon, and cast himself at the feet of Paul and Silas. "What must I do to be saved?" begged the jailer. "Believe in the Lord Jesus,"[22] replied Paul. Eagerly the jailer accepted the terms of salvation. Then, in the dim light, the two prisoners baptized their Roman keeper and all his household. Finally, they went to the jailer's house, where Paul and Silas were no longer unwelcome law-breaking Jews but honored guests. Far into the night, they ate the love feast with their rejoicing host.

With the return of daylight the magistrates sent their lictors to the prison with the contemptuous order, "Let those men go." Evidently something had made them uneasy. When the jailer reported to Paul and

Silas what he thought was good news, he exclaimed, "Now therefore come out and go in peace." But Paul defiantly replied, "They have beaten us publicly, uncondemned, men who are Roman citizens, and have thrown us into prison; and do they now cast us out secretly? No! let them come themselves and take us out."[23] These were the words of one whose course of action was determined not by a desire for personal safety, but by the wish to protect the honor and welfare of his Lord's church. To have taken shelter under his Roman citizenship by crying out, "I am a Roman citizen," to save himself from a beating, would have nullified his martyr doctrine and inoculated the Philippian Church with ruinous instability. There would be times to hide, to flee, and even to appeal to Rome, but this was not one of them.

The magistrates had revealed their weakness: They had been undignified in the conduct of their court, they had failed to inquire into the status of their prisoners, and they had given them no opportunity to defend themselves. Without legal procedure they had ordered a beating. By their hasty indifference they had violated Roman laws that rendered them liable to punishment, ranging from ordinary penalties to the forfeiture of life.

When the lictors returned with their message, the two praetors hastened to the prison and apologized to Paul and Silas. Then, as if fearing to display any sign of authority, meekly "asked them to leave the city."

After their release, Paul and Silas went to Lydia's home to rest. Later they called the brethren of the church together for parting instructions. Doubtless the church had been fully organized before the arrest of Paul and Silas and was safe under the care of its elders, deacons, and teachers. Certainly it continued to prosper and became the strongest supporter of Paul's European work. The permanent bond of love that existed between it and its founder was exceptional and beautiful.

REFERENCES
Chapter 9

1. Acts 23:16.
2. Acts 16:4.
3. Acts 16:5.
4. Acts 16:1.
5. II Tim. 1:5.
6. Gal. 5:6.
7. Acts 16:4-5.
8. Acts 16:6-8.
9. Col. 4:14.
10. Heb. 11:8.
11. Acts 16:10-17.
12. Acts 20:6.
13. Cf. Juvenal, Satire III, Lines 23-24, 296; cf. also Ps. 137:1; Ezek. 1:3.
14. Acts 18:2.
15. Strabo. *The Geography*. XIII. 4. 14.
16. Acts 16:14.
17. Cf. Clement of Rome, *Recognitions* 31.
18. Acts 16:16-19.
19. Acts 16:23.
20. Acts 16:28.
21. Josephus. *Wars*. IV. 4. Sec. 5; Tacitus. *The Annals*. XII. 43. Sec. 58; XIV. 27; XV. 22; Seneca. *Works. Exhortations.* Sec. 91.
22. Acts 16:30-31.
23. Acts 16:37.

Paul and Lydia in Philippi

Second Missionary Tour: Philippi — Athens

THE PARTING SERVICE at Philippi, including the observance of the agape and the eucharist, must have occurred in the evening several days after the beating. On the following morning Paul and Silas took Timothy and departed for Thessalonica. Luke perhaps remained in Philippi, though he may have been absent at the time of the arrest.

It was a cold morning in late December when the three evangelists began their ride. Paul and Silas felt the weight of their winter garments upon their wounded backs, but they were traveling in the joy of victory, when wounds were but badges of honorable conflict. Their sufferings had made them bold, as Paul wrote later "but though we had already suffered and been shamefully treated at Philippi, as you know, we had courage in our God to declare to you the gospel of God in the face of much opposition."[1]

Toward evening they reached the narrow neck of land betwen Lake Cercinitis and the Strymonic Gulf, across which the Strymon River had cut its way, and on which stood Amphipolis, a Greek city built upon an older town called Ennea Hodoi, the Nine Ways. The city stood on a promontory that thrust into a deep bend of the river and was walled on the

119

land side only. After at least one night's rest, the travelers crossed the Strymon, perhaps at the point where Xerxes had offered his sacrifice of white horses to the river and where he had buried alive nine youths and maidens. Much of their route lay along a plain, with a view of the sea to the left, and of Mt. Athos fifty miles away.

Wearily they passed the marble milestones along the great Roman military highway. As the day advanced, they crossed another river that severed another neck of land between the sea and a second lake, and in the evening came to Apollonia, where they rested and then continued westward through a long valley that almost severed the Chalcidic peninsula from the mainland. To the left were imposing heavily timbered mountains and to the right, the quiet waters of Lake Bolbe. Before nightfall they ascended a low ridge, and after passing through a defile came into view of the Thermaic Gulf, the Plain of Axius, and Thessalonica, at their feet.

It was the old city of Thermae, so named from the hot springs in the vicinity, and renamed, perhaps by Cassander, in honor of his wife, Thessalonica, the daughter of Philip of Macedon and half sister of Alexander the Great. Within the city, the Roman road became a long straight street, spanned by a great triumphal arch celebrating the victory of Octavianus and Anthony at Philippi.

When Paul and his companions came to the eastern gate, they inquired for the Jewish quarter and then sought a man who may have been known to Paul and Silas; Joshua, or Jesus, or, as he was known to the Greek city, Jason. He may have been a manufacturer with whom Paul hoped to find employment.[2] Jason, like Lydia of Philippi, seems to have received the evangelists gladly and his home became their headquarters.

Paul did not stumble as a refugee upon Thessalonica, but mapped it on his itinerary as an important center from which the gospel might radiate. Amphipolis and Apollonia, like other cities, had been left to become out-stations for the other laborers.

Thessalonica, five or six miles in perimeter, stood impressively on a remarkably calm and beautiful harbor. The great walled city was the metropolis of Macedonia, a busy commercial and manufacturing center. It had been honored with self-government, for which it was careful to be loyal to Rome. The opportunities it offered for business attracted large numbers of Jews.

Paul and his companions could not have been in the city long without becoming aware of some of its historic past, nor could they have remained ignorant of their proximity to the scenes of ancient myths. From several points about the city, Mount Olympus, the home of the gods, could be seen fifty miles away. Beyond it could be seen Ossa, upon which the giants would pile Pelion in order to scale heaven. And between Ossa and

Olympus lay the valley of Tempe, that deep and rugged gash where Orpheus opened the gates of death and where Apollo atoned for slaying the Python.

As usual, Paul began his work in the synagogue, and for three Sabbath days reasoned with the Jews in an effort to convince them from their own scriptures that the Messiah they sought would have to fulfill prophecies that required him to suffer, die, and rise again from the dead. From the fact that Jesus had fulfilled these conditions, he proclaimed him to be the Messiah. Some of the Jews and a multitude of Greek proselytes and prominent women believed and met with Paul and Silas for instruction and worship. But after the third Sabbath Day, the synagogue was closed against the messianic preachers, and Paul proceeded at once to organize his church, perhaps at the home of Jason.

For five months or more the evangelists labored, winning Gentile converts from those who had been trained in Judaism, and others directly from idolatry. While the chill of winter lasted, they did most of their preaching in the homes of converts, but with the return of inviting weather they must have made frequent visits to the agora, to the neighborhood of the great hippodrome, and out to the famous thermal baths. Perhaps they even went to the little temple where sailors who had been initiated into the secret mysteries of the Kabeiri congregated. But everywhere men were becoming tired of their ancient gods, and many turned welcoming ears to the new gospel of salvation.

For many days, Paul toiled with his hands at his trade of tentmaker, weaving, cutting, and sewing to support himself and his helpers. In this way he would not be chargeable to the church, which, in its infancy, would have been suspicious of any man who attempted to profit by his preaching.[3] Besides, the Jews were watching him. Their own rabbis had trades and worked at them—shoemaker, tailor, potter, baker, carpenter, and others. Paul did not wish to lose favor with his own race to the injury of his church. His toil, however, was eased somewhat by gifts that were sent to him from his beloved church at Philippi.[4]

As converts from paganism to Christianity increased, the synagogue grew jealous of the church. They collected a band of ruffians from the idlers of the market square, who paraded the streets until a crowd had collected and the city was thrown into an uproar. They then rushed to the house of Jason, seeking Paul and Silas. Not finding them, they seized Jason and the prominent leaders of the church and haled them before the rulers of the city.

There they prefaced their charge by saying, "These men who have turned the world upside down have come here also"[5]—words that were unintentionally complimentary to Paul and Silas. The charge was then so framed that it included not only Paul and Silas, but Jason and his companion, and the whole church. Luke states it thus, "and Jason has received them; and they are all acting against the decrees of Caesar, saying that there is another king, Jesus,"[6] It was a sweeping charge of treason by which they hoped to expose the founders and leaders of the church to the penalties of the Julian laws.[7] The officials and others present felt a shock of anxiety from the nature of the charge, and evidently suspected ulterior motives in the accusation, for after taking security from Jason and his companions, they let them go. A case of sedition could not have been treated so lightly.

The politarchs of the Greek free city, like the praetors of the Roman colony of Philippi were now anxious to be rid of the two men. Out of respect to the officials, who had acted benevolently, and to protect Jason and the officers of the church, Paul and Silas decided to leave at once. But they had already founded a church that would make history through the centuries.

Before Paul left the city, he received the disheartening news that his Galatian churches, Derbe, Lystra, Iconium, and Antioch, and perhaps others, were being swept away from his gospel back to Judaism. This defection was brought about by certain Judaizers who were dissatisfied with the decisions of the Jerusalem council and who trailed Paul on his second tour, maligning him and frightening his converts. It is possible that these men went out with the connivance of James, the head of the church in Jerusalem.

The success of these men was so alarming that someone dispatched full particulars to Paul. The news struck deep into the apostle's soul. His indignation became explosive; his defensive instincts surged for expression; and his abhorrence of religious narrowness on one hand, and of instability on the other, drove his emotions from rage to pity. In that mood he wrote a letter, the earliest of all preserved Christian documents, that reveals its author as a fearless, masterful leader who could be graciously just while necessarily severe.

Conscious of his power, he expressed no doubt about the effect of what he wrote and presumed he would be obeyed. The wolves that had entered the Galatian folds said that Paul was only a man-made apostle from Antioch, that he pilfered his gospel from the true apostles, that he preached for the applause of men, and that he was inconsistent in his attitude toward circumcision.

Of course Paul was human enough to be angry, and angry enough to subject his enemies to smarting irony and humiliating sarcasm. Of the false preacher he said: "But even if we, or an angel from heaven should preach to you a gospel contrary to that which we preached to you, let him be accursed."[8] Of the cringing church officials at Jerusalem he said: "And from those who were reputed to be something, what they were makes no difference to me; God shows no partiality."[9] And of the radical circumcisionists he said in disgust: "I wish those who unsettle you would mutilate themselves."[10]

In his salutation to the Galatians, Paul asserted the divine origin of his apostleship and then defended the origin of his gospel, which he claimed had come to him through revelation of Jesus Christ. He excluded all human sources, even that of the Jerusalem apostles. He did not refer to the so-called apostolic council of Jerusalem, because it occurred after his first missionary tour and therefore had no bearing on his preaching at that time.

The letter next turns to the great subject of the ceremonial law and pleads the cause of spiritual liberty. Though necessarily rabbinical in its reasoning, the discussion nevertheless reveals to the Jew, and to the world, a new and satisfactory way into perfect righteousness. It stands today as a withering rebuke to all those religionists who adulterate faith by injecting into it certain ecclesiastical practices and making them essentials of salvation. The law proclaimed man a sinner and condemned sin, but it had no power to save. Though imperfect, weak, and temporary it did, however, point to a messianic Savior. It led the world to the Christ. With the approach of the Christ, the function of the Mosaic law ceased, and man came under the law of faith and the operations of divine grace. And even circumcision, the seal of the Jew, for which the Judaizing Christians contended so rabidly, lost its original significance and gave way to the new seal, the seal of the Spirit. All people were to become one in Christ Jesus, in whom none would be known as Jew or Greek, slave or free, male or female, circumcised or uncircumcised.[11]

The firm decisiveness of this letter reveals a man who understood men and who knew his own mind. The expressions of surprise and doubt show tactical approaches to difficult subjects: "I am astonished that you are so quickly deserting him who called you;"[12] "O foolish Galatians who has bewitched you?"[13] And there is just enough tenderness, appreciation, and confidence to excite obedience and restore order: "Brethren, I beseech you;"[14] "My little children;"[15] "You would have plucked out your eyes and given them to me."[16]

After giving certain orders and warnings about conditions in general, Paul closed his letter with emphatic finality: "Henceforth let not man trouble me; for I bear on my body the marks of Jesus"[17]—and it was final, for the Galatians turned again to their spiritual liberty in the gospel.

With this new anxiety heaped like Pelion upon Ossa, Paul and Silas prepared to leave Thessalonica immediately. They decided that Timothy should remain behind to stabilize the disturbed church, and later to follow and make his report. The brethren, knowing the danger from the stones of the Jews and the daggers of the ruffians to which the two men would be exposed, sent them away by night to Beroea, fifty miles onward in the direction of their proposed tour.

Shortly after Orion had disappeared below the western horizon and the Twins, Castor and Pollux, were entering the mists just behind him, Paul and Silas and their escort left some quiet home beyond the walls of the city and entered the Via Egnatia for the first half of their secret journey. At midnight the Northern Crown, studded with starry gems, hung exactly overhead. Paul was striving for a heavenly crown;[18] was this an omen of success? Dawn, and then the glowing sun—and Pella was in sight. Here was food, and short rest. Beroea was one daytime ride distant on a road of varied scenery that led southward from the Egnatian Way. Beroea was a secluded city, a half-day's journey back from the sea. It stood upon a mountain slope, and looked out from beneath great plane trees down the wider fertile valley of the Haliacmon far towards Thessalonica.

It was evening when the little company crossed the bridge below the city and rode up to the gate.

It was not long until the men were made comfortable in the home of some prominent Jew recommended by the brethren back in Thessalonica. At their first opportunity they visited the synagogue, where they were heard with great respect and openness of mind, unlike their reception in Thessalonica, where they had been confronted with an attitude of doubt and suspicion. Of the Beroean Jews Luke said: "These Jews were more noble than those in Thessalonica, for they received the word with all eagerness, examining the scriptures daily to see if these things were so."[19] This compliment has left an imperishable halo about the name of Beroea.

There was immediate success in this field of refuge. Many of the Jews believed, and many women of high standing.

After perhaps a few weeks, Timothy came down from Thessalonica and reported that the church there was still steadfast and growing. With this encouragement the three men toiled joyfully, and converts continued to multiply. But back in Thessalonica the elders of the synagogue scowled heavily. Many of their proselytes had gone over to the church, and the receipts of their treasury were falling off. They hated Paul, and, hearing that he had gone to Beroea, they sent emissaries there hoping to disorganize the church and to destroy Paul. Whatever trouble the emissaries may have made, they failed in their main purpose, for the brethren promptly conveyed Paul to another field, keeping Silas and Timothy with them to complete the organization of the church.

It was perhaps near the middle of October when Paul gave his parting instructions to Silas and Timothy about the infant Beroean Church. There could be no delay. The enraged Jews were ready with stones, and the assassins with daggers. A merciless death awaited him if he should be discovered.

A little company of brethren on horses escorted Paul down to Dium, a

Roman colony seventeen miles distant. It was the intention of the escort to return after seeing Paul aboard a ship bound for Athens, but some new danger arose, and at least two of the brethren accompanied him all the way to Athens.

The sail may have been accomplished in three days, or three times three, or more, according to the winds and weather and the possibility of night sailing. The course lay through waters and along shores laden with the events of history, tradition, and myth; enriched by the gifts of poets, orators, and philosophers; and adorned by the works of engineers, architects, and sculptors.

Athens, like many other ancient cities stood back from the coast. Piraeus, its port, stood on the Saronic Gulf, five miles distant. Port and city were once connected by a broad and densely populated avenue between two many-towered walls. But when Paul passed that way, these were in ruins.

Paul was not wholly ignorant of Athens, for he had heard enough about the city to form a mental outline of its site, architecture, and inhabitants. He had heard of its famous philosophers and knew of its reputation for gossipy learning. Athens was a self-centered city, inordinately proud of its past and unconscious of its present decadence. Paul had no intention of wasting his gospel on its infertile soil but from Corinth he would soon undermine its worldly wisdom. The city was simply a place for waiting until he could assemble his helpers and move onward.

As he passed through the gates between the Pnyx and Museum hills, he became conscious of an atmosphere and spirit different from that in any other city he had ever known. Tarsus was gay and boastful; Antioch, transparent and vulgar; Jerusalem, azure and ritualistic; but Athens was pale and insincere, a city of altars, temples, and gods, where many worshiped without believing, and others, fearing unbelief, propitiated gods unknown; a city of ivory and silver, bronze and marble, gardens and fountains; a city where exquisite art imposed itself upon every eye, and gaiety paraded itself as the universal solace.

Paul was not embarrassed; he was saddened. He knew that when men glorify their own wisdom and their own works, they become blind to God, lose the consciousness of His personality, and become callous to His infinite attributes.

Within the gate, Paul easily recognized the members of his own race — dark-bearded men in loose simlahs—and was at once on his way to the Jewish colony. Having decided upon a place where he could be found, he dismissed his escort with instructions to Silas and Timothy to come to Athens.

There was a synagogue at Athens, and into it the Jews withdrew as from a noisome pestilence—a pestilence of gods. Despite the skepticism of philosophers and the sacrilegious jest of poets, playwrights, and satirists, the twelve gods of Olympus still kept sanctuaries in Athens.

One altar in particular may have attracted Paul's attention. It was dedicated to "an unknown god." It was perhaps the votive offering of some citizen who could not determine what god had befriended him in some emergency. Petronius,[20] who wrote somewhat later than Luke, said in his satirical way that it was easier to find a god than a man in Athens.

Tarsus had its gods, but they were not associated with the development of art, and were therefore less conspicuous. Jerusalem had but one God, the "Lord of heaven and earth."[21] No craftsman could carve his likeness. Paul the Jew did not think the better of an idol because it was a work of art. To him an idol had "no real existence,"[22] but the sight of a city forever in an attitude of adoration before dumb images—and that city the boastful Athens—agitated his soul to its depths.

When Paul returned to the synagogue he found himself swayed by an almost furious moral urge; Athens had robbed him of needed rest—he must preach. Regularly in the synagogue he reasoned with the Jews and devout Greeks, and daily he took his place in the agora to proclaim the Christ to all who would hear. In the agora he was commanding and forceful enough to attract the attention of certain philosophers of the two chief schools of the city, the Epicureans and the Stoics.[23]

As these men were parading in front of the shops and temples around the great marketplace they heard Paul's earnest voice, and saw an unusually attentive audience gather close around him. They drew closer, and in their customary scurrilous way said, "What would this seed-picker,[24] this dung-pecking finch, this chatterer, this babbler say?" As they listened, someone remarked, "He seems to be a preacher of foreign divinities." They caught only sentences without context, and words without definitions: Christ, Jesus, resurrection.

Soon they decided that he was worth hearing, but that the agora was not a suitable place for their purpose; so they took him to the Areopagus, or the open-air court close by, on the summit of Mars Hill. It was there that Socrates, four hundred and fifty years before, had stood charged with the crime of introducing strange gods.

Judging from Luke's description of the scene on Mars Hill, Paul must have been treated with at least cautious respect. At least one member of the court was present, and, perhaps, a large number of those educated idlers, citizens, and strangers, who "spent their time in nothing except telling or hearing something new."[25]

Beckoning for order, one of the philosophers addressed Paul with shallow politeness saying, "May we know what this new teaching is which you present? For you bring some strange things to our ears; we wish to know therefore what these things mean."[26] Paul was well acquainted with the principal tenets of both the Stoic and Epicurean philosophies, for they were taught openly in his home city of Tarsus, and doubtless were discussed in Gamaliel's school in Jerusalem. He knew in advance that a part of his address would invite sharp dissent or even ridicule, yet he was as bold to proclaim what he believed to be true as his hearers would be to defend the ancient doctrines of the "Porch" and the "Garden" or of the Academy and the Lyceum.

Luke has prepared an outline of what he thought would be an appropriate exordium to Paul's address, but breaks off just where the Apostle would introduce his proofs of the resurrection of Jesus. It is an admirable approach that feels its way cautiously among the conflicting views of the sophisticated critics of Mars Hill.

All eyes were turned on Paul. He was aware of a suppressed judgement that in a moment might express itself in ridicule; an intense coolness that in an instant might release itself in violence. But Paul was not a coward; he was not ashamed of his race or of his Jewish education and not ashamed of his gospel which carried more power than all the philosophies of Athens to give solace to the human heart. He knew that the scholastic assumptions and dialectic methods of Athens differed so greatly from the Jewish fundamentals and the rabbinical reasoning of Jerusalem that he would be at a disadvantage as a speaker. And yet he knew that his gospel had a universal appeal that might break down any barrier, or any "dividing wall of hostility."[27]

Therefore without undue deference, without self-abasement, and without false pretensions, he stood before the august court of Mars Hill half as an honored guest and half as a possible subject of legal apprehension. Paul was as calm as the soft October air. Beckoning with his hand for attention, said: "Men of Athens, I perceive that in every way you are very religious. For as I passed along, and observed the objects of your worship. I found also an altar with this inscription, 'To an unknown God.' What therefore you worship as unknown, this I proclaim to you. The God who made the world and everything in it, being Lord of heaven and earth, does not live in shrines made by man, nor is he served by human hands, as though he needed anything, since he himself gives to all men life and breath and everything. And he made from one every nation of men to live on all the face of the earth, having determined allotted periods and boundaries of their habitation that they should seek God, in the hope they might feel after him and find him. Yet he is not far from each one of us, for 'In him we live, and move and have our being;' as even some of your own poets have said. 'For we are indeed his offspring.'

"Being then God's offspring, we ought not to think that the Deity is like gold, or silver, or stone, a representation by the art and imagination of man. The times of ignorance therefore God overlooked, but now he commands all men everywhere to repent, because he has fixed a day on which he will judge the world in righteousness by a man whom he has appointed, and of this he has given assurance to all men by raising him from the dead."[28]

At the mention of the resurrection, the Epicureans and some others laughed aloud and scoffed. Those with closed minds arose and left. Paul was not surprised at this interruption. In his speech, however, he cleverly cleared himself of the possible charge of introducing new gods by quoting an inscription from an authorized altar and by appealing to the poets, Aratus and Cleanthes.

But some who had listened to the apostle wished to hear him no more, others wished to hear him again, and still others heard and believed. Of these last Luke names but two; one from the noblest blood of Athens, and the other a common woman; Dionysius the Areopagite and Damaris. Both must have achieved prominence later in the Athenian church, otherwise Luke would not have named them. In fact tradition says that Dionysius became the first bishop of Athens.[29]

Paul probably continued preaching for several days after his contact with the interrogators of Mars Hill, and also probably confined his preaching strictly to his own message. He was too wise a man to waste time as the Athenians were doing in interminable debates for the mere sake of discussion. It would be a serious misunderstanding of the apostle, and an erroneous interpretation of Luke, to suppose that Paul was disillusioned or discouraged by his contact with the Athenians. He knew Athens before it knew him, and Luke was not telling a melancholy story of failure, but one of skillful triumph.

While Paul was still awaiting the arrival of his two helpers from Beroea, he received news of a most distressing nature from his churches in Macedonia. Persecution had begun, and he was sorely troubled that the faith of his converts should fail them. Therefore immediately upon the arrival of Silas and Timothy they were sent back to Macedonia; Timothy to Thessalonica,[30] and Silas perhaps to Philippi, both with instructions to report at Corinth.

This was one of the darkest periods in the apostle's history. The Judaizers and the unbelieving Jews were on his trail, determined to undo his work. The former had almost taken Galatia from him, and now the latter were seeking his life and undermining the faith of his converts in Europe. A dark despair[31] was creeping over his soul; faith in his apostolic power was ebbing out like a tired sea; and his tongue began proclaiming only a cautious gospel—the inoffensive half that Peter preached. A messenger of Satan more terrible than fever was humbling the apostle of Christ. Paul dared not rush back to Macedonia; certain death awaited him there. His only hope lay in what Silas and Timothy might be able to do for the churches by encouraging them to remain steadfast under persecution.

Immediately after the departure of Silas and Timothy, Paul met for the last time with the little group of believers that he had gathered from the synagogue, the agora and the Areopagus; and, after delivering a farewell exhortation, he sailed for Corinth.

REFERENCES
Chapter 10

1. I Thes. 2:2.
2. Cf. I Thes. 2:9.
3. I Thes. 2:9; II Thes. 3:8.
4. Phil. 4:16.
5. Acts 17:6.
6. Acts 17:7.
7. Cf. Luke 23:2; John 19:12.
8. Gal. 1:8.
9. Gal. 2:6.
10. Gal. 5:12.
11. Gal. 3:28; Col. 3:11.
12. Gal. 1:6.
13. Gal. 3:1.
14. Gal. 4:13.
15. Gal. 4:19.
16. Gal. 4:15.
17. Gal. 5:17.
18. I Cor. 9:25.
19. Acts 17:11.
20. Petronius. *Satires.* 17.
21. Acts 17:24.
22. I Cor. 8:4.
23. Acts 17:18.
24. Cf. Aristophanes. *The Birds.*
25. Acts 17:21.
26. Acts 17:19-20.
27. Eph. 2:14.
28. Acts 17:22-31.
29. Eusebius. *The Ecclesiastical History.* III. 4; IV. 23.
30. I Thes. 3:2.
31. I Thes. 2:17-18; 3:5.

Mars Hill, Athens

Second Missionary Tour: Athens — Antioch, Syria

IT WAS ABOUT FORTY MILES from Piraeus, the northern port of Athens, to Cenchreae, the eastern port of Corinth. As Paul's vessel passed out into the open sea, the great bronze statue of Minerva, the protectress of Athens, gradually rose into view from her pedestal high on the great rock of the Acropolis. Phidas had fashioned her from the broken shields and spears gathered from the awful carnage of Marathon. She looked westward over the sea towards Corinth as if warning Aphrodite, who watched the ports of her own city from the Acro-Corinthus, that Paul the foe of the gods was approaching.

But Paul was heavy of heart, and the very majesty of the sea that he loved and the beauty of the ever-changing coastlines only deepened his sadness. He knew that if his converts weakened under persecution, his work as an apostle would be a failure.[1] There was some relief however in the thought of new adventures in a new field, especially in a city that was making history instead of looking back complacently on history already made.

It was perhaps about the middle of November when Paul crossed the Saronic Gulf and rode up from Cenchreae to Corinth. The weather in that month was usually humid and chilly and not at all favorable to one suffering from depression and anxiety. Somewhere he found a temporary lodging, but his expenses had been heavy and he had to find employment at his old trade. Somehow he met Aquila and Priscilla, a Jewish couple who had come lately from Italy because of an order of Claudius expelling all Jews from Rome. With them he found a home and employment, for like himself they were tentmakers. It is possible that Aquila and his wife were already Christians and that they were as glad to receive Paul as he was to find them.

The Corinth of Paul's day was an effective center from which to spread the gospel. It stood at the western end of the long narrow isthmus of rock that prevents the lower end of Greece from breaking away into a great island. Thus it stood near two seas, and by Horace was called the "city of two seas."

Corinth had two ports: Lechaeum, on the western sea about a mile and a half north of the city and connected with it by a broad fortified avenue like that connecting Piraeus with Athens; and Cenchreae, nearly nine miles away on the eastern sea. The city therefore commanded the only land route from north to south through Greece and had sea connections with both the east and the west.

Corinth was the wealthiest city in all Greece and the capital of the Roman province of Achaia. It had its temples and altars, its schools and library, its bath and theaters, its agora and its parks. The population, though predominantly Roman[2] and Greek, was extremely heterogeneous; and though a city of trade and manufacture, it took a degree of pride in the arts and encouraged at least the appearance of learning. Its promiscuous character however brought to it the vices of many countries, until to live like a Corinthian was to yield both body and mind to the foulest excesses of lust. The Aphrodite of Corinth, the beautiful Venus, had lost all her modesty and had become the mother of a thousand harlots, who as her courtesans, entertained the slaves of passion from every land.

In fact Corinth had all the vices, not only of a cosmopolitan city, but of a new city and of a seaport. It had lain waste for a whole century, and scarcely a century had passed since its restoration by Julius Caesar, who in 46 B.C. planted a colony of Roman freedom on the old site. The prospect of great wealth attracted to it ambitious men from many other cities; merchants, builders, and manufacturers; and with them a great mass of parasites: thieves, gamblers, fortune-tellers, and prostitutes, who preyed upon the weaklings of the city and lay in wait for incoming strangers.

The famous Isthmian games, conducted nearby, were an additional attraction that periodically filled the city with excitement. Gladiators came with their swords, and horsemen with their chariots; men came to fight with men, and men with beasts; runners and wrestlers, musicians and poets, and others famous for endurance, strength, or skill came hoping to wear away the crown of pine. Paul could never have found satisfaction for his compelling energy in a slow-moving town. He needed the sight and sound of strenuous activity, he needed obstacles and opposition, he needed strain and suffering.[3] Corinth offered him all these, and he accepted its challenge.

In the garments of toil, Paul the scholar followed Aquila to his dingy goat-scented tent factory and seated himself among the workmen to earn money for the spread of the gospel of the Kingdom of God. On the Sabbath days he reasoned in the synagogue, persuading not only the Jews but also the Greeks, or Gentile adherents. His message however was softened to avoid conflict with the Jews until he could hear from the persecuted churches of Macedonia.

Weeks passed. Silas and Timothy returned from their mission and sought Aquila's workshop. Before their tongues could command a word, Paul knew by their countenances that they had come with a good report. It was one of the happiest moments of the apostle's life—a moment in which his spiritual agony was transmuted into joy. The report of his helpers convinced him that his work was acceptable to his Lord, and reassured him of his apostolic call. He could not rest; the hitherto restrained gospel now demanded full utterance. Galatia was safe, Macedonia was safe, and now Achaia must be brought into the fold.

Encouraged by the faith and loyalty of the persecuted Macedonians, Paul now threw off all restraints and boldly preached Jesus as the Messiah. But the emotional pendulum that had reached one extreme now swung to the other; and whereas he had begun his work "in weakness, and in much fear and trembling,"[4] he now became almost defiantly aggressive. In the synagogue he had proved from the scriptures and the signs of the times that the Kingdom of God was at hand;[5] now he proclaimed Jesus as the promised messianic King and urged His immediate acceptance as the Savior of all who should believe. The Jews became enraged and began to blaspheme the name to which "every knee should bow."[6]

When Paul saw that the Jews had definitely rejected Jesus, he stood before them and exclaimed: "Your blood be upon your heads! I am innocent. From now on I will go to the Gentiles."[7] Paul might have been handled roughly for his exasperating act had not the Jews remembered their recent expulsion from Rome for fomenting riots. Nevertheless vengeance lurked in the shadows.

This ominous lowering found its way into the apostle's dreams, but there it encountered a supreme faith that stripped it of its terrors. Paul dreamed and, as usual, dreamed so realistically that he saw his Lord, who said to him: "Do not be afraid, but speak and do not be silent; for I am with you; and no man shall attack you to harm you, for I have many people in this city."[8] Such a dream-like vision must have been the product of long continued importunate prayer in which the apostle constantly pictured the presence of his Lord. Accepting the vision as a pledge of divine aid and protection, he brought it to fulfillment by casting his own mighty energy into his work.

After the rupture with the Jews, Paul took his converts to the house of Titus Justice near the synagogue, where, perhaps, he organized the Corinthian church. Titus Justice may have been a Roman and, like Cornelius,[9] was a worshipper of the God of the Jews.

Among those who went over with Paul and received baptism, was Crispus, the ruler of the synagogue, and with him all his household. This fact, together with the irritating proximity of the new church and the loss of many Gentile adherents, increased the rage of the Jews. The church, however, flourished, for "many of the Corinthians hearing Paul believed and were baptized."[10] Silas and Timothy were kept busy with the affairs of organization, the instruction and baptism of new converts, and the oversight of brotherhood meetings. Paul gave himself chiefly to apostolic duties, "prayer and the ministry of the word."[11] Even the administration of baptism was committed to the hands of his assistant, he having performed that rite only for Crispus and Gaius and the household of Stephanas.[12]

For a year and a half the apostle and his aides toiled in Corinth and its environs, preaching and teaching wherever groups of hearers could be attracted.

They doubtless visited the great theater, ascended the Acro-Corinthus, went out to the temple of Poseidon where the Isthmian contests were held; visited the portage where small vessels were drawn by oxen across the isthmus from sea to sea; went up through the long-walls to Lechaeum, and down by the fortified road to Cenchreae. Certainly a church was organized at Cenchreae, for one of its members, Phoebe, was later commended by Paul to the church at Rome,[13] perhaps as the bearer of his letter to that church.

Paul had not been in Corinth many months before news began drifting in from Macedonia and elsewhere about the heroic faith displayed by the Thessalonian Christians under persecution by both Jews and Gentiles. He had forewarned the followers of Christ that they should be prepared to suffer for their faith, and now the news of their heroism was spreading everywhere—from city to city, from synagogue to synagogue, and from church to church. It was a revival of the old Hebrew martyr spirit[14] in a new setting; a new courage at which all the world was soon to wonder.

Paul longed to see the brethren to comfort and advise them but he could not interrupt his work at Corinth and would not subject the Thessalonian Christians to new dangers by going to them. Twice he had almost decided to visit them, but "Satan hindered."[15] He therefore wrote them an affectionate letter, the First Thessalonians of the New Testament. He perhaps dictated his message to one of the professional scribes in the cloisters of the marketplace, since such a man would be provided with writing materials while Paul would not. The scribe may have been a convert, but if not, he must have been intensely interested in this remarkable dictation.

Since the occasion of this letter was the good news that had reached Corinth, Paul wrote very informally, dealing with practical affairs rather than with doctrine. He did, however, state his views concerning those who die in the faith before the return of the Christ. He devoted but six verses to the subject,[16] yet nothing more beautiful has ever been offered for the comfort of those who sorrow for their dead. Death had occurred in the homes of some of the Thessalonian Christians, and those who sorrowed feared that their loved ones would be separated from them at the coming of the Lord. Paul assured them on the authority of a revelation that the dead would rise to rejoin the living and that both would then meet the Lord to dwell with him forever. Also, the letter urged the duty of harmonious churchlife, brotherly love, industrious self-support, obedience to the officers of the church, and abstinence from immoral heathen practices.

Paul had heard that his enemies were working to ruin his church by bringing him into disrepute. He had heard that he was charged with covetousness, with the use of flattery, and with the ulterior motive of carrying on a religious campaign to glorify himself. These charges he met by simply reminding the Thessalonians of his model manner of life while among them.

His letter caused a flurry of excitement; for the church thought from some of his statements that the Christ might return at any moment, day or night. Some were stricken with terror, while others waited in a state of mingled fear and joy. There were some even who abandoned their work to live off the church commissariat or to wander from house to house getting free meals while they speculated about the Lord's coming. It appears, too, that tricksters took advantage of the excitement in the church to increase fear by exaggerating the terror of the last day and even by forging letters in Paul's name.

As soon as the apostle heard about this agitation, he wrote another letter, being more specific about the time of the advent and the signs that were to precede it. In his first letter he had mentioned the early return of the Lord, not to frighten, but to give comfort and courage to those who were ill-treated, insulted, persecuted, and tortured by showing that their sufferings would soon end in joyful deliverance. He repictured the scene of the Lord's coming and the awful disasters that would overtake unbelievers and he assured his readers of the security of those who should be found worthy of salvation.

He then reminded the church of what he had taught them of "the man of lawlessness," "the son of perdition," who, through the instigation of Satan would exalt himself even to deity,[17] and who "with all power and with pretended signs and wonders, and with wicked deception"[18] would bring about a great apostasy, or a falling away from the faith. This person was at the time temporarily restrained by someone whom Paul for prudent reasons refrained from naming; but upon the removal of that power the man of sin would be revealed, whom Jesus would "slay with the breath of his mouth and destroy him by his appearing and his coming."[19]

No other passage in Paul's letters is so obscure to modern readers as this one. It omits certain details that must have been already known to the Thessalonians, it avoids the use of names, it excludes the time element as it crowds together prodigious events. Whatever or whomever Paul may have meant by "he who now restrains," and the "man of lawlessness," it is evident that he expected the one to be "revealed" at some unknown hour within his own lifetime.

Paul's doctrine of the man of sin, or the Antichrist, as John calls him,[20] was his own adaptation to the Christian church of current Jewish speculations that rested upon the apocryphal passages in the book of Daniel.[21] Rome was then deifying her emperors, a practice so loathesomely abhorrent to a Jew that the apostle evidently saw in it a portent of speedy world disaster.*

Of course there has never been a literal fulfillment of the visions of Daniel, or of the revelations of Paul, although the character of Antichrist has been ascribed to such men as Antiochus Epiphanes, Herod the Great, Caligula, and others. But human history is such that in course of time coincidences can occur that might, by some degree of straining, be interpreted to fit any possible prophetic speculation.

Nothing, however, has yet occurred that corresponds literally to Paul's prediction, and certainly did not occur within the time expected. For this reason the authors of Mark, Matthew, and Second Peter later stressed the unpredictableness of the time of the Lord's advent;[22] and later theologians subjected the whole scheme of New Testament eschatology to mystical interpretation.

---

* Rome was not the only country in the Near East that deified her emperors. Most countries thought their king or emperor was God's apostle or son. See S. Mowinckel, *The Psalms in Israel's Worship*, tr. D.R. Ap-Thomas (in 2 vols; New York: Abingdon Press, 1962) I, 48-49, 54, 60, 62-63, 125. Jesus was also called the Son of God, which meant Christians believed he was God's apostle and destined to be king. The argument Christians had with the Romans was that the two groups disagreed on the identity of the true Son of God. Romans said it was Caesar; Christians said it was Jesus. (GWB)

In his letter, Paul displayed one of the traits that made him a beloved leader. With a background that would have bred austerity and aloofness in some men, he showed a humility that won for him the willing cooperation of his converts. "Brethren pray for us," he wrote, "that the word of the Lord may speed on and triumph, as it did among you, and that we may be delivered from wicked and evil men."[23] Thus every member of the church was taken into partnership with him and was made to feel that the success of the gospel depended upon the prayers of the brotherhood. Silas and Timothy were included in the authorship of the letter; and after the professional scribe had finished his task, Paul took up the pen and added a salutation in his own handwriting, that the Thessalonians might know the letter to be genuine.

Corinth now engaged the undivided attention of the apostle and his assistants. Paul, Silas and Timothy were now well known throughout the city. Every Jew knew them; and many hated them, spat out at them, shouted at them, and interrupted their preaching.

In the early summer of the year A.D. 52, the Jewish foes of the church that had now grown prosperous became increasingly insolent. About the first of July (judging from the inscription on the famous Delphic stone), Gallio, a brother of Seneca the Stoic philosopher, and an uncle of Lucan the poet, had arrived and had taken office as a proconsul of Achaia. The superlative complaisance of the man apparently led the Jews to believe that he would adjudicate their complaint against Paul in their favor, since Judaism was entitled to protection as a *religio licita.*

Accordingly, under the leadership of Sosthenes, who seems to have succeeded Crispus as ruler of the synagogue, they "made a united atack upon Paul and brought him before the tribunal."[24] Gallio was then holding court in the agora or marketplace.

When Sosthenes was asked to state his complaint, he replied: "This man is persuading men to worship God contrary to the law."[25] He of course meant the God of the Jews, and the Mosaic, not the Roman law; and Gallio knew it. Instantly the amiable proconsul revealed the shrewdness of his judgment. He was angry because the Jews presumed upon his gentleness to trick him into their service.

As Paul was about to begin his defense, Gallio prevented him by exclaiming: "If it were a matter of wrongdoing or vicious crime, I should have reason to bear with you, O Jews; but since it is a matter of questions about words and names and your own law, see to it yourselves; I refuse to be a judge of these things."[26] Then, he ordered the Jews driven from his presence.

As the Jews were rushing through the ranks of the spectators, the mob seized Sosthenes, their leader, and flogged him before the judgment-seat. The Jews were very unpopular at that time, and Gallio, knowing of their recent expulsion from Rome by Claudius, paid no attention.

It is not likely that either the proconsul, or the crowd that made the assault, cared anything for Paul at the time, though the fiasco of arraignment may have brought him a degree of popularity as well as a season of safety. It may even have led to a possible acquaintance with Gallio and, ultimately, to a meeting with Seneca.

For six months or more, Paul, Silas, and Timothy continued their ministry at Corinth, from which place as a base they doubtless sent out workers or went themselves to surrounding cities. Luke does not attempt to enumerate all of Paul's movements, nor does he name many of the apostle's emissaries, who doubtless went out by land and sea proclaiming the Day of the Lord.

A second fall and winter passed, bringing the Corinthian church to such a state of prosperity that it could be entrusted to the care of others. Paul therefore decided to visit Jerusalem to keep his own work bound up with that of the other apostles, for in the Kingdom of Heaven racial distinctions would disappear—Jew and Gentile would be one.[27] His love for his own people, whether they were in the brotherhood of the church or out of it, had never waned.[28] He believed that notwithstanding their present rejection of the Messiah, God would find for them a way of salvation.[29] It was through them that divine grace had been extended to the Gentiles, and now the Gentiles would be an instrument in the salvation of the Jew.[30] To save the Gentiles therefore was to save the Jew. In the compelling consciousness of that fact Paul toiled incessantly, and now his thoughts have turned towards Jerusalem, and there must he go.

Luke is extremely elliptical, and even ambiguous, in his account of the closing months at Corinth, leaving his readers to solve in their own way the questions that are sure to arise. Aquila and his wife may have agreed to move their business to Ephesus and there be ready to receive and aid Paul on his next missionary tour. Certainly a church was later organized in their house in that city.[31] Silas, who now drops from history, perhaps returned to Jerusalem to rejoin his brethren there.[32] Timothy may have returned to his home in Lystra with the understanding that he would rejoin Paul somewhere for the next tour. And perhaps the church was left in the care of Crispus. And among his helpers may well have been Gaius Titus Justice (if these names in fact belonged to one man), Fortunatus, Achaicus, and certainly Stephanas.[33]

On a day near the end of February A.D. 53, Paul, Silas, Timothy, Aquila, and Priscilla could have been seen leaving the east gate of Corinth and riding down the long busy highway towards Cenchreae and the Saronic Gulf. They went of course to the house of Phoebe, the liberal, popular, and loveable deaconess, to spend some time with the church in her house.

In Cenchreae, Paul had his head shorn in the performance of a vow, if, indeed, Luke's hurried Greek really applies to Paul instead of to Aquila. In either case there is no clue to the purpose of the vow, and little reason for its mention, unless it was to show that Paul did not regard the act as inconsistent with his view of the Mosaic Law. If Aquila took the vow, he of course went up to Jerusalem to burn the cropped hair upon the altar under a peace offering. But it is easier to assume that the book of Acts is in error about the vow than it is to account for the conduct of either Paul or Aquila. It would have been a strange sight to one of Paul's Galatian converts to have witnessed him among the legalists with his head shaved, offering the three sacrifices of the Nazarite—the burnt-offering, the sin-offering, and the peace-offering.

After the farewell with the church, the five travelers, all bound for Ephesus, two hundred and fifty miles due east of Corinth, sailed out between the two temple-crowned promontories that sheltered the harbor over which Poseidon the god of the sea presided in colossal Corinthian bronze. It was a season of contrary winds, when the necessary tacking increased both time and mileage enormously. Cicero once made the same voyage when it required fifteen days. Perhaps Paul and his companions were more fortunate.

As the ship threaded its way through the frayed coast and island remnants of an older Greece, through Cyclades and Sporades, it never passed beyond the sight of land. Island after island lifted itself from a low bank to a towering bulk.

Ephesus sat upon the banks of the Cayster three miles back from the Ionian Gulf, and there the travelers separated. Timothy went overland to Lystra. Silas, Aquila, and Priscilla continued by sea, perhaps with other Jewish pilgrims, eager to reach Jerusalem for Pentecost. Paul paused in the city to prepare for a future visit. The Levitical Sabbath having come, Paul went to the synagogue and proclaimed the day of the Messiah but without discussing his views that would have antagonized his hearers. He was asked to stay longer but he declined, promising to return on his next tour. He then sailed for Caesarea to go up to Jerusalem.

On this long voyage, through the ever changing beauty of the Sporades, past Cos and Rhodes, into the open sea, and past Cyprus, may have occurred one of the shipwrecks mentioned in the second letter to Corinthians. If Luke's purpose had been to recount all the thrilling incidents of Paul's travels, it is almost certain that the voyage from Cenchreae to Caesarea would have furnished a lively chapter.

At Caesarea, where Cornelius was stationed at the time of his conversion, Paul perhaps spent a short time with Philip the evangelist, one of the seven original deacons of the church in Jerusalem, whose four virgin daughters prophesied in the church at Caesarea. From him, Paul would learn particulars about the progress of the gospel in Syria and the attitude of the Jews towards his work among the Gentiles.

At Jerusalem he knew where to find friends and it is not likely that he exposed himself to unnecessary danger in that city. He knew that his enemies there kept the flame of hate alive; and he knew that foes were there from Damascus, Lystra, Philippi, Thassalonica, and elsewhere, picturing him as the arch-foe of Judaism. There was nothing to be gained by flaunting his presence in the streets or in the Temple. Besides, the evangelization of Jerusalem belonged to the Twelve and he was willing to leave it with them.

"He went up and saluted the church," says Luke, and that was at least a gesture of good will. If he went up for the Feast of Pentecost or for some other festival, as certain old manuscripts imply, he perhaps hoped to meet one or more of the Twelve, though there is no sign in the whole New Testament that any of them ever showed much desire to meet him.

After meeting with the Church and relating the amazing story of his labors, Paul went down to Antioch, his adopted home, and the starting point of all his tours.

REFERENCES
Chapter 11

1. I Thes. 3:5.
2. Cf. Strabo. *The Geography*. VIII. 6.
3. Cf. II Cor. 12:10.
4. I Cor. 2:3.
5. Cf. Matt. 10:7.
6. Phil. 2:10.
7. Acts 18:6.
8. Acts 18:9-10.
9. Acts 10:2.
10. Acts 18.8.
11. Cf. Acts 6:4.
12. I Cor. 1:14-15.
13. Rom. 16:1.
14. Heb. 11:35-38; II Maccabees 6:7-11.
15. I Thes. 2:18.
16. I Thes. 4:13-18.
17. Dan. 11:36.
18. II Thes. 2:3-10.
19. II Thes. 2:8, 22; 4:3; II John 7.
20. I John 2:18, 22; 4:3; II John 7.
21. Dan. chaps. 7-11.
22. Mark 13:32-37; Matt. 24-36; II Pet. 3:8-10.
23. II Thes. 3:1-2.
24. Acts 18:12.
25. Acts 18:13.
26. Acts 18:14-15.
27. Gal. 3:28; I Cor. 12:13; Rom. 10:12; Col. 3:11.
28. Cf. Rom. 9:3.
29. Rom. 11.
30. Rom. 11:11, 25, 26.
31. I Cor. 16:19.
32. Cf. Acts 15:22.
33. I Cor. 16:15, 16.

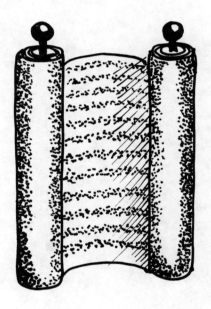

Philippi Neapolis
Thessalonica
Berea Apollonia
Assos Troas
Mitylene Pergamum
Athens Smyrna Antioch
Corinth Ephesus Iconium
Samos Lystra
Miletus Derbe CILICIAN GATE
Cos Taurus Tarsus
Rhodes Patara Antioch

CYPRUS

CRETE

Mediterranean Sea

Sidon

Caesarea
Antipatris
Jerusalem

Third Missionary Tour: Antioch, Syria — Ephesus

PAUL WAS NOW PERHAPS fifty-three years of age. His apostolic labors had covered twenty years; a score of cities had heard the gospel from his own lips, and many more had heard it from his converts. His Jewish prejudices had broadened into a worldly sympathy and his doubts and fears had subsided in the consciousness of an approved and successful apostleship. His Jewish habit of meditation, the exigencies of a varied experience, together with an occasional "revelation," had expanded and coordinated many of his theological concepts. He correctly thought he was the leader of the Christian movement. His liberal views had saved the Church from extinction. Peter and James would have made all Gentiles become Jewish first and then Christian, whereas Paul would have inducted them into Christianity first that they might afterwards inherit the Jewish promises. The Antiochian church must have seen a difference in Paul at the time of his last visit. There was undoubtedly an impressive maturity of authority, a richer parental tenderness, and a more restless urgency of purpose.

In this short last visit to Antioch very much of great interest may have happened, but history is silent, and Luke rushes onward to new scenes of conquest.

Paul soon set out on his third tour to confirm all his Asiatic churches from Antioch in Syria to Antioch of Pisidia, and to bid farewell to each until "our assembling to meet him,"[1] upon the coming of the Lord.

Certainly Paul paused in Tarsus; it was full of memories. But the stay was short, for after satisfying himself that his church in his beloved city was safe, he bade what was to be his last farewell and hastened onward to Derbe, Lystra, Iconium, and Antioch, "strengthening all the disciples." Although it is extremely doubtful, he may even have visited Tavium, Ancyra, and Pessinus, if Luke's words "upper country"[2] may be strained to include the region of these cities. South Galatia was of course "upper country" with references to Ephesus, which city was apparently in Luke's thought. It seems almost unfair, however, to exclude Paul from north Galatia where great churches certainly sprang up; but the ricocheting accounts for his second and third tours as given by Luke[3] make the question one of pure conjecture.

Evidently Paul's Galatian letter, written while on his second tour, had quieted the churches to which it had been addressed and had repulsed their disturbers, the Judaizers; for Paul on his third tour ordered the collection of a fund[4] to relieve the poor among the saints at Jerusalem, who had gathered there by the thousands to wait for the Messiah. It was assumed that the Gentiles were in debt to the Jews for spiritual benefits and should therefore "be of service to them in material blessings"—a rather businesslike argument bluntly enunciated by Paul to the Romans.[5] But Jerusalem had once requested such gifts.[6]

With all his prodigious energy, Paul, and much less the Twelve, could never have made Christianity take root if it had not been for the belief that Jesus would return to the earth at some near moment and for the great doctrine of grace that put all moral and religious conduct on an entirely new basis. It was the insistence upon the imminent cataclysmic return of the Lord that gave to the gospel its initial power. Men had only time enough to repent and establish allegiance with the Messiah in order to be saved. And it was the great doctrine of grace, that doctrine which in some form must ever remain a cornerstone of theology, that steadied the church when the days of its watching[7] grew long, and no response was heard to its cry "Come, Lord Jesus!"[8]

From the edge of the "upper country," or the great Phrygian tableland, from Antioch, if not from Pessinus, Paul was carried by his biographer at a single bound down to Ephesus. Apparently the best route for the apostle would have been over the great Roman highway down the valley of the Meander, through Apamea, Colossae, Laodicea, Hierapolis, and Tralles. If he took this road, he did not preach along the way, at least not in Colossae or Laodicea.[9] But these cities, like Smyrna, Sardis, Philadelphia, Thyatira, Pergamos, and others were doubtless regarded by him as possible out-stations to be reached from Ephesus by trained workers;[10] or, some of them may have been left to men upon whose work Paul would not intrude.[11]

Timothy, perhaps, had rejoined Paul at Lystra and was his companion on the two-hundred-mile ride from Antioch to Ephesus. Silas perhaps remained in Jerusalem.

It was late in October when the two men entered Ephesus and began their inquiries for Aquila, who had moved his business from Corinth. He may have done this to accommodate Paul. It was, in any event, a transaction that would seem altogether reasonable for one who believed that the end of the age was near.

Everywhere the signs of approaching winter were present: The day was becoming shorter, the shadows longer, the sunlight weaker, and the midnight sky strewn with wintry stars. The fruits of autumn were now in the stalls of the old Greek agora and the Roman forum; the great woodyards near the walls were heaped with fragrant oak and pine; and the ships with naked masts were made fast in the artificial basin below the city.

Aquila was easily found; the Jews all knew him. Prisca had rooms ready for her guests. She was always "Prisca," the esteemed matron, to Paul, the gentleman;[12] but a hint of her agreeable nature is dropped by Luke who calls her "Priscilla," the affectionate diminutive form of "Prisca." She was one of a trio of women in the early Church: Lydia of Philippi, Phoebe of Cenchreae, and Prisca of Ephesus.

Ephesus, the metropolis and capital of the Province of Asia, ranked third in population and importance after Rome and Alexandria. It was at the center of numerous converging sea and land routes, and a kind of queen to a swarm of towns and smaller cities. Ephesus stood on a plain that had been formed through the ages by silting at the mouth of the Cayster river. It nestled against the side of a two-peaked mound called Mt. Coressus, and on the south against a range of hills called Mt. Prior, or the "saw." The plain was about five miles long and three wide.

The principal public buildings of the city lay to the south and west of Mt. Coressus, and could be visited by following the great avenue over which the religious processions from the temple of Diana—or Artemis— were accustomed to pass. The avenue curved westward from the Magnesian Gate, turned northward near the agora, and eastward at the stadium. The great temple of Artemis that did more than anything else to make the city famous stood in the plain about a mile northeast of the city wall. Paul, of course, soon became familiar with all these buildings, labored in their vicinity, and experienced a variety of reactions from the sight of them; yet he is named in connection with but two—the great theater and the temple of Artemis.

Paul must have been well aware of the fact that he was in the very cradle of Hellenic culture, the center of the region in which poetry and music, art and science, history and philosophy had flourished from far back in the centuries. But with his belief that the age in which he was living was near its end, he could not have wasted his time on that which was about to perish. As usual, Paul began his work in the synagogue, appealing first to the Jews and the Gentiles who affiliated with them. His hope, of course, was that the Jews would hear and believe, and that the synagogue would then become the church into which the Gentiles could be drawn.[13] The opposition of the Jews, however, was everywhere too great to permit this, and the church had to become a separate institution.

Before Paul had reached Ephesus, a brilliant Jewish scholar and orator named Apollos visited the synagogue of that city and preached Jesus as the Messiah. By his eloquence and earnestness he won a respectful hearing and persuaded about twelve men to accept Johannean baptism, that is a baptism of repentance, a preparatory rite instituted by John the Baptist before he had acknowledged the Messiahship of Jesus,[14] and to which Jesus had submitted himself.[15]

But when Aquila and Priscilla heard the eloquent rabbi, they recognized his value to the church, invited him to their home, and "expounded to him the way of God more accurately."[16] He then crossed over to Corinth bearing letters of enthusiastic recommendations from the brethren in Ephesus. But when Paul met the twelve converts he inquired of them whether they had received the Holy Spirit. Upon learning that they had not heard about the Spirit being given to believers, he baptized them in the name of the Lord Jesus; and when he "had laid his hands upon them, the Holy Spirit came on them; and they spoke with tongues and prophesied."[17] Luke's report of this occurrence, like his account of the first use of tongues[18] and like the first bestowal of that gift upon the Gentiles,[19] appears to place a higher evidential value on glossolalia than is conceded by Paul in his first letter to the Corinthians.[20] Paul accepted glossalalia on the rabbinic interpretation of a passage in Isaiah[21] and regarded it not as a sign to believers, but as a rebuking sign to the unbelieving Jews who would not heed their own prophets. It would have no significance if unbelieving Jews were not present.

But out of erroneous ideas, mental excitement, bewilderment, and the confusion of emotions, the overjoyed converts found relief in unintelligible and incoherent utterances that may have consisted of meaningless syllables, a mixture of words from two or more languages, or even a purely foreign tongue. Thus glossolalia was simply an incidental that attached itself to the early Church and had its counterpart in other religions.

For three winter months, the Jews of Ephesus listened to Paul's arguments and persuasions concerning the great theme of "The Kingdom of God"; but some of his hearers who were not convinced gradually became hardened and then openly before the synagogue denounced the whole Christian way. Paul was aware of the growing opposition and wisely withdrew from the synagogue, though not until he had administered a fearless rebuke for unbelief.[22]

No man in Ephesus toiled with such superhuman endurance as Paul. Long hours were spent at his trade in the shop of his friend Aquila, with whom he had a business understanding: "these hands ministered to my necessities, and to those who were with me," he said later to the elders of the church.[23] Wherever an audience could be attracted, Paul's clear voice could be heard telling the story of salvation by grace through faith in Jesus.

Weightier still was the task of organization and extension. At the school of Tyrannus he trained the teachers and the prophets or preachers who were to carry the gospel to other cities. His church was a theological school, and the headquarters of a vast missionary enterprise, "so that all the residents of Asia heard the word of the Lord, both Jews and Greeks."[24] Paul was a skillful organizer and a firm administrator. He did not plant churches and leave them to an uncertain fate, but watched over them as a parent over children. To the Corinthians he said, "There is the daily pressure upon me of my anxiety for all the churches."[25] He must have made many unrecorded tours, written many unpreserved letters, and ordained many unremembered men. Records are brief, but Paul's achievements were great.

Paul was passing his middle fifties when he began the evangelization of Ephesus. Toil and suffering[26] were slowly reducing his physical reserve. The burdens of the ever expanding church were gradually absorbing his social impulses. And the unceasing machinations of Judaists and Judaizers were slowly turning his thoughts towards impending catastrophe. But his years of experience had given him more than he had lost, and he was ready for the greatest task of his life.

Nearly all nationalities and races had mingled in Ephesus, although the city was essentially Greek, highly orientalized, and obsequiously Roman. This latter fact must have given Paul a feeling of security, for the Roman proconsul of the province had his residence in Ephesus—and Paul was a loyal Roman citizen.

There was perhaps no better way of obeying the command, "Go into all the world and preach the gospel to the whole creation"[27] than to establish a center of proclamation in Ephesus. Luke's picture of Paul at work there is confined to five or six exciting incidents, such as would appeal to the readers of his day. But they were incidents that reveal the impelling faith, the moral force, and the heroic courage of the mighty apostle.

Luke says that "God did extraordinary miracles by the hands of Paul."[28] There must have been miracles of healing and exorcism, or cures, however performed, that satisfied the universal demand for miracles. When his reputation as a healer began to spread beyond the church, persons believing that some potent virtue emanated from his body carried away his handkerchiefs or sweat mops, and even his work aprons, or sought to touch him with their own, hoping to bear away healing virtue to their sick ones at home. Luke asserts that diseases were thus cured and evil spirits expelled.

Whatever medical aids were used at any time by the apostle, they were applied in the name of the Lord Jesus, whom he regarded as the source of all healing power. But the mystical use of the name "Jesus" caught the ears of the seven sons of a Jewish high priest named Sceva. These men were exorcists and had been relying upon the mystical number "seven" and other ancient formulas. Now they would try out that name so constantly upon the lips of Paul—"Jesus."

Having found a patient who had an evil spirit, they entered the room where he was confined, heedless of that fact that he was a dangerous maniac. After placing olive branches before the man, they stepped behind him to avoid the fleeing spirit, and began their incantations over his head. But when they commanded the evil spirit to come forth, saying, "I adjure you by the Jesus whom Paul preaches," the madman exclaimed, "Jesus I know, and Paul I know; but who are you?" Then instantly he sprang upon the exorcists, and before they could escape, wounded them and tore off their garments. The story soon spread over all Ephesus; though Luke, or even Paul and Timothy may have seen the humor of it, yet everywhere it was taken so seriously that "fear fell upon them all; and the name of the Jesus was extolled."[29]

Ephesus overflowed with magicians and with all manner of tricksters who found an easy livelihood by playing on the credulous. High and low, Greek and Roman, Jew and Egyptian—everyone believed in magic, and everyone resorted to its aid. But the ignominious defeat of the sons of Sceva brought the Christian gospel into such high repute that many persons who owned books on magic brought them together and burned them publicly. Then for the third time in the space of eleven verses,[30] Luke is constrained to comment on the great success of the gospel: "So, the word of the Lord grew and prevailed mightily."

One of the clearest glimpses of Paul's activity in Ephesus, and incidentally of his warmth of heart, can be obtained from the last chapter of his letter to the Romans. The editor of that letter had found a scrap of manuscript that did not seem to belong anywhere else, so he attached it where something like it seemed to have been lost. It belonged, however, to some almost totally destroyed letter to the Ephesians. So numerous are the workers named in the little scrap, so tender the greetings, and so evident the mention of several groups of churches, that the editor's error turns out to the modern reader's advantage. No one can read through this list of names[31] without feeling his heart warming towards Paul, and his admiration swelling toward the Ephesian Church.

But success did not come by an untroubled road. "There are many adversaries,"[32] wrote Paul in one of his letters. The Jews were always denouncing him, insulting him, and meddling with his converts. Though afraid to stone him, they opposed him with such vicious treachery that the conflict with them was like a fight with "beasts."[33] Perhaps in his first year at Ephesus, he and Timothy met with some overwhelming misfortune that filled both men with despair. In writing to the Corinthians,[34] he spoke of his suffering but did not say how it was caused. His readers of course knew what had happened. While the most searching textual criticism fails to give a clue to their experience, a reasonable conjecture would be that the men had suffered almost death from a Jewish scourging or from violent abuse by a Gentile mob.

After his work had been well established in Ephesus, Paul felt a yearning to visit his church in Corinth,[35] just across the Aegean Sea. The young congregation there had been left in the care of elders and, for a time, had been under the ministry of the brilliant Apollos; but the apostle became uneasy, evidently having received disquieting news through Apollos. Leaving Timothy in charge at Ephesus, he sailed for Cenchreae and then hastened up the long avenue to the great city where the lewd Aphrodite dictated the morals of the populace.

The visit perhaps lasted only a few days or, at most, a few weeks. But it revealed the fact that many of the Corinthian converts, while still professing faith in Christ, had returned to their old immoral habits and contentious manners. In their assemblies they had fallen so far away from the grace of brotherhood that some of their numbers became puffed up with offensive self-importance, while others subsided into jealousy. Some went about whispering suspicions, and others who were a little less cautious resorted to backbiting. Then followed anger and strife, resulting in factions and tumults.

To these irregularities some members of the church had added the notorious Corinthian sins of "impurity, immorality, and licentiousness,"[36] contending perhaps, after the Gnostic mode of thought, that if the "spiritual man" were the all-important concern of the Christian life, and the body but a prison, then it mattered not what the flesh did towards its own destruction. It would have been quite easy, too, for a philosopher of the Epicurean type to justify any kind of conduct.

The discovery of these conditions sickened Paul's soul and humiliated him to tears before his Jewish and other foes. But he remembered that his church had been gathered out of ignorant paganism and that men of very diverse origins had been brought together and were expected to live in fellowship and harmony. Therefore, shocked and pained as he had been, he dealt leniently with the offenders, exhorting them to repentance.

Some time after Paul's return to Ephesus, reports began to reach him that the evil beyond the Aegean was still at work. He had displayed leniency only to be accused of weakness and cowardice. There are times when only strong men conscious of a safe reserve of power can afford to be gentle. Paul's gentleness had exposed the weakness of his Corinthian critics and he could now be severe without seeming to be merciless. Moved by indignation and grief, he wrote a letter to the church commanding its officers to chastise the mischief-makers. To make discipline effective, he gave orders that no member of the church should eat or keep company with any other member who was "guilty of immorality or greed, or is an idolater, reviler, drunkard, or robber."[37] In his salutation, as was his custom, he must have revealed the depth of his love and the sincerity of his purpose, but the body of the letter was firm and ominous. That letter disappeared and never has been recovered, but Paul's references to it in his other letters give a clue to its contents.

Very soon the Corinthians sent a letter to Paul. Some of them were deeply sorry, but like many other wrongdoers, were too reluctant about their confession. Their letter, too, has been lost, but its contents are known in outline from the questions they had asked, and which Paul answered in his second letter, the extant First Corinthians.

When Paul was about to reply to this letter, certain Christian slaves, members of the household of Chloe, returned to Ephesus after a business trip to Corinth and gave Paul an account of conditions there. Very soon these men were followed by Stephanas, Fortunatus, and Achaicus, three members of the Corinthian church who confirmed what the others had said and gave additional facts of an encouraging nature. Paul, with his usual good diplomacy, mentioned these men in his next letter, but in such a manner that they could not be accused at home of being talebearers.[38] He did not permit them even to carry the letter that mentioned their names.

The slaves certainly reported about the four factions into which the Church had become parted: "I belong to Paul, or I belong to Apollos, or I belong to Cephus, or I belong to Christ."[39] They perhaps told also about a nauseous case of immorality, and about certain persons who had dishonored the church by going "to law before the unrighteous instead of the saints."[40]

In poignant distress at all that he had heard, Paul's first impulse was to hasten across the sea, but the pressure of work in Ephesus was great. Besides, it was better that the elders in Corinth should feel the weight of responsibility and learn by experience how to deal with their own problems. Paul therefore wisely decided to write a second letter (the First Corinthians), dealing with the reports that had reached him. He promised them, however, an early visit, thinking to go directly to them, and then after a short stay to make a hasty tour of Macedonia, return again to Corinth, and from there sail for Jerusalem.[41] But after the letter was written and after it had reached the church, he changed his plan, wishing to spare them the embarrassment of a hasty visit and himself the sorrow of beholding their disorder and disobedience.[42] He therefore decided to go through Macedonia first and then, after visiting Corinth, to sail from its western port for Jerusalem.

His second letter (First Corinthians) had hardly reached the church when the apostle began to regret either something he had written or the way he had written it.[43] This uncomfortable self-censure clouded his joy for many weeks. It was not until after he had left Ephesus that he discovered the needlessness of his regrets.[44]

Thus it was the unbecoming conduct of the Corinthian church that called into existence two of the greatest theological documents ever composed—the First Corinthians and the Second Corinthians. These letters were not intended to be chapters on systematic theology, they dealt only with the immediate needs and current problems of a particular church. Nevertheless they contained scraps of doctrine that with others from other letters have since been pieced together, with much straining of parts and distortion of pattern, into a variety of theological systems.

But the Corinthian letters are like focused light upon the very soul of Paul himself. He is always led, drawn, constrained, impelled by the fixed conviction that he is an apostle of the Messiah, that the Messiah had appeared to him, and would soon return to earth to gather out of it those who were worthy of the Kingdom of Heaven. He plunged into his tasks without regard to their difficulties or to his personal loss, suffering, or safety. Belief with him was always transmuted into instant and constant action. Unlike the noisy fanatical enthusiast who contends for merely an opinion or a creed, he spoke and labored with that awful intensity, directness, and purposefulness that should characterize any man who claims to believe in either the first or second advent of the Christ.

The pendulum of Paul's emotions swung between wide extremes— and he permitted it to swing with good effect. His mental states were always under control and came regularly to perfect equilibrium. He said of himself, "afflicted in every way, but not crushed; perplexed, but not driven to despair; persecuted, but not forsaken; struck down, but not destroyed."[45]

Before Paul replied to the letter that he had received from Corinth, he probably spread it out before him and knelt and prayed for guidance. But even then his answer was not easily composed, especially since it involved a defense of Paul himself. Certain members of the church had been belittling him because he neither wrote nor spoke in the style of the fame-seeking orators who were frequent visitors in Corinth. The Jewish Christians of the Jerusalem type who were still legalists, and who had crept into the church to trouble it, accused him of ulterior motives because he did not preach for money, and they even hinted that he might have been dishonest in handling gifts. They said that he was "beside himself" and that he preached a "veiled gospel" instead of the gospel of a personal knowledge of Jesus in the flesh. They charged him with cowardice, asserting that he wrote threatening letters and then postponed the execution of his threats, and they pretended that his leniency was nothing else than fear. These absurd charges, which Paul may have hyperbolized somewhat in order to strengthen his defense, are answered in four chapters that still have practical value. Two chapters are then devoted to the moral conditions prevailing in the church, nine to questions that had been asked, and one to the benevolent offering then being taken in all the Gentile churches for the saints in Jerusalem, called "the poor" who were waiting for the coming of their Lord.

The Corinthian letter contained six major questions bearing on the subjects of marriage,[46] sacrificial meats,[47] feminine attire,[48] the Lord's Supper,[49] spiritual gifts,[50] and the resurrection of the dead.[51] Paul's reply to the first deals intimately with various problems. In the light of the awful suffering that the saints would undergo at the hands of their enemies, and in view of the belief that the end of the world was at hand, he advised against marriage but did not forbid it.

His answer to the second question introduced the great law of Christian liberty and the limitations of its use. Some members of the church in Corinth believed it to be a defiling sin to eat meat that had been dedicated to an idol.* Others, knowing an idol to be an impotent thing, saw no harm in eating such meat even at a feast in a heathen temple. Paul agreed to some extent with the latter view, but said that the man of knowledge should not so use his liberty as to offend the conscience of his weaker brother.

The third question relates to the use of the veil by women at public worship. Evidently some progressive member of the church had overlooked the spiritual significance of head coverings and thought that they should be abandoned. Paul replied to him in terms of the Jewish teaching about the place of woman in the social order, and in terms of local custom. The book of Genesis subordinates the woman to the man in her

---

*   Food that was not sold at a *kasher* meat market was probably sacrificed to some other deity than Jehovah. Jews considered this idolatrous, but some broad-minded Jews were willing to eat food not sold at a Jewish meat market.

Then as now Jews were in conflict about the propriety of eating food sold at popular meat markets. (GWB)

very origin and subjects her to the arbitrary rule of her husband. Paul, of course, had been brought up in this belief, which was still accepted in universal practice. On it, therefore, he defended in rabbinic style the use of the veil in his churches. Notwithstanding his uncomplimentary views, it was Paul more than any other who paved the way for woman's emancipation. It was not his business to reorganize society, but to preach the gospel of salvation. The rapidly approaching Kingdom of Heaven would have its own social order, and earthly customs would be at an end.

The question relating to the manner of observing the Lord's supper must have brought agony to Paul's soul. Within the space of months, the most sacred institution of the church had been degraded to the level of a mystery-cult feast. Just as the Christians of Jerusalem assembled for common meals, so did those of Corinth and other places, the members of the church contributing food so that the poor might share equally with the rich. These evening meals were followed by the Eucharist, or perhaps, at a later date were preceded by it. Instead of waiting for one another and conducting an orderly meal, some of the Corinthians fell into the habit of plundering their individual baskets and drinking to drunkenness, to the neglect of the poor and the late arrivals.* Thus the love-feast became a scandal, and the Eucharist a mockery. But judging from Jude,[52] these disorders may have been brought about by men who were working secretly to scandalize the church and thus to discredit Paul.

In his reply to the Corinthian church, the apostle outlines an order of service for the Last Supper which he claims to have received directly from the Lord. He makes no reference to the other apostles though, of course, it was their practice that had infiltrated as a revelation into his mind. Even if Paul's virtuous self-sufficiency had permitted him to accept authority in the gospel from another apostle, he dared not do so, for both Judaists and Judaizers would have used the fact to his quick undoing. His own claims as an apostle "untimely born" had to be supported by visions and revelations, both of which were ready products of his intense nature and religious inheritance.

Incidentally, Paul's description of the Last Supper seems to confirm

---

* The situation in Corinth was probably centered around a Passover Seder. Passover is a very important festival for Jews. No Jewish family may deny another Jew the privilege of joining in this meal. The minimum requirements for Passover duties is an olive's bulk of the Passover offering, an olive's bulk of bitter **herbs, an unspecified amount of unleavened bread, and four glasses of wine** (Mishnah Pesahim 2:6; 8:3; 10:1).

Following Jewish custom, Paul was horrified that this basic concept was neglected. Paul said that those who observed the feast unworthily, not only would not receive merit from God for their observance, but would be punished instead. Unless they perceived the body, that is, unless they took into account the entire body of Christ, the whole community, they ate and drank to their own damnation (I Cor 11:29). (GWB)

the fact that Jesus claimed to be the Messiah. If Jesus had not said, "This is my body," "This cup is the new covenant in my blood,"[53] then Peter or any other apostle could have denied that such words had ever been spoken.

The unqualified acceptance of Jesus as Messiah and Savior was supposed to be coincident with the gift of the Holy Spirit, who in turn conferred gifts on all believers according to their capacities. One became useful in the church body for his word of wisdom, and another for his word of knowledge; one had the faith to heal diseases, and another the power to work miracles; some could prophesy or proclaim the gospel, and others could discern between good and evil spirits; some could speak with tongues, and others interpret tongues.

Evidently some members of the church took advantage of the diversity among these gifts and vaunted themselves to the discouragement of some of their less talented brethren. This sin, which still plagues religious and other organizations, Paul condemned by comparing it to a disagreement among the coordinated necessary parts of a human body.[54] And then, because condemnation is not of itself a cure, he prescribed the greatest antidote of all for moral ills, the greatest of the three graces—love. If any one word could have invited the "heavenly Muse," it was that one. So, in the midst of a long argument, Paul broke into song in praise of love.[55] In this rhetorically beautiful eulogium Paul throws open a great window into his own soul. His hastily written letters, usually controversial or admonitory and intended for the day only, were never composed as formal literature, though often displaying literary power; but for a moment in his "Psalm of Love", his gift bursts forth into brilliancy, revealing the qualities of a poetic genius. What might Saul of Tarsus have achieved in another sphere had he not become Paul, the apostle to the Gentiles!

The Psalm of Love reveals the broadmindedness of a great man adjusting himself to a crude and supposedly vanishing age. Customs and beliefs that were not wholly ideal had come over naturally into the church from Jewish and Gentile sources and were permitted to remain; but Paul saw beyond their transitory use to a time when incomplete knowledge, though useful for a season, would be swept away by incoming floods of truth. He saw the day approaching when such spiritual aids as glossalalia, that early object of ridicule,[56] would be heard no more. He saw but "darkly" and knew only "in part," yet he pursued such light as he saw and led mankind into an energizing hope that has remade the world. He was in error about much but had discovered the deepest cravings of the human soul and was able to preach a gospel that brought into conscious activity man's finest virtues.

It was out of the depths of an intense personal experience that Paul sang of faith, hope, and love. These were the characteristics of the man himself. His faith gave him a Savior, his hope promised him eternal life, and his love established right relations for him with God and man. Paul loved profoundly and beautifully, and was ardently loved by multitudes. His own letters, and Luke's references to him, set this fact beyond dispute. Of course many of the Jews hated him, but that was because of his liberal attitude towards their law and the effect of his Gentile work upon their treasuries.

His answer to the sixth major question is an affirmation of the fundamental creed of Christendom, the resurrection of Jesus,[57] and a refutation of the Sadducean and Epicurean contention that there is no resurrection of the dead.[58] His discussion closes with a joyous outburst of his own compelling hope—more effectual perhaps than all his logic, for the greatest things of life lie beyond the limited realm of explanation.

It was perhaps in March A.D. 57, shortly before the Passover, or days of unleavened bread, that Paul completed his letter and sent it by Titus and two companions to Corinth. He had sent Timothy and Erastus on a tour of the churches of Macedonia, with orders to proceed to Corinth in his place, supposing that they would reach that city soon after the messengers would arrive with the letter.[59] Other workers were out among the churches, and the apostle was left alone in Ephesus with Sosthenes, his secretary.

The Pauline gospel was now spreading faster than its founder could follow, but everywhere was meeting with corrupting pagan influences and bitter Jewish opposition. Its hold, however, upon the hearts of men had already insured perpetuity so that Paul was planning to extend his conquest to Rome and Spain.[60] His labor in Asia had prospered, but as converts to the gospel increased, the adversaries of the Pauline church multiplied.[61] He decided therefore to tarry in Ephesus until Pentecost to strengthen the church for its independence. His work in all Asia would then be turned over permanently to trained leaders.

Before Paul was ready to leave Ephesus, his enemies, of whom he was watchfully aware, began plotting his overthrow. It was Paul's rule to avoid giving unnecessary offense to the Gentiles[62] even by denouncing their gods. But his work in Ephesus was undermining the authority of the goddess Artemis, whose beautiful temple, one of the seven wonders of the ancient world, stood a short distance beyond the city walls. When this deflection began to affect the business of a prominent silversmith named Demetrius, who manufactured miniature shrines of the goddess for sale to the worshippers, then the wrath of the whole city was turned suddenly upon Paul.

Demetrius called a meeting of his fellow craftsmen and pictured to them in heated words the gloomy outlook for their trade. In a few minutes the whole guild was out upon the streets bellowing the warning cry, "Great is Artemis of the Ephesians!"[63] Soon the whole city was in confusion, not knowing the cause of the disturbance. Somewhere the smiths and the potters and the carvers happened upon "Gaius and Aristarchus, Macedonians who were Paul's companions in travel"[64] and rushed them into the theater—that great place of public assembly near the agora carved out of the rocky western slope of Mt. Coressus.

When Paul heard of the capture of Gaius and Aristarchus, he wanted to rush to their aid, but the brethren held him back, and some of the Asiarchs, who were his friends, sent him word that he should not "venture into the theater."[65]

During all this time the crowd was increasing and making an uproar by shouting questions back and forth. Very few knew the purpose of the gathering, but when the suspicion arose that it had something to do with the Jews, then the Jewish enemies of Paul became alarmed and put forward one of their number, Alexander, perhaps a coppersmith,[66] to offer a defense. As soon as he beckoned for attention the crowd discovered that he was a Jew and instantly drowned his voice with the cry, "Great is Artemis of the Ephesians!" For nearly two hours this noisy acclaim was shouted back and forth until exhaustion accomplished what no orator could have achieved. The town-clerk then took advantage of the lull, and with a few peaceful words, respectful to the crowd, reverent to Artemis, and lawfully just to Demetrius, quieted the mob, and then dismissed it.[67]

Paul was not a blasphemer of the gods, not even of Artemis. He never indulged in defamatory or mocking gibes, but simply presented a better way. Broad-minded and sympathetic, he recognized the fact that even in idolatry, as well as in philosophy, men in their darkness might be "feeling after God." He had never insulted the priests of Artemis, never hurled anathemas at their gilded temple, nor offended the Asiarch who had the oversight of the great religious festivals.

It is reported in the gospels that a disciple once called the attention of Jesus to the beauty and magnitude of the Jewish temple and that Jesus replied saying: "Do you see these great buildings? There shall not be left here one stone upon another which shall not be destroyed."[68] Had Paul made such a prophesy concerning the temple of Artemis he might have been classed with Hierostratus the incendiary who laid waste the former temple, and whose loathsome name was condemned to oblivion. But the words of Jesus came true, and the preaching of Paul gradually dimmed the glory of Artemis until her temple became a ruin, its stones carried away, and the place of its foundations forgotten.

REFERENCES
Chapter 12

1. II Thes. 2:1.
2. Acts 19:1.
3. Acts 16:6-8; 18:23; 19:1.
4. I Cor. 16:1-4.
5. Rom. 15:27.
6. Gal. 2:10.
7. Matt. 24:42.
8. Rev. 22:20.
9. Col. 2:1.
10. Cf. Col. 1:7.
11. Cf. Rom. 15:20; II Cor. 10:15; I Cor. 3:10.
12. Rom. 16:3; I Cor. 16:19.
13. Cf. Isa. 2:2-3.
14. Cf. Acts 19:2-5; Mark 1:7-8; Matt. 11:6.
15. Mark 1:9.
16. Acts 18:26.
17. Acts 19:6.
18. Acts 2:1-13.
19. Acts 10:46.
20. I Cor. chaps. 12-14.
21. I Cor. 14:21.
22. Cf. Acts 18.
23. Acts 20:34.
24. Acts 19:10.
25. II Cor. 11:28.
26. II Cor. 11:25-31.
27. Mark 16:15.
28. Acts 19:11.
29. Acts 19:13-17.
30. Acts 19:10, 17, 20.
31. Rom. 16:3-16.
32. I Cor. 16:9.
33. I Cor. 15:32.
34. II Cor. 1:8-11.
35. II Cor. 12:14; 13:1-2.
36. II Cor. 12:20-21.
37. I Cor. 5:11.
38. I Cor. 16:17-18.
39. I Cor. 1:12.
40. I Cor. 6:1.
41. II Cor. 1:15, 16.
42. II Cor. 1:23.
43. II Cor. 7:8.
44. II Cor. 7:11.
45. II Cor. 4:8-9.
46. I Cor. 7:1-40.
47. I Cor. 8:1; 11:1.
48. I Cor. 11:2-16.
49. I Cor. 11:17-34.
50. I Cor. 12:1; 14:39.
51. I Cor. 15:1-58.
52. Jude 4, 12.
53. I Cor. 11:24-26.
54. I Cor. 12:12-27.
55. I Cor. 13.
56. Acts 2:13; I Cor. 14:23.
57. I Cor. 15:3; 4, 13.
58. Acts 23:8; 17:32.
59. I Cor. 16:10.
60. Rom. 1:13; 15:23; 24.
61. I Cor. 16:9.
62. I Cor. 10:32.
63. Acts 19:28.
64. Acts 19:29.
65. Acts 19:31.
66. Cf. II Tim. 4:14.
67. Acts 19:35-40.
68. Mark 13:2.

Amphitheater at Ephesus

Third Missionary Tour:
Ephesus — Jerusalem

PAUL'S WORK IN EPHESUS came to a close several weeks earlier than he had intended, very soon after he had sent his second letter (First Corinthians) to Corinth, and a short time before the May festival which was to be held in honor of Artemis. Paul knew that the fiasco of Alexander's attempt to clear the Jews of suspicion before the mob in the theater would deepen the hatred of his countrymen. Immediately, he called the church together. After advising them, he took affectionate leave and embarked for Troas. There, he hoped to meet Titus, who would bring him news of Corinth about the effect of his letters.

Three large islands, Samos, Chios, and Lesbos marked his northward course. Samos had been an ancient naval base where the first triremes were built[1] and on which stood a temple dedicated to an Asian goddess who had been equated with Hera or Juno. It was the birthplace of Pythagoras and had been the home of great engineers, architects, and sculptors. It was an enormous mass of mountain cut from the mainland by a narrow strait and, like a great door, it stood at the entrance of the Sinus Ionius, once open to admit Paul to Ephesus, and now open to permit his escape.

Until Paul was aboard his ship, perhaps in disguise, he was constantly alert lest he should be secretly assaulted. Being cautious, as well as courageous, he took no needless risks. Even on shipboard there was danger, though the chances of surprise were supposed to be less. Paul was now fully persuaded of the fact that his enemies would never cease to trail him until they should have him in their power.[2] He was willing, however, to meet with any fate, and even rejoiced at the prospect of suffering for his Lord's sake;[3] but there was one thing that would have been unendurable— the collapse of his apostolic mission.

As the peaks of Samos swung astern, the craggy shores of beautiful Chios drew near, fragrant with orange blossoms, flowing with purple wine and amber oil, the ancient home of epic poets and other literary men.

At the chief port on the narrow channel, five miles from the mainland, the ship harbored for the night. Favorable winds would bring Paul in another day to Mitylene on Lesbos, where Sappho sang. Lesbos was one of the chief cradles of Hellenic civilization, and its shore the fruitful mother of poets and historians. Its equable and salubrious climate would have tempted any other man than Paul to rest in its beautiful and fertile highlands.

But the ship sailed for Assos on the south coast of the Troad, the land of Homer's great epic poem, the Iliad. Thence it doubled Cape Lechum and came to Troas within a day. A group of disciples doubtless welcomed with enthusiasm the apostle's arrival, for he wrote to the Corinthians that a door was opened to him there.[4]

After a brief time, Paul began to grow restless because Titus had not come from Corinth and nothing had been heard from him. The picture that filled the apostle's imagination must have been extremely distressing: Had the Corinthian church renounced his leadership? Had it broken into quarreling factions under the leadership of legalists, Gnostics, and Epicureans? What had become of Timothy, gentle Timothy? Had dependable Titus been murdered? As anxiety grew into torture, Paul took leave of his church to sail for Macedonia, hoping thus to make quicker contact with Titus.

On leaving Troas he sailed by a route already familiar to him, and disembarked at Neapolis. A long ride across the country then brought him to Philippi on the great Roman highway, the Via Egnatia. He, of course, went at once to the house of Lydia, the wealthy Thyatrian Jewish proselyte, his first convert in Europe. "Have you any word from Titus?" would be his first question—and his hopeful expectancy would fade back into disillusion. Before Paul could prepare for another stage of his journey he heard the excitement of arriving guests—and a little later was listening eagerly to the glowing reports of his "brother" Titus and his "son" Timothy. From the protracted anxiety that had involved everything worthwhile in the apostle's life to the sudden knowledge of a great victory was like a leap out of despair into ecstatic joy: Corinth was safe, Corinth was loyal, Corinth was penitent. There was much still that needed correction and purification, but the church had passed safely through an almost ruinous crisis.

Paul now saw that he could soon entrust the care of all his churches to their own officers,[5] while he should press onward in his apostolic duty towards the western limits of the world. It would appear that he had long before[6] selected four central stations from which to radiate his gospel: Ephesus, which he was unable to reach on his first journey,[7] Corinth, Rome, and perhaps Ispalis (Seville).[8] From these four stations the thrilling story of the new plan of salvation would flow out upon the channels of trade to "the end of the earth."[9] Now that his work in the first two centers was almost completed[10] he was eager to reach the third, but never dreamed of how his desire was to be fulfilled.

Soon after his long conference with Titus and Timothy, he wrote a letter, the Second Corinthians, addressed to "the church of God which is at Corinth, with all the saints that are in the whole of Achaia."[11] Much of the letter is devoted directly or indirectly to the defense of his own character as a man, a preacher, and an apostle, but it is done with such modesty, frankness, and honesty that no one could have charged him with egotism.

There runs through the whole letter such an intense solicitude for the welfare of the church and its members, and such a repugnance for the need to defend himself that the ground upon which his enemies had based their criticisms is swept away. The letter reveals anew the fact that Paul's most persistent foes in Corinth, like those in Galatia, were Christian Jews who insinuated themselves into the churches by means of letters of recommendation, perhaps from Jerusalem, and if not from James, at least under his connivance.[12]

Timothy perhaps acted as amanuensis, and inserted his own name in the salutation, and Titus was made bearer of the letter. It must have been with great relief that Paul then arose to begin the work of strengthening his churches on the European side of the Aegean Sea. He planned to devote nine or ten months to this task, and then to go up to Jerusalem for the next observance of Pentecost, and later, to sail for Rome. His heart was again light in the belief that God "in Christ always leads us in triumph."[13] He had bowed before the raging storms of human passion, but was again standing erect in the ineradicable faith. No man with doubt in his heart about the gospel he was preaching would have endured all the apostle suffered, and then, continue his work without the slightest halting, knowing almost certainly that it would terminate in his death.

Lydia's house was no doubt restful, and the city of Philippi somewhat friendly. Certainly, no one of all Paul's recorded churches was more loyal to its founder than that of Philippi. There three or four weeks spent with that congregation must have been as spiritually invigorating to the apostle as to the people. The love-feast with the sacred ceremony of the Last Supper took on a lively freshness that seemed to hasten the messianic approach; and the prayers and the hymns and testimonies and the tongues became eloquent proofs of the presence of the Holy Spirit.

But Paul's program was heavy, and he left his friends as if he should not see them again until they should be "caught up together . . . in the clouds, to meet the Lord in the air."[14] Of course the Philippian jailer, who once clamped the stocks on Paul's feet in the dungeon, was present at the parting and, perhaps, also a magistrate or two. Certainly the women of the riverside place of worship would have been represented and, last of all, Lydia and her household.

Besides Philippi, Paul's tour certainly included the churches of Thessalonica and Beroea, and he may have visited others along the Via Egnatia as far west as Illyricum, or on the roads southward into Greece. He surely revisited Athens also before sailing across to Corinth, where he had planned to spend the winter.

Luke omits all details about his important journey through Macedonia and Achaia,[15] leaving a hiatus that might have been filled with thrilling experiences. Even about the events of the three months in Corinth, where Judaism had its teeth in the throat of the church and Gnosticism was injecting poison into the gospel, Luke's pen is inactive until Paul is about to sail for Jerusalem. He says nothing about the effect of the apostle's three letters to the Corinthians, nothing about the scandals that had broken out in the church, nor the disciplinary measures adopted by Paul to check them. He says nothing about the apostle's ironic refusal to play the sophist in presenting his gospel, or his refusal to satisfy Jewish curiosity by posing as a thaumaturgist,[16] nor does he mention the great letter to the Romans which must have been written from Corinth near the end of his visit.

Phoebe, the beloved deaconess down at Cenchreae, was planning a business trip to Rome,[17] and when Paul heard of it he called in Tertius, an epistolarian, and drew up a letter to the Christians of that city. Many of them had gone there from Greek-speaking communities where Paul had labored and were his cherished friends. He wrote in Greek, even though the letter was going to a Latin-speaking city. When Phoebe came up the crowded avenue to Corinth to sail from Lechaeum, the western port, Paul entrusted his letter to her care. It contained an introduction that would make her a welcome guest in a strange city.

Paul's previous letters to other churches had been drawn from his pen by conditions that required immediate attention. They dealt with local problems only and, therefore, presented only particular phases of certain truths and displayed only those characteristic traits of the apostle that such problems called forth. But the letter to the Romans sprang from the heart of its author unprovoked by such annoyances as heresy, internal disorder, and external interference. The polemical element, except in a single remark,[18] is only what was necessary in explaining his gospel; it is not entirely without directness, but burns with sacrificial love.[19] For many years Paul had wished to reach Rome[20] to make it a center of labor, but his gospel had traveled faster than he could, and a large group of Christians had found their way to that city. Certain Jews, like Aquila and Priscilla had returned after the death of Claudius, and numerous Greeks well known to Paul had gone there for business reasons. All these were on Paul's prayer list, and he sent them affectionate greetings.

Rome was Paul's legitimate missionary field. It lay on his great line of conquest—Jerusalem to Illyricum, Illyricum to Spain.[21] Its church, so far as it existed in an organized form, was of the Pauline type, not the Petrine. The Christians of the latter type had been dispersed with the other Jews by Claudius, and if any returned they still affiliated with the synagogues. One of the most improbable conjectures of history is that Peter was ever at any time in Rome; and no assertion could be more absurd than that he at any time had held office there.* There is no reliable evidence for either belief; and besides, it was not the privilege of an apostle to become stationary. Peter was domestic and provincial, and hugged Jerusalem and its environs; but even then he did not assume the papal tiara in that city, though it was the apostolic meeting place and the headquarters of the Church. Paul makes no reference to Peter in his letter, as he most surely would have if that apostle had been in Rome before A.D. 58; and Luke could not have failed to speak of him if he had been there four years later. Since Paul refused to build upon another apostle's foundation,[22] the church at Rome must have been the indirect product of his own labors; and Aquila and Priscilla may have been sent back to that city from Ephesus to provide headquarters for him.

Paul's purpose in writing to the Romans was to pave the way for his visit and to furnish the church, which already had a reputation for sturdy faith, with the fundamentals of his gospel in case Judaism or heresy should

---

* The tradition that Peter was at Rome is very strong. There was a church at Rome before Paul arrived, and it was to that congregation that Paul wrote Romans. That congregation was evidently a Jewish Christian group of some kind, because Paul had to emphasize his Jewishness in his attempt to be accepted there. Marcion was a strong Paulinist, who had no apparent problems in Asia Minor, but when he went to Rome, he was excommunicated by that Church. It seems likely that the name "Peter" was attached to all churches belonging to the Petrine branch of the church, just as Luther's name is attached to all Lutheran churches, even though Luther had never seen most of the locations where these churches exist. It seems very likely that the first Roman church was Petrine, even though Peter was never there. (GWB)

attack it before his arrival. For the instruction of both Jew and Gentile, though writing to the latter, he reasons through the ancient scriptures in his rabbinical style. He shows that all men are under God's wrath against sin, and that the only way to salvation is through faith by which access is obtained through Jesus Christ into God's saving grace, and that the way is open to both Jew and Gentile. He wrote a letter, not a formal theological treatise, and yet he has given to the world its greatest single piece of religious literature. Its doctrines of limitless grace and exhaustless righteousness through faith have done more than all the philosophies of all time to sweeten and beautify life. But he knows from unpleasant experience what the tendency of the extremists always is. Paul therefore meets their arguments in advance.[23]

He grieves deeply over the inability of the Jew to grasp the full significance of Israel's mission—the Jews, his own kinsmen, "who are Israelites, and to them belong the sonship, the glory, and the covenants, the giving of the law, and worship, and the promises; to them belong the patriarchs, and of their race, according to the flesh, is the Christ."[24] He finds consolation, however, in the hope that the Gentile, who should have been brought into the Messianic Kingdom by the Jew, would eventually be the means by which the Jew himself was brought in: a hope that evidently led the apostle to extend indefinitely the time of his Lord's return.

Twice in the course of his letter, Paul rose above the level of his argument and soared towards the summit of his faith. In the fifth chapter he thrills his readers by revealing the results and the joys of justification by faith; and in the eighth, shows the believer how under the reign of the Spirit and the love of Christ he will be more than conqueror, even in the bitterest conflicts of life.

While Paul was preparing to sail for Jerusalem, someone discovered a plot to take his life. Apparently the Jews of Corinth found themselves unable to intimidate the apostle and were afraid to make any attack on him where his Roman citizenship might give him protection. They made plans to do away with him at Cenchreae, where their deed might be charged to the ruffians of the port. Or, failing in that, they would hire an assassin to follow him to sea.

Paul had required a liberal collection to be taken in all the churches for the relief of the indigent saints in Jerusalem. He had emphasized the fact that the Gentiles had received salvation through the Jews and that as an act of gratitude they should willingly aid those who aided them. Members of the churches had been requested to lay aside on the first day of each week a portion of their earnings, and to choose trustworthy men to carry their gifts to Jerusalem. Several of these men had assembled at Corinth, expecting to sail from Cenchreae with Paul. But when the murderous plot was discovered, Paul and the delegates left secretly by way of the Isthmus and traversed Macedonia to sail from another port. At Philippi, Paul spent the Passover season with friends.

On leaving Philippi for Troas, Paul was accompanied by Luke, "the beloved physician," who appears to have been identified with that city, and who may be traced with Paul by the pronouns "we" and "us," as they occur from the sixteenth chapter of the Acts to the end of the book.[25] The northeast winds doubtless caused a delay of five days and prolonged the time of landing beyond both the Sabbath and the Lord's Day. For this reason perhaps, Paul decided to remain seven days with the disciples of Troas so he could be with them for the weekly agape and for the celebration of the Lord's Supper. The Lord's Day of course began in the evening just at the time when the Jewish Sabbath ended.

A large well-lighted upper room on the third floor had been engaged by the disciples for their last meeting with Paul. At the appointed hour the room had become crowded. It was Paul's night, and the linguists and the exhorters and the prophets kept silence in his honor. The apostle told the story of God's chosen people, the promise of a Savior Messiah, the fulfillment of that promise in the sending of Jesus, the opening of the messianic Kingdom to penitent Jews, and the extension of that Kingdom to include the Gentiles. He explained the fulfillment of the Jewish ritual law, the place of faith in the salvation of men. He spoke of the early return of the Messiah in the power and majesty of heaven, of the awe-inspiring spectacle of a world that had run its course, and of the joyful reunion of saints triumphant through faith.

At midnight, just before the celebration of the Lord's Supper, a boy who had found a comfortable seat in an open window and had fallen asleep fell to the ground. The thud of his body brought a shudder of horror to those who saw him disappear, and when someone cried out that Eutychus had fallen from the window, Paul was among the first to reach his side. Luke pronounced him dead, but Paul took charge and declared that his life was still in him, and the congregation returned to its place for the breaking of the bread.

Paul was now hunted like a wild beast. He must never reach Jerusalem—the man who had placed faith and grace above the ceremonial law, who had enticed the rich proselytes away from the synagogues and had reduced the flow of benevolence into the coffers of mercenary priests. The man who had ignored the seal of God by making uncircumcised Gentiles heirs of the Kingdom of Heaven must die; if not by Jewish stones or the assassin's dagger, then by the Roman Sword.

The next morning after Paul's great address, Luke, Timothy, Sopater, Aristarchus, Secundus, Gaius, Tychicus, and Trophimus[26] went aboard a coastwise ship sailing for Patara, the port of Xanthus in Lycia. But Paul had reasons for believing that assassins were ready to go aboard the ship if he should be seen to embark at Troas. As at Cenchreae, Paul remained behind and secretly took the oak-shaded road across the country to Assos, while the ship sailed around Cape Lectum to the same port. Even the land route was dangerous for him, since Jews from all parts of the world were just then crowding the caravans and ships in order to reach Jerusalem for Pentecost.

"Go to Assos and break your neck," the seamen used to say. Assos stood on a rocky eminence overlooking the Bay of Adramyttium, and was reached from the sea by a steep ascent. Its scenic outlook through the great channel between Lesbos and the mainland would have halted the most indifferent traveler; and its own picture from the sea could never be forgotten.

The ship came into port at about the same time that Paul entered the city, and remained overnight. On the next day, with Paul aboard, it sailed for Mitylene, the chief city of Lesbos. Thus sailing by day and putting into harbor or anchoring at night, they came from Lesbos to Chios, and then to Samos. If tradition is reliable, it anchored for the night off the promontory of Trogyllium, that mountain terminal from which the island had broken away.

The next day the ship put in at Miletus which, though nearly thirty miles away, had become one of the ports of Ephesus after silting of the Cayster River had made navigation difficult. The stay at Miletus extended over two or more days, and Paul took advantage of the time to send to Ephesus for the elders of the Church. Being anxious to reach Jerusalem before Pentecost, and having already suffered long delays, he could not take the risk of missing his ship by leaving the port. It was a day's journey between the two cities, and perhaps two days elapsed before the arrival of the elders. Paul wished for news of the Ephesian Church and its outposts, and, in turn, to impress upon the presbyters, or "bishops," as they are called in Paul's address, the responsibilities of their office. Luke was doubtless present at the meeting and long years later gave the substance of what he had heard as nearly as it could be recalled. Paul is thus represented as reminding the elders of his life and work when among them for three years and of insisting that his example be followed—an ideal of emulation for all who would preach the gospel.[27]

The elders were then warned against two dangers: fierce wolves from without that would attempt to destroy the flock and disputants within who would divide it by "speaking perverse things." Luke's words may have been *ex post facto*, but if not, they became history by fulfillment.

In his farewell words, Paul told his friends that they should see his face no more, a distressing announcement that if *ex post facto* almost proves that he never left Rome after his "first" imprisonment there.

It was a hurried meeting, intense, and weighted with heavenly business. It revealed Paul in the beauty and strength of his character and the Ephesian elders in the loyalty and tenderness of their hearts. Prayer, embraces, tears marked the last moments, and then Paul was escorted to the ship.

The next port was Cos, on the island of the same name, a short sail on a straight course before a favorable wind. Paul and his companions, Luke, Timothy, and the money carriers, could see the island long before reaching it—a great rounded mass of limestone seventy-five miles in circumference, famous for its wine and for its delicate textile fabrics. It was the birthplace of Apeles the artist and Hippocrates the physician, the site of a medical school, and of a great temple of Aesculapius that had become a museum of votive offerings representing human afflictions.

After one night at Cos, the ship put in at Rhodes, on the island of the same name, that famous dark green fragment of a mountain dropping away from the southwest corner of Asia Minor; or, as fable has it, drawn up from the sea by the attraction of the sun. It was the place from which the Greeks reckoned latitude and longitude, famous for its healthful climate, and on which once stood one of the ancient wonders of the world: the Colossus of Rhodes. The huge bronze statue of the sun god, Helios, had been shaken from its pedestal by an earthquake and, after nearly three hundred years, when Paul passed that way, was still sprawling by the sea.

From Rhodes, the little vessel sailed for a few hours in the open sea and then put in at Patara, the port of Xanthus, the capital of Lycia. Here Paul and his companions embarked at once on a larger and speedier vessel sailing directly for Tyre in Phoenicia. This change relieved the apostle of some of his anxiety that had been caused by long delays. He could now reach Jerusalem and have time to spare. But at every port and on every ship he still had reason to fear the presence of enemies—enemies who were his own countrymen and for whose salvation he was in constant prayer.

Evidently the winds and the sky were favorable for night sailing, otherwise the vessel would have remained in port until morning. The ship carried no compass, but its course would lie so near to well-known landmarks that by taking a general direction it could sail safely between them; and on clear nights there was always one star that never moved.

Eventually, Paul reached Tyre, where the ship had to put in for seven days to unload its cargo. Paul had been in Tyre before; and Jesus had once visited that city and had paid a tribute to its possible faith. It was the city of King David's friend, Hiram, King of Tyre, and one of the places to which the followers of Jesus fled when Paul was terrorizing Jerusalem. Paul and his companions sought out the disciples in Tyre and met with them in their weekly services. Among the number were certain prophets who through the spirit were warned of Paul's danger and told him "not to go on to Jerusalem."[28] But the apostle's purpose outweighted all arguments and no warning could deter him from making one last appeal to the heart of Judaism.

The seven days had warmed the heart of the church and, when the time for sailing arrived, the brethren with their wives and children accompanied Paul and his delegates out of the city and down to the beach, where they prayed together.

It was a beautiful sail from Tyre down the coast to Ptolemais, the old Canaanite city of Acco.[29] Paul and his company left the ship there and, after a day with the church in that city, set overland for Caesarea. The road was not new to Paul, but may have been to some of the men who were with him. There was undoubtedly some good reason for choosing the land route. The delegates may have believed themselves trailed by robbers, or the apostle may have received warnings at Ptolemais.

At Caesarea the travelers went directly to the home of Philip the evangelist, who had once served as one of the seven deacons in the church at Jerusalem until Paul's furious persecution there caused him to flee to the city of Samaria. Philip, like others of the Christian dispersion, began preaching Jesus as the Messiah, and soon won great renown as an evangelist and wonder-worker. Later he chose for his home the beautiful city built by Herod the Great. In his family were four daughters who, perhaps expecting the early return of the Messiah, foresook marriage and devoted themselves to religious teaching.

After a few days, a visitor named Agabus arrived at Philip's home. Evidently he had heard in Judaea that Paul was in Caesarea, and, being a prophet, he hastened down to warn the apostle of his danger if he should venture into Jerusalem. In the presence of Philip's household and all their guests, Agabus removed Paul's girdle,[30] and with it, in the dramatic manner of the ancient prophets, tied his own feet and hands and said: "Thus says the Holy Spirit, 'So shall the Jews at Jerusalem bind the man who owns this girdle and deliver him into the hands of the Gentiles.' " The minds of those present was filled with fear and horror. No one doubted the words of the prophet, but all began urging Paul to abandon his purpose. But Paul was adamant: "What are you doing, weeping and breaking my heart? For I am ready not only to be imprisoned but even to die at Jerusalem for the name of the Lord Jesus." Thus seeing their persuasions to be of no avail they ceased and said, "The will of the Lord be done."[31]

Paul probably took the words of Agabus literally, and therefore instead of acting on a chance, he deliberately faced a definite situation. In some way he expected to fall into the hands of the Romans, but further than that he could not see. But whether prison or death or both awaited him, he was constrained for the name of the Lord Jesus to clear his ministry before all Jerusalem of the unjust accusations from which it had suffered. By his great gift from the Gentile churches to the needy saints, he hoped to silence the Judaizing element of the church, and by his very presence in the city on a great festival occasion, he hoped to show all Jewry that he had sought the fulfillment of the law, not its destruction.

Paul never wavered in his faith. He believed that the crucified Jesus had risen from the dead, that more than half a thousand people had seen him alive after he had left the tomb,[32] and that his resurrection was an undeniable proof of his messianic character.[33] The risen Christ was now an objective reality to him, and with this starting point of personal knowledge he began to interpret that future in vivid literal terms, in which he regarded himself as a chosen actor who could not fail without everlasting disaster to himself, if not to the world. Once he said to King Agrippa, "I was not disobedient to the heavenly vision."[34]

Laboring under such an impelling conviction, a man like Paul would have gone to Jerusalem in spite of the steaming rage of fierce Sanhedrists, the unjust charges of misguided saints, and the brutality of mobs. After a few days with Philip, Paul and his fellow travelers, together with a number of brethren from Ceasarea, set out on the seventy-mile journey to Jerusalem.

REFERENCES
Chapter 13

1. Thucydides. *A History of the Peloponnesian War.* 1. 13.
2. Acts 20:23.
3. II Cor. 12:10; Rom. 5:3; 8:25-39.
4. II Cor. 2:12.
5. Acts 20:28.
6. Rom. 15:23-24.
7. Cf. Gal. 4:13.
8. Rom. 15:24, 28.
9. Cf. Acts 1:8; Mark 16:15; Col. 1:23.
10. Rom. 15:23.
11. II Cor. 1:1.
12. Cf. II Cor. 3:1.
13. II Cor. 2:14.
14. I Thes. 4:17.
15. Cf. Acts 20:1-3.
16. I Cor. 1:17-25; 2:13.
17. Rom. 16:1-2.
18. Rom. 16:17-19.
19. Rom. 9:1-5.
20. Rom. 15:23.
21. Rom. 15:24.
22. Rom. 15:20.
23. Rom. 6:1, 2, 15.
24. Rom. 9:4-5.
25. Acts 16:10-17; 20:5-15; 21:1-18; 27:1 28:16.
26. Acts 20:4.
27. Acts 20:18-38.
28. Acts 21:4.
29. Judg. 1:31.
30. Acts 21:11.
31. Acts 21:13-14.
32. I Cor. 15:5-8.
33. Cf. I Cor. 15:14.
34. Acts 26:19.

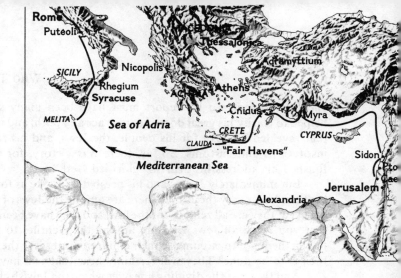

A Prisoner of Rome:
Jerusalem — Caesarea

IT WAS EVENING of the second day when the company reached Jerusalem. Some loyal brethren were awaiting them, and they received them gladly. It was not long, however, until the conversation turned to the subject of Paul's grave danger in Jerusalem. In whispers of caution the apostle was told that both the church and the city regarded him as an outlaw, and that if he should be discovered, only a miracle could save him from death.

But duty prevailed over danger; and on the following morning, Paul, accompanied by the delegates from the Gentile churches, visited the headquarters of the Jerusalem Church, where James—the Lord's brother—had assembled all the presbyters. If any of the apostles or other persons were present, there is no record of the fact. The occasion, however, did not require their attendance. When the bags of Gentile gold for the relief of the poor of the church were accepted by these officials, the church was at once compromised in Paul's favor and had to extend him a courteous though secret hearing. Paul then arose and gave a detailed account of his work. It was a thrilling story. Nothing approaching it in sacrifice, suffering, and achievement had ever been reported by another

171

apostle. Woven into his report must have been many statements that
helped to clarify his great doctrines of grace and faith, and many assertions
that revealed his love for his people, the Jews, and his respect for their
institutions and customs. So far, there was victory, for when Paul had
finished his address his hearers "glorified God."

But immediately James and his presbyters spoke as follows: "You see
brother, how many thousands there are among the Jews of those who have
believed; they are all zealous for the law, and they have been told about you
that you teach all Jews who are among the Gentiles to forsake Moses,
telling them not to circumcise their children or observe the customs. What
then is to be done? They will certainly hear that you have come."[1]

And that was the dividing line over which the Jewish church could not
pass—they were "all zealous for the law," Pharisaically zealous, because
they believed it to be still in force, and because its observance protected
them from prosecution. It was therefore evident that Paul could not
appear before the whole Jerusalem church, or any part of it, or be seen
upon the streets without risking his life. He might have left Jerusalem and
have gone secretly to Rome, but his enemies would then have mocked his
cowardice to the jeopardy of his work, and the breach he longed to close
would have been permanently widened.

There remained one hope: He might disprove, at least in part, some of
the charges made against him if he could perform some rite that would not
compromise his faith. He was not an enemy of Moses, but his great
doctrine of grace left no room for the works of the law as an instrument of
salvation. Under grace, good works of all kinds were but products, not
means, of salvation. Paul, however, practiced circumcision, vows, and
fastings, yet never as encroachments upon grace. He circumcised Timothy
to make him unobjectionable to the Jews; he made a vow at the close of his
second missionary tour; and he resorted to fasting on many occasions.
James knew this and, therefore, suggested that Paul take the Nazarite vow,
which should be sufficiently spectacular to disprove the charges made
against him. But regularly, the minimum time for such a vow was thirty
days, a period too long for the present purpose. Fortunately there was a
short way, one by which Agrippa I had won favor in the sight of the Jews.[2]
He could join himself to other Nazarites who were completing the
prescribed time, purify himself with them, and pay all their expenses
incident to shaving, sacrifices, and priestly fees.

It happened that James knew of four men who were under a vow and
who were doubtless unable to meet the temple expenses.[3] These vows Paul
took, and the next day purified himself with the four, and after reporting to
the priests at the temple, took quarters in the court of the Israelites to
complete the seven days of purification. It was on the great day of
Pentecost when the five men entered the Temple. For several days, crowds

from all parts of the world had been thronging the city and its suburbs, and many would remain for several days longer. All these, on visiting the court of the Israelites, would pass near Paul, who was not in hiding, but was wishing to be seen by all as a law-abiding Jew. It had long been his practice to adjust himself to other men by conforming to their conventions in things non-essential to his faith. He had once written: "To the Jews I became as a Jew, in order to win Jews; to those under the law I became as one under the law—though not being myself under the law—that I might win those under the law . . . I have become all things to all men, that I might by all means save some."[4]

Apparently there was no sign of trouble until the fifth day when certain Jews from the province of Asia, evidently from Ephesus, and very likely under the leadership of Alexander the coppersmith,[5] tracked the apostle to the Temple Court and, finding him, set up a cry that brought forth a mob. Gloating with revenge, Alexander cried out: "Men of Israel, help! This is the man who is teaching men everywhere against the people and the law, and his place; moreover he also brought Greeks into the temple, and he has defiled this holy place."[6] Alexander did not hesitate about manufacturing images of Diana and now he was ready to declare in fact what was only an evil wish in his heart. Somewhere in the city, he and his associates had seen Trophimus, a Greek of Ephesus, one of Paul's traveling companions, and on that ground claimed that Paul had taken him into the sacred precincts of the temple.

Nothing could have enraged the Jews more than such an act of sacrilege. On marble blocks in the balustrade that surrounded the inner courts was carved a warning that death was the penalty for aliens who ventured within the enclosure. Alexander and his associates made the most of their opportunity. In a moment the whole temple area was aflame with excitement. Quickly the temple police surrounded and seized the apostle.

Paul was dragged out like a beast, his body thumping down two or three flights of marble stairs, while surging crowds subjected him to every possible indignity. According to the law, he deserved death, if the charges against him were true. Therefore, the instant he was out of the temple, his enraged countrymen began beating him. But Herod's fortress of Antonia, teeming with Roman soldiers, adjoined the northwest corner of the temple area and communicated directly with the outer court and with the roofs of the porticoes. On feast days, when the Jews were likely to be turbulent, soldiers patrolled the roofs to keep watch below. When they saw the excitement over Paul, they reported at once to the military tribune, Claudius Lysias, who rushed down from the fortress with centurions and soldiers.

By this time, rumor after rumor was spreading over the city, and the people were rushing together. Hurriedly the temple doors were closed and at the same time the centurions marched their companies to strategic positions. But the military tribune himself, accompanied by soldiers, went directly to Paul and reached him just as the mob began beating him. Slowly the raging crowd pressed back upon itself as the chief captain in polished armor approached with his cool and highly trained veterans. The temple police abandoned their arrest.

The Jews knew that it was Paul whom they had seized. But word had circulated through the Roman fortress that a notorious Egyptian prophet,[7] who a short time before had led a band of followers to the Mount of Olives with the purpose of capturing Jerusalem, had been discovered in the temple. The Romans had slaughtered many of that band, but the prophet himself had escaped. Claudius believed he had captured the imposter prophet and ordered Paul bound with chains. He had now escaped death at the hands of the Jews and knew that he could appeal, by his Roman citizenship, for further protection.

As Paul was being led to the tower stairs, the crowd surged so violently that the soldiers had to carry him. As he passed beyond the reach of blows, his ears were filled with the savage death-demanding yells of the multitude: "Away with him!" "Away with him!" It was the cry that had once filled the ears of his Lord[8] nearly thirty years before. On the balcony above, Paul spoke for the first time. Addressing the chief captain, he said, "May I say something to you?" He spoke in Greek. The captain would have expected Aramaic, the current Hebrew, such as the prophet would have used. In surprise, Claudius Lysias replied: "Are you not the Egyptian then, who recently stirred up a revolt and led four thousand men of the Assassins out into the wilderness?" "I am a Jew of Tarsus in Cilicia," said Paul, "a citizen of no mean city; and I beg from you, let me speak to the people."[9]

Something in Paul's manner and appearance was utterly inconsistent with the character of a ruffian. His respectful address, his superior self-command so impressed the officer that he granted Paul's request. With swollen face Paul appeared, his clothing torn and soiled and, looking down upon the people, signalled with his shackled hand that he was about to speak.

A great silence followed. Paul spoke in Hebrew, whereas some of his hearers at least were expecting him to use the Greek of the Tarsian shops. According to the narrative in the Book of Acts, which is Luke's idea of what was said, Paul gave a brief outline of his life—his birthplace, his schooling, his acts as a persecutor, his conversion, and his vision in which he was commissioned as an apostle to the Gentiles.

It was an entertaining story, but as its intimation grew more and more personal, a deepening cloud of disapproval spread over the sea of upturned faces. When it reached the point where Paul claimed that the Lord had told him to leave Jerusalem and go to the Gentiles because the Jews would refuse to hear his gospel, the storm broke. In rage the Jews cast off their clothes and waved them above their heads. "Away with such a fellow from the earth! For he ought not to live," the crowd shouted.

The tribune, not being able to determine from either the speech or the shouting why the crowd was so enraged, ordered Paul to be taken into the castle for examination by scourging. Paul knew the full meaning of that order. In its mildest form it would be an awful ordeal, and, in its severest, might result in death. Within a few moments the soliders had him stripped to the waist, revealing the scars of former stripes and rods on back and breast.

When Paul had been tied up, he said to a centurion: "Is it lawful for you to scourge a man who is a Roman citizen, and uncondemned?" The centurion went to Claudius Lysias and said: "What are you about to do? For this man is a Roman citizen." The tribune went to Paul and inquired: "Tell me, are you a Roman citizen?" "Yes," Paul replied. To which Claudius Lysias responded doubtingly: "I bought this citizenship for a large sum." "But I was born a citizen,"[10] returned Paul, who knew that a false claim of citizenship was punishable with death.

Immediately the scourgers were dismissed, and Paul was released. Claudius Lysias was uneasy. Without inquiry he had bound a Roman, and Paul, or someone else, might report the incident. There was doubtless a conference between the officially stern military tribune and the fearlessly calm apostle of Christ that was to the advantage of both. Paul, however, was returned to the care of his two guards for the night.

Next morning Lysias, wishing to know why the Jews were accusing his prisoner, commanded the chief priests and all the members of the Jewish Council, or Sanhedrin, to assemble. The Sanhedrin was not assembled in its judicial capacity, but rather as a party in a dispute, and as having something to explain. It was the duty of the military tribune to report the tumult of the previous day to the governor of the province and he chose this plan to discover the necessary facts that, so far, had been extremely elusive. He wished to deal justly with Paul, and, at the same time, to give the least possible offense to the Jews, who at that period of their history were in almost constant ferment.

The council—perhaps seventy or more in number—having assembled, notified Claudius Lysias, who brought Paul down from the castle. Temple police guarded the prisoner. As a young man Paul had once occupied a side bench in this court, but a quarter of a century had passed since then. He now scanned the whole semicircle for familiar faces. There were but few, and not one a friend.

The charge against Paul had been proclaimed in the temple the day before by Alexander the coppersmith of Ephesus. In substance it was now repeated and Paul was given an opportunity to explain his actions.

Unperturbed and at the same time emboldened by the coincidence of duty and opportunity, Paul began: "Brethren, I have lived before God in all good conscience up to this day."[11] Instantly the high priest Ananias ordered Paul to be struck on the mouth. Micaiah,[12] Jeremiah,[13] and Jesus[14] had suffered similar indignities. All that was human in Paul rose in one violent impulse and he shouted back, "God shall strike you, you white-washed wall! Are you sitting to judge me according to the law, and yet contrary to the law you order me to be struck?" Instantly the guards reproved him saying, "Would you revile God's high priest?"[15]

Ananias had in fact been high priest, but was no longer in office, except that he usurped privilege and authority whenever possible. He was not in official robes, so Paul did not know him. With appropriate words Paul apologized to the Court saying, "I did not know, brethren, that he was the high priest; for it is written, 'you will not speak evil of a ruler of your people.'"[16] Luke knew at the time when he was writing the Acts that Paul's epithet, "whitewashed wall" was fully justified, for Ananias was both false and cruel. He finally perished at the hands of the *sicarii*, or nationalistic terrorists,[17] who at that time were numerous even in Jerusalem.

As Paul continued his defense, he observed that some of the Sanhedrin were Sadducees and some were Pharisees. He took advantage of this to divide his adversaries into opposing groups, calling out dramatically: "Brethren, I am a Pharisee, a son of Pharisees; with respect to the hope and the resurrection of the dead I am on trial."[18] The Jews had been vague and false in their charges, and Paul in a single sentence forced the attention of his hearers to the fundamental issue. The Sadducees hurled anathemas at Paul, and ridicule at the Pharisees.

But there were several courageous scribes among the Pharisees who replied hotly; and, at the risk of a beating, attempted to defend Paul by shouting, "We find nothing wrong in this man. What if a spirit or an angel spoke to him?"[19] The Sadducees could endure no more. They did not believe in angels or spirits, nor in the resurrection of the dead, as the Pharisees did. The great court that should have been a model of dignity, order, and justice now became a mob intent upon murder. So savagely was Paul assailed that Lysias ordered a company of soldiers to bring him into the castle.

Once more the apostle was under the protection of Rome; but this time he was aware of a certain respect and sympathy that made the garrison seem safe and hospitable. That night he dreamed—dreamed with all the vividness of reality. By his side stood Jesus, his Christ, who said, "Take courage, for as you have testified about me at Jerusalem, so you must bear witness also at Rome."[20] The apostle's tremendous faith colored all his dreams with encouragement and made them veritable incidents.

When morning came, the whole castle of a thousand soldiers

wondered at the calm self-possession of its remarkable prisoner. But with the new day, while Lysias was struggling over the report that he should make to Felix, the governor at Caesarea, more than forty Jews met secretly and vowed not to eat or drink until they had killed Paul. Among them probably were several religious insurrectionists, or *sicarii*, who were dedicated to the Gentiles and Jews who considered on matters of the land. Having agreed upon a plan they reported it to the chief priests and elders, who promptly agreed to become partisans.

Their part was to call a meeting of the Sanhedrin for the following day and to request Claudius Lysias to send Paul to them again so they might "determine his case more exactly." The assassins were then to take their places nonchalantly near the foot of the tower stairs and, when Paul arrived, would jostle around him until a skillful *sicarius* with his dagger hidden in his robes could kill his victim with a secret thrust. The others of the forty, all purposely unarmed, would then crowd around in mock innocence until they could cover the retreat of their guilty comrade.

But before the request was sent to Lysias, the proposed assassination became known to Paul's sister's son. With the terrible secret, the boy fled to the castle and told Paul, who called a centurion and told him to take the boy to Lysias, who received him kindly. When the lad revealed the plot, Lysias quickly summoned two of his centurions and issued orders that an escort be fitted out immediately to convey Paul in safety to Felix at Caesarea.

That night at nine o'clock, after all Jerusalem had fallen into its first sleep, two hundred legionary soldiers, two hundred spearmen, and seventy horsemen quietly fell in line beyond the Damascus Gate and began a forced march northward. With the cavalry rode Paul the Hebrew-Roman, the persecutor, the persecuted. He had been taken secretly from the castle, and the luggage that he had collected for his intended journey to Rome had been brought from the home of his host.

The great size of the escort may have been partly for military discipline, but the restlessness and treachery of the times would alone have fully justified such precaution. For three hours or more, Paul was on the road over which he had once planned to lead men and women in chains. About midnight the escort reached Gophna, beyond Bethel, and, after a halt, turned to the left and passed down through Timnah to Antipatris. As the risk was now small for the remainder of the journey, the legionnaires and spearmen turned back for Jerusalem, while the cavalry proceeded alone with Paul, marching northward through the plain of Sharon, a vast stretch of rolling land whose fertile acres were clothed in wheat and barley.

During this journey, Paul must have wondered about his fellow travelers, who had accompanied him from Assos to Jerusalem; about James and the elders, who trembled with the fear of death; about Peter and the other apostles, who were afraid to be seen with him; and about Claudius Lysias, who was now secretly his friend. He may have thought, too, of Alexander the coppersmith, who had betrayed him with a falsehood; of Ananias, the "whitewashed wall;" and of the *sicarius*, with his unused dagger. He must have thought also of his own people, the chosen Israel.

Paul did not blame the Jews for wishing to kill him, for they had law that could be construed to justify such a deed. But Paul did blame them for rejecting his gospel and thus delaying the return of the Messiah. He may even have thought of them in terms similar to those used by Jesus and reported by Matthew in a scathing but just arraignment of them.[21]

But Paul never dwelt unnecessarily long upon the past; to him the call of the future was loud and clear, and the past had served its purpose. Though a prisoner, he was nevertheless planning to declare his gospel in Caesarea, and ultimately to bear witness for his Lord in Rome. His constraining motto left him no time for either idleness or lamentations. He said, "This one thing I do, forgetting the things which are behind, and stretching forward to the things which are before, I press on toward the goal unto the prize of the high calling of God in Christ Jesus."[22]

It was but an easy day's journey from Antipatris to Caesarea, but Paul was glad when the two long aqueducts, the city walls, and the towers of the praetorium came into view. It was at least the fourth time that he had approached the city; twice within a few days.

REFERENCES
Chapter 14

1. Acts 21:20-21.
2. Josephus. *Antiquities.* XIX. 6. 1.
3. Num. 6.
4. I. Cor. 9:20-22.
5. Acts 19:33, 34; II Tim. 4:14-17.
6. Acts 21:28.
7. Josephus. *Antiquities.* XX. 8. 6; *Wars.* II. 13. 4.
8. Luke 23:18; John 19:15.
9. Acts 21:37-39.
10. Acts 22:25-28.
11. Acts 23:1.
12. I Kings 22:24.
13. Jer. 20:2.
14. John 18:22.
15. Acts 23:3-4.
16. Acts 23:5.
17. Josephus. *Wars.* II. 17.
18. Acts 23:6.
19. Acts 23:9.
20. Acts 23:11.
21. Matt. 23; Cf. Josephus. *Antiquities.* XVIII. 8. 1, 2.
22. Phil. 3:13-14.

Paul a prisoner at Caesarea

A Prisoner of Rome:
At Caesarea

THE CENTURION IN COMMAND of the escort carried an explanatory letter from Claudius Lysias to Antonius Felix, the procurator at Caesarea. Upon reading the letter, Felix ordered Paul to be brought before him at once. All Judaea had been seething with crime: robbery, assassination, confiscation of property, and petty insurrections, so that all men, high and low, were living in constant fear.[1] Felix therefore had seen all kinds of criminals and had received complaints against both suspected and innocent persons.

But Paul's case was unusual. Lysias had found Paul had been "charged with nothing deserving death or imprisonment"[2] so far as Roman law was concerned, but reported that he was accused by the Jews "about questions of their law," and that a plot had been made to take his life. This letter made a favorable impression upon Felix, and Paul, knowing something of its charitable contents, was at ease when the centurion presented him before the court. Felix looked him over—nearly sixty, respectful, unperturbed, intelligent, honest. "Of what province are you?" he inquired. "Cilicia," Paul replied. The tribune's letter said that Paul's accusers had been ordered to take their complaint up to Caesarea. Felix said therefore: "I will hear you when your accusers arrive." He then commanded that Paul be kept in the Praetorium, Herod's palace.

When the chief priests in Jerusalem went to Lysias with their treacherous request, they were told that Paul had been sent to Caesarea and were commanded to go there and lay their cause before Felix. Ananias, still smarting under Paul's prediction that God would smite him, hastily selected a delegation of Sanhedrists and hired a Roman barrister named Tertullus, who was noted for his eloquence.

After five days from the time of Paul's arrest, Ananias and his deputies arrived in Caesarea and reported to Felix. Roman law was supposed to act without delay, and the court convened promptly. Paul was brought into the judgment hall and placed so that he and his accusers faced each other. At the signal of the court, Ananias rose and stated his charges against the prisoner. Felix then beckoned to the orator advocate, who arose and began his speech with a panegyric that was supposed to feed the vanity of the procurator. He then argued the three charges that the Sanhedrin had framed as most likely to convince the court. The underlying facts, however, had been concealed, and those were distorted into falsehoods. The high priests and Sadducees hated Paul because his work was affecting the revenues of the temple treasury.

After Tertullus had showered praise upon Felix, he pointed to Paul, and with scornful invective said: "We have found this man a pestilence."[3] With that one word he characterized the hated apostle to the gloating elation of Ananias and his associates. He then stated the three charges in terms that, if true, would have justified the death penalty. He accused the apostle of being "an agitator among all the Jews throughout the world," a charge that was equivalent to treason against Rome. He accused him of being a "ringleader of the sect of the Nazoreans," which might have implied disloyalty to Rome. He accused him also of having attempted "to profane the Temple,"[4] a serious charge punishable by death, according to Jewish law, and recognized as a crime against Roman law.

After Ananias and the other Jews had declared these charges to be true, Felix beckoned to Paul, who then with courteous dignity made his defense by giving an account of his conduct during the twelve days since his arrival in Jerusalem. In addressing the judge he used a factual compliment that greatly outweighed the flattery used by the advocate and invited judicial respect instead of displaying a guilty obsequiousness. Then in unimpassioned words and manner, he denied the charges brought against him saying, "they did not find me disputing with anyone or stirring up a crowd, either in the temple or in the synagogues, or in the city. Neither can they prove to you what they now bring up against me."[5]

While Ananias and his subalterns were lowering like storm clouds, Paul seized their attention by adroitly adding the words, "But this I admit to you." He then stated his creed and his practice: "according to the Way, which they call a sect, I worship the God of our fathers, believing everything laid down by the law or written in the prophets; having a hope in God which these themselves accept, that there will be a resurrection of both the just and the unjust. So I always take pains to have a clear conscience toward God and toward men."[6]

Paul had not gone to Jerusalem to incite discord, but, as he said, "I went up to worship at Jerusalem," and "to bring to my nation alms and offerings." It was a visit of conciliation, of unification, and of yearning compassion, like that once suffered by Jesus his Lord.[7] His accusers could not give direct testimony against him, for they had seen nothing, and yet they brought no witnesses with them. Even Alexander the coppersmith and his associates, who pretended that Paul had defiled the temple, had not been summoned. Perhaps the accusing Sanhedrists thought that their word alone was sufficient; and Alexander, after his disorderly conduct in Ephesus, doubtless felt reluctant to appear before a Roman procurator to swear to a falsehood. He was safer back amongst the votaries of Artemis.

Finally, noting the absence of witnesses, Paul exclaimed, "Or else let these men themselves say what wrongdoing they found when I stood before the Council." Then, as if seizing reluctant testimony from their lips, he made his own confession, which was more incriminating to them than to himself, and which turned their thoughts to their own disorderly conduct. He reminded them that his only offense at that time was his one exclamation: "With respect to the resurrection of the dead I am on trial before you this day."

But Felix had heard enough. He knew the reputation of Ananias, and was exceptionally well informed about the doctrines and character of the Christian sect.[8] Not wishing to offend the Jews or to mistreat Paul, he dismissed the court, saying to the Sanhedrinists, "When Lysias the tribune comes down, I will decide your case." There is no evidence that Lysias ever came down.

Again the enemies of the apostle failed. Their charges of treasonable acts against Rome seemed to excite no interest. Their efforts to get their prey into their own hands for conviction by the Sanhedrin, or more likely for exposure to assassination, were again abortive. Felix ordered the centurion to keep Paul in custody, but with indulgence, and not to forbid any of his friends to help him. Evidently Felix was impressed by the superior personality of his prisoner and doubtless believed him innocent of any greater misconduct than becoming involved in some dispute about Jewish legalism. He could have thrown the whole matter out of the court as Gallio the proconsul of Achaia once did, but his own interests were always paramount to any other consideration, and he was already wondering how he could make his prisoner profitable.

It was better for Paul that Felix did not release him. Zealous nationalists kept watch over the castle gates, hungry for the blood of one they considered an apostate. Felix was an unscrupulous tyrant, notorious for his greed, lust, and cruelty, to whom justice was impossible except as an instrument of personal advantage. His contributions to public order, mentioned by Tertullus, consisted of quelling certain seditions, breaking up bands of robbers, and punishing *sicarii*. But even these acts were no better than the outbursts of cruelty, for he was quite willing to enrich himself by the aid of any of these agents of plunder and murder. He and his brother Pallas had been slaves in the household of Antonia, the mother of the emperor Claudius, but were later made freedmen. Pallas rose to eminence under his friend Claudius and, in turn, secured the appointment of his less able and less scrupulous brother to the procuratorship of Judaea.

When Felix, listening to Paul's defense, caught the words "I came to bring alms to my nation, and offerings," his lust for gold flamed up, and he thought that here was a man who has money, or who could at least command it. Perhaps his thousands of ardent followers would give a great sum to obtain his freedom. Thus Paul fell into favor and escaped many of the miseries of prison life. He was not a public burden, for Philip's household and the church at Caesarea supplied him with food and other comforts.

A few days after Paul's imprisonment in Herod's castle, Felix came to the audience chamber bringing with him his wife Drusilla, a beautiful young Jewish woman who was scarcely twenty years of age, and sent for Paul to hear him concerning the faith in Christ Jesus. Aside from their mercenary motives, both the procurator and his wife were probably sincere in wishing to know more about the new faith. Felix, to prepare himself for legal questions that might arise later, and Drusilla, to satisfy her curiosity about the new sect. Drusilla's life had been none too happy. She was the youngest of three sisters, daughters of Agrippa I. Before she was six years old, her father had betrothed her to Epiphanes, son of Antiochus, King of Commagene, who later broke his troth by refusing to be circumcised. After her father's death, when she was about fourteen years old, her brother, who then governed northern Palestine, gave her in marriage to Azizus, king of Emesa, who was willing to submit to the required Jewish rite. But Drusilla being unhappy with her husband and annoyed by the jealousy of her less beautiful sister, Bernice, yielded to the machinations of Simon, a Cyprian magician, whom Felix had employed to entice her away from Azizus with a promise of happiness.

Felix and Drusilla, the court attendants, and the invited guests heard more than they expected to hear. Besides the story of Paul's own experiences, they heard the gospel of God's love and grace, of a Savior who had conquered death and who could be received by faith, of the gospel of the Kingdom of God whose gates were open to Jew and Gentile alike upon the condition of allegiance to the Christ. When Paul spoke of the moral standards of the Kingdom and "reasoned of righteousness, self-control, and the judgment to come," Felix, staggering under visions of his own immorality and its consequences, became terrified and cried out: "Go away for the present; when I have an opportunity I will summon you."⁹

Drusilla's overpowering beauty must have paled under the awful earnestness and soul-piercing eloquence of the apostle. Did she recall that her father had been a persecutor, had killed James the brother of John with the sword, and had imprisoned Peter? Did she harden her heart with delay?¹⁰

Slowly the weeks of confinement became lengthy months, and Paul thought more and more about the vision that had appeared to him in the Tower of Antonia in Jerusalem, and wondered when it would be fulfilled. But Felix was in no hurry to decide Paul's case, knowing that a just decision would make him unpopular with the Jews. Besides, he was deceitfully cultivating Paul's good will in the hope of obtaining money from him or from his churches. He was even willing to listen to the gospel, which he feared, but also rejected.

Luke says nothing about Paul's daily activities during his confinement in Caesarea but, judging from the apostle's habits, it would have been impossible for him, unless prohibited by orders, to refrain from proclaiming his gospel to all those around him who were willing to hear. And it is equally certain that he would have displayed none of that self-refuting tendency that accompanies shallow convictions, and none of that odious impertinence that accompanies self-righteousness—Paul was strong, commandingly so.

Paul was always chained to a soldier by his right wrist. The soldiers who took turns sharing the apostle's chain had the fortunate privilege of observing intimately the spiritual life of the greatest exemplar of the Christian faith. They saw him at fasting, at prayer, and perhaps in ecstatic vision. They heard him singing the old psalms of the scriptures—and the new hymns and spiritual songs of the church. They heard him pleading for Israel, for his churches, for the Roman state, for Felix, and for the soldiers in the castle. They heard him pray for his helpers and for multitudes of others, calling them all by name. They heard him pleading with Jesus to hasten the coming of his Kingdom. It need not be doubted that conversions occurred in the castle or that the church of Caesarea profited by the near presence of the apostle.

After a time, an occasional visitor arrived at the castle bringing news and greetings from the churches. These were friends closer than brothers, who were received with affectionate embraces, men whom the soldiers had heard mentioned in the apostle's prayers. Perhaps relatives came over from Tarsus, and his sister and nephew from Jerusalem.

When Paul realized that his imprisonment was dragging along indefinitely, he probably wrote letters to some of his evangelists and churches. If so, these letters have all been lost, unless Ephesians, Colossians, Philippians, and Philemon can be shown to belong to the Caesarean imprisonment instead of the Roman.

For two slow years Paul wore his chain and prayed for freedom that he might carry his work into Rome and Spain. In the meantime Felix was growing unpopular, and when complaints reached Rome, the young emperor, Nero, recalled him and, in A.D. 58 or 59, sent Porcius Festus to take his place. Felix, wishing to carry with him a little of the good will of the Jews, left Paul in bonds.

Three days after his arrival in Caesarea, Festus hastened to Jerusalem to inform himself about conditions at the heart of Judaism. Scarcely had he settled in his quarters in the castle of Antonia when the chief priests and the leading men of the city came fawning upon him to ask a favor. The Jews at this time, though living in hourly terror of assassins and brigands left among them by Felix, told Festus the favor that would please them most. They wanted Paul to be sent to Jerusalem so they could ambush and kill him on the way. Festus, however, was not to be tricked into haste. He replied that Paul would be kept at Caesarea, and gave orders that those having complaints to make should prepare their charges, secure their witnesses, and accompany him back to that city, where he would take up their case at once.

After about eight or ten days, Festus, with a pompous equipage, passed through the crowds and out of Damascus gate, followed by the high officials of Jerusalem with their attendants, and then by the common travelers who kept near for the benefit of the military protection. After two days, the gates of Caesarea came into view, and promptly on the following day, Festus in his robes of white and scarlet and in gold-embroidered sandals, ascended the judgment seat surrounded by his council. Nearby stood the very flower of Judaism; men in the spotless raiment of wealth, girded with costly sashes; men familiar with power, whose hard eyes shot out beneath dark brows. These "men of authority" wished to impress Festus and to overawe the object of their hatred.

Promptly Festus commanded that the prisoner be brought in to face his accusers. A moment of silence—a metallic sound as of a chain; and there entered in full uniform a centurion, and at his left, the unperturbed object of undying Jewish hatred. Instantly there was a triangular battle of eyes—Festus and Paul, the accusers and Paul, Festus and the accusers. Was this the first meeting between Paul and Festus? Were these the same accusers who had appeared before Felix?

At the procurator's signal, the spokesman for the accusers came forward and in his most vehement and denunciatory style brought "many serious charges" against the defendant. In substance the charges were the same as those that had been preferred by Tertullus two years earlier, which briefly were: annulment of the law, defilement of the temple, and treason against Rome.[11] The arguments of the Sanhedrinists reflected so unfavorably upon their own conduct that the procurator evidently believed Paul innocent, though he did not wish to gain the enmity of the Jews by telling them so. He therefore asked Paul if he would be willing to have his case transferred to Jerusalem to stand trial there before the full body of the Sanhedrin. This weak evasion of prompt justice was so offensive to the fearless straightforward apostle that he replied with firmness and a trace of fire, saying: "I am standing before Caesar's tribunal, where I ought to be tried; to the Jews I have done no wrong, as you know very well. If then I am a wrongdoer, and have committed anything for which I deserve to die, I do not seek to escape death, but if there is nothing in their charges against me, no one can give me up to them. I appeal to Caesar."[12]

It was an intensely dramatic moment. With a wave of his hand and two words in Latin or Greek,[13] Paul the Roman slipped from the grasp of his astonished enemies and took refuge with his emperor. It was a last resort. No other course was then open by which to escape death. Festus, too, saw an escape for himself from his annoying dilemma and, after a short conference with his council, replied: "You have appealed to Caesar: to Caesar you shall go." Disappointed and angry, the Jews consoled themselves with the fact that Paul was still a prisoner, and that a death sentence might yet be obtained against him even in Rome.

When biography becomes too inquisitive, it is sure to be mocked by a multitude of unanswerable questions, and this is certainly true about many details of Paul's life. Thus the question arises about where he obtained the money to make his appeal to Caesar, a course impossible to a poor man. Felix knew something about Paul's financial circumstances because he wished to coax a bribe out of him; and when the apostle finally reached Rome, he had money with which to hire a house in which he lived as a prisoner. It is evident, however, that he held his appeal in reserve as a last act of self-defense, and that he had previously discussed the matter with friends, who promised him aid out of their own wealth or through an appeal to the churches. It is even possible that he had come into an inheritance and that the fact had become known in Caesarea.

In escaping one perplexity, Festus fell into another, for when he attempted to prepare a formal report of Paul's case for transmission to Rome, he could not grasp the Jewish viewpoint clearly enough to draw up a strong argument for the apostle's appeal. However, after a few days,

Agrippa II, king of Batanaea and Trachonitis, a near neighbor of the new procurator, came to Caesarea with Bernice his sister to make a friendly official visit. Festus told him about the remarkable prisoner Felix, his predecessor, had left in bonds, about the accusations of the Jews, the appeal of the prisoner to Caesar, and about the difficulty of explaining the appeal to the higher court. Agrippa had been educated at the court of Claudius in Rome, and in A.D. 48, when about twenty-one years of age, he was given the principality of Chalcis. With it came the superintendency of the temple and its treasures at Jerusalem, which carried the right to nominate the high priest. Four years later he received, with the title of king, the tetrarchies that had been under the rule of his great-uncles, Philip and Lysanius, to which Nero a year later added several cities of Galilee.

Since Agrippa, an Idumean, had been brought up as a Jew and held the presidency of the temple, it was natural that Festus should consult him about Paul's appeal. It appears that Agrippa already knew something of the apostle's activities and fame[14] and that he had been wishing to hear him. "Tomorrow you shall hear him," Festus promised. The king and his sister were making a long stay, and the procurator felt obliged to have the days seem short to his guests by providing a number of exciting entertainments. The suggestion that Paul be put on exhibition pleased Festus, and he proceeded at once to make it a brilliant affair. The palace auditorium was set in order and decorated, and invitations were hurried out to the leading citizens of Caesarea.

At the appointed hour when the auditorium was filled with expectant guests, Festus entered with the king and his sister. With great pomp Agrippa ascended to his temporary throne, apparently forgetful that pomp had been fatal to his father in that same place scarcely fourteen years before.[15] Agrippa was barely more than thirty years of age, and his sister a year younger. Both were tarnished by the incestuous immorality of the Herodian house, and were at that moment subjects of a nameless scandal. Bernice had been married at the age of thirteen to her Uncle Herod, king of Chalcis, who died six or seven years later leaving two sons. She afterwards made her home for a time with her brother, and was now seated where her even more beautiful sister, Drusilla, two years before had listened to Paul as he explained his gospel to the trembling but impenitent Felix.[16]

At the command of Festus, Paul was brought into the audience chamber, his face pale from long imprisonment and his hands white and soft from the abandonment of toil. For a moment the gorgeous king was forgotten and all eyes were centered upon the famous prisoner; the whole scene being an unconscious tribute to a remarkable personality.

Festus then arose and explained Paul's presence in the following words, as Luke reports them: "King Agrippa and all who are present with us, you see this man about whom the whole Jewish people petitioned me, both at Jerusalem and here, shouting that he ought not to live any longer. But I found that he had done nothing deserving death: and as he himself appealed to the emperor, I decided to send him. But I have nothing definite to write to my lord. Therefore I have brought him before you, and especially before you, King Agrippa, that, after we have examined him, I may have something to write. For it seems to me unreasonable, in sending a prisoner, not to indicate the charges against him." Agrippa then said to Paul, "You have permission to speak for yourself."[17]

It was a great moment for the apostle. With unwavering faith, he stood with the grace of one who could live or die for a great cause. Stretching out his hand for attention he replied: "I think myself fortunate that it is before you, King Agrippa, I am to make my defense today against all the accusations of the Jews: because you are especially familiar with all customs and controversies of the Jews: therefore I beg you to listen to me patiently."[18]

Paul then declared that he was not a stranger in Jerusalem, that all the Jews there knew his history from the time when he began his studies under Gamaliel, and that everyone knew how blamelessly he had lived among them as a Pharisee. They knew, too, how with their own sanction, and even at their own instigation, he had persecuted the young church and how he had voted for the deaths of Stephen and others. He spoke of the Messiah for whom all the Jews were looking, and proved from the Scriptures that in Jesus all the Messianic promises were being fulfilled. He declared that the power of God to raise the dead could not reasonably be denied and that the resurrection of Jesus to which hundreds of living persons could testify was, because of its very improbability, the irrefutable proof of Messiahship. "And now," he said, "I stand here on trial for hope in the promise made by God to our fathers, to which our twelve tribes hope to attain, as they earnestly worship night and day. And for this hope I am accused by Jews, O king!"[19]

He then told the story of his conversion, of his apostleship to the Gentiles, on his instant obedience to his call, and gave a summary of his gospel as he proclaimed it. His cultured civility, his strength, and his eloquent earnestness won the respect of his hearers. But the incredulous procurator cried out, "Paul, you are mad; your great learning is turning you mad." And Paul replied, "I am not mad, most excellent Festus; but I am speaking the sober truth." Then looking towards Agrippa he continued: "For the king knows about these things, and to him I speak freely: for I am persuaded that none of these things has escaped his notice; for this was not done in a corner."[20] And then with the skill of a practised orator, and still facing the king he added: "King Agrippa, do you believe the prophets? I know that you believe."

Agrippa, being a Jew, could not say "no;" but to say "yes," would be almost an acceptance of Paul's gospel. He therefore parried by saying, "In a short time you think to make me a Christian!" He did not say "Nazorean," but used the Roman word "Christian," and spoke it with the contempt of its original implication. Paul seized his words: "Whether short or long, I would to God that not only you but also all who hear me this day might become such as I am—except for these chains."[21]

A procurator and a king, who, with two words, "*mainomai*" and "*Christianos*," had extinguished a spiritual flame that might have consumed the aristocracy of Caesarea, now separated themselves from the fawning multitude and exchanged their charitable opinions: Festus, as a Roman, said, "This man is doing nothing to deserve death or imprisonment;" and Agrippa as a Jew, replied, "This man could have been set free if he had not appealed to Caesar." Festus stumbled at the suggestion of a resurrection, Agrippa weakened at the thought of choosing a name of reproach. Paul was placed at a serious disadvantage, as had been his experience in Athens. In both instances, he was required to present his sacred gospel as an entertainment; the one audience hardened by its love of ostentation, and the other puffed up by an undue regard for its own wisdom. But it is not the fault of sunshine if it does not enter a darkened room.

REFERENCES
Chapter 15

1. Josephus. *Antiquities.* XX. 8. 5; *Wars.* II. 13. 2.
2. Acts 23:29.
3. Acts 24:5, rendering *loimos* "Pestilence", which is its normal meaning and the one Dr. Johnson chose. (GWB)
4. Acts 24:6.
5. Acts 24:12-13.
6. Acts 24:14-16.
7. Matt. 23:37.
8. Acts 24:22.
9. Acts 24:25.
10. Drusilla and her son, Agrippa, may have been killed in the eruption of Vesuvius. See Josephus, *Antiquities.* XIX. 9. 1-2; Suetonius. *The Lives of the Caesars, Life of Tiberius Claudius Drusus.* Chap. 28.
11. Acts 24:1-3.
12. Acts 25:8-11.
13. "Caesarem appello," or "Kaisara epikaloumai."
14. Acts 26:26.
15. Acts 12:21-23.
16. Acts 24:24.
17. Acts 25:24-27.
18. Acts 26:2-3.
19. Acts 26:6-7.
20. Acts 26:24-26.
21. Acts 26:29.

Paul's ship, storm-tossed

Perils of the Sea:
Caesarea — Puteoli

NOT LONG AFTER the visit of Agrippa and Bernice, a large coastwise vessel from Adramyttium on the Aegean Sea put into port at Caesarea, and Festus seized the opportunity to send Paul and certain other prisoners of a different class[1] to Rome. These were delivered to a centurion named Julius, of the Augustan Cohort who engaged passage for them and his soldiers as far as Myra, a transfer point on the Lycian coast. Paul, with the joyous emotion of a great prospect, began preparing for the voyage, and Luke and Aristarchus, who perhaps had spent much time with him in Caesarea, made arrangements to go with him and obtained Julius's permission to enter the convoy.

In the meantime, excitement spread throughout the local church and many of the brethren went to the praetorium to speak a parting word. Indeed it is possible that Paul was permitted to conduct a farewell service of council and prayer such as the one held with the elders of Ephesus or with the church of Tyre.

Again the clank of chains was heard in the praetorium. A long line of prisoners with their guards awaited the order of Julius. With them, the last in line, but not one of them, stood Paul. Julius had heard him when he

189

stood before Agrippa and believed him to be an innocent and persecuted man. Along the line of march from the praetorium to the ship, many curious and noisy spectators ran together shouting ridicule and finding sport in misery: "The Mamertine dungeon for you," "A feast for Nero's lions," "The poison cup for you," and to Paul, "Your head for the Emperor's sword." As the long line approached the ship, it passed by a quiet group of men and women—Philip and his daughters and other members of the Church of Caesarea. If they tried to touch Paul to treasure the memory of the fact, it would have been an act consistent with the manners of the age. Certainly there must have been many exchanges of affectionate encouragement.

Out on the sea a great square sail on a tall central mast, such a sail as Paul may have helped to weave in his father's shop in Tarsus, bellied in the wind that was already frilling the waves of the blue sea with white and then whipping them against the Syrian coast. Slowly the ship of Adramyttium crept northward past Ptolemais and Tyre to the ancient city of Sidon.

Paul had found a good friend in Julius the centurion, who, when the ship had put into port, permitted him to go ashore "to go to his friends and be cared for." These, perhaps, were converts made many years before or possibly some very near relatives who could provide him with articles of comfort, now necessary because of the threatening weather. It was on the second day, after a sail of less than seventy miles, that the ship had put into port and, because of the uncertainty of the weather, the discharge and loading of cargo was done quickly.

The direct course from Sidon to Myra lay south of the island of Cyprus, at a distance of about three hundred and sixty miles; but the wind being unfavorable at that time, the course was changed to the north to take advantage of the sea current, coast shelter, and shore winds. It was a slow sail but Paul and his companions found entertainment in watching the continuous transformation of the familiar coasts of Syria, Cyprus, Cilicia, and Pamphylia.

The September night sky that had spoken of heavenly wisdom to David, the shepherd,[2] doubtless made itself audible to Paul, the "prisoner of Jesus Christ," and to his two companions. Even if seen through rifts in the clouds, there could be no mistake made about the ruby-tinted Antares of the south or the amber-tinted Arcturus of the West.

No other three men on the ship had more to occupy their minds than Paul and his companions. Theirs were the affairs of the Kingdom of God; there were hours of meditation, hours of prayers for the churches, and hours of conversation about the endless questions arising from the expected return of Jesus as the triumphant Messiah. Paul was making plans for the best use of his time in Rome before his accusers could get there to prefer charges against him. Aristarchus was attending upon the apostle with a loyalty that offset some of the lost honor of his native city.[3] Luke, who was an acute observer, kept a diary, portions of which he incorporated many years later in the *Acts.*

Myra, situated two and half miles back from the coast at the entrance of a gorge that served as a gateway to the interior of the province of Lycia, was a city of importance. Its port was frequented not only by coastwise vessels, but also by great ships that touched there on their way from Alexandria to Italy. Myra was almost on the same meridian with Alexandria but nearly three hundred and fifty miles farther north. Ships sailing on that part of the course had only to watch the sun by day and the North Star by night, correcting their errors when the conspicuous heights behind Myra came into view.

When Julius arrived with his prisoners, he found one of these Egyptian ships in port and immediately engaged passage on it. After the handling of cargo had been completed, the great ship, weighted down to its loadline, put out to sea.

It was a daring defiance of wind and wave, costly in time and patience. They sailed north of Rhodes, hoping to cross the Aegean, but after "a number of days" in which they had covered scarcely one hundred and thirty miles, they came under Cnidus. Here the ship was met by Etesian winds that were blowing hard from the northwest and had to change its course to the southward towards Crete.

On reaching Cape Salmone, they coasted along with great difficulty under the lee of the island until they came to Fair Havens, an exposed harbor not far from the small city of Lasea. Here, the sorely overworked sailors had a short respite. The owner and the captain of the vessel knew that dangerous winds were likely to be encountered at that time of year. They decided to put into port somewhere for the winter but were not satisfied with Fair Havens. Nearly forty miles farther west, the city of Phoenix offered a good harbor, though to reach it the ship would have to round Cape Matala and there perhaps would encounter winds as stubborn as those that had driven it from the Cnidian peninsula. The centurion, who was responsible for his prisoners and soldiers, was then brought into the conference. He listened to the arguments of the captain and owner and agreed with them that an attempt should be made at once to reach Phoenix.

At this point, Paul, with the assurance of one who knew ships and the seas, yielded to his bent for leadership and gave his advice against the risk, saying: "Sirs I perceive that the voyage will be with injury and much loss, not only of the cargo and the ship, but also of our lives." Though he received a respectful hearing, his counsel was rejected, even by his friend, the centurion, who, as might have been expected, "paid more attention to the captain and the owner of the ship." When a general vote was taken, the majority favored sailing at the first lull of the wind.

It was in October, shortly after the Jewish fast of the Atonement, when the south wind was blowing softly, that the ship of Alexandria weighed anchor and abandoned Fair Havens. The weary crew was joyful at the prospect of reaching a satisfactory port, and while some manned the great sail, the helmsmen seized the two great steering paddles to control the ship while it sailed close inshore.

The soft wind should have been regarded as a precursor of storm, as Paul doubtless knew. Scarcely had they rounded Cape Matala, only four or five miles away, and had entered the Gulf of Messara, when a violent wind burst upon them from the northeast. The great ship rolled and plunged and "could not face the wind."

When it became evident that the haven of Phoenix could not be reached, the captain, thinking no doubt of Paul's warning, gave orders to yield more to the wind, but to hold the course of the ship to the west. Scudding thus, they dropped twenty-three miles south of Phoenix and came under the lee of the little island of Cauda, where they found sufficient temporary shelter.

From the mild sea at Fair Havens the ship's boat had been towed through the raging waters beyond Cape Matala. Since it could not have been taken aboard after the storm began, it became the first concern of the crew when they reached Cauda. It had filled with water, and, as it was being drawn in, the waves threatened to smash it to pieces against the side of the rolling ship. After a great struggle, the seaman hoisted it to its place on deck with the help of some of the passengers.

The relentless torturing that the ship had endured for many days had caused a leak, with other signs of weakness in the hull. To prevent further damage, it was then undergirded, or frapped. This involved dropping loops of cable or chains over the bow and then drawing them along under the vessel to its widest part. There, they were tightened and clamped.

A new danger now threatened the voyage: The ship could not remain under the lee of the island, and if it should sail, there was great fear that it might be driven upon one of the horrible Syrtis. These were seas of quicksands and marsh off the coast of Africa, from which there could be no rescue. As a precaution against such a calamity, all movable objects on deck were lowered so as not to catch the wind or affect the steering.

Little by little they were now driven from the shelter of Cauda out into the open Sea of Adria, and into the night. The only clue to direction was the wind itself, against which the sailors exhausted themselves as they tried to hold a northwesterly course, hoping to touch Italy or Sicily.

In the dull light of a sunless day, the ship was again inspected and was found to have suffered further damage. The crew was then ordered to tighten the frapping and to throw overboard a large quantity of freight.

The ship was still seven hundred miles from Rome and was advancing scarcely a mile and a half in an hour. With its human freight of two hundred and seventy-six souls, the vessel again tunneled into the blackness of night.

On the third day, everything that could be spared was thrown into the sea. All possible precautions had now been taken and the crew devoted itself to the exhausting tasks of bailing water and holding the ship against the wind. Day after day, their eyes were strained upon the empty horizon and night after night, hearts were sick at the thought of foundering in coastless depths.

The story of the ship of Alexandria is the story of an incident in a man's life. What was Paul doing during the long days after leaving Fair Havens? Did he suffer more or less than other men? Did faith prevail over fear, and hope over despair? It is certain that Paul was neither a physical nor a moral coward. As despair crept into the hearts of those around him, he became more and more conscious of his own strength. He prayed, not through fear and dread, but in submission to the will of God. And yet he prayed for his own deliverance and for the escape of those who were in danger with him.

Days passed, a week, and more. The storm never abated. Impenetrable clouds closed down on the horizon making a dungeon of Adria. No man knew where he was. The great ship groaned as the waves heaved it skyward only to plunge it again into the yawning chasms of the sea. Men's hearts sank. But Paul and Luke and Aristarchus still had spiritual reserve. They remembered the words of the Psalmist:[4]

> Some went down to the sea in ships,
> doing business on the great waters;
> they saw the deeds of the Lord,
> his wondrous works in the deep.
> For he commanded, and raised the
> stormy wind,
> which lifted up the waves of the sea.
> They mounted up to heaven, they
> went down to the depths;
> their courage melted away in
> their evil plight;
> they reeled and staggered like
> drunken men, and were at their wits' end.
> Then they cried to the Lord in their
> trouble,
> and he delivered them from their distress.

That night after exhaustion had forced sleep upon Paul, he dreamed that an angel of God stood by his side and said, "Do not be afraid Paul; you must stand before Caesar; and lo, God has granted you all those who sail with you."[5] An angel bringing a message in the blackness of a starless night to a lost and leaking storm-tossed ship was not an incredible thing to Paul. He accepted the vision of the angel as truly objective, and acted accordingly. At Crete, when he warned the officers of the ship not to leave Fair Havens, he spoke out of his own knowledge of the freakishness of autumnal storms. Now, he arises from a dream and speaks with the authority of one who has received a revelation.

The storm was raging in a fresh outbreak of fury, and the owner and officers of the ship, with the pallor of death showing through the bronze of their cheeks,. were waiting for the breaking up of the ship, when Paul appeared, glowing with the lingering radiance of the angel's visit. "Men," he said, "you should have listened to me, and should not have set sail from Crete, and incurred this injury and loss."[6] Paul spoke with authority but not with irony. He knew that a momentary reminder of the past would add force to what he was about to say.

"I now bid you," he continued, "to be of good heart; for there will be no loss of life among you, but only of the ship." He then told of the angel's visit and closed with a second exhortation, saying, "So take heart, men, for I have faith in God that it will be exactly as I have been told."[7]

Soon the message of hope and cheer reached the last man on the ship. If any disbelieved, he at least hoped secretly that a benevolent spirit had truly visited Paul. It was a choice between credulity and despair. Hope, however, was rekindled.

In the cold and rain and wind the ship of Alexandria still floundered about in the Sea of Adria; zigzagging onward in an unknown course above a thousand feet of water. When would Paul's dream come true? They were now thirteen nights of horror from Crete and were beginning the fourteenth, and still the stars refused to shine and the sounding line failed to pierce the depths. But at the approach of midnight they met certain signs of land, such signs as only a sailor might detect in the behavior and sounds of the sea. Immediately a sounding was taken, and bottom was found at twenty fathoms.

A second sounding showed fifteen fathoms and excitement took on fear. To prevent the ship from crashing against rocks in the darkness, four anchors were dropped from the stern and the rudders were lashed.[8] Day was still five long dark hours away and the longing for its light was like a tired impatient prayer.

Some of the sailors, forseeing the destruction of the ship, tried to escape by stealing the ship's boat while pretending to lay out anchors from the bow. Paul, discovering their purpose, immediately warned the centurion that no one could be saved if the sailors were allowed to leave the ship. The boat had already been lowered to the water and the sailors were ready to leap into it. But the soldiers drew their swords, cut the lines, and let it drift away.

As a master mind was now needed to insure order, Paul assumed that role. Just as dawn approached, he tried to dissipate the new fear of being dashed to death on the rocky coast. He declared that not a hair from the head of any one on the ship should perish. Then, since no one had eaten for fourteen days, he urged them to do so to maintain their strength and to be of good cheer. But the cave of despair is a strange refuge from which men are not easily driven. Paul, therefore, took bread, and giving thanks to God before them all, began to eat. His example became contagious, and fear gave way to cheer, and fasting to eating.

As the light of morning increased, all eyes were strained across the white-frilled waves to get a sight of land, but what was seen, no one could recognize. As the morning advanced, a bay with a beach was discovered in the far distance. Into this they prepared to thrust the ship. The last of the cargo of wheat was now cast overboard to lighten the ship for beaching, the anchors were cut loose and left in the sea, the rudders were released from their bands for immediate use, and the foresail was hoisted to the wind. As if released from an unwilling delay the ship drove forward through the turbulent sea while the helmsmen with their oars held it to its course.

The ship, however, struck a shoal and went fast aground. There was now great excitement about getting to shore. The ship's boat had been left at sea, the waves were dangerously violent, and some of the passengers were unable to swim.

Again, death stalked the ever elusive apostle. Roman guards had to pay with their own lives if they let their prisoners escape. The soldiers proposed that their charges including Paul, be killed at once, lest they swim away to liberty. It was a chilly moment for the prisoners, and even Paul must have paled at the sight of the wicked unsheathed sword in his guard's hand. The centurion, who wished to save Paul, promptly forbade the deed and ordered all soldiers who could swim to leap overboard and get first to land where they could recapture their prisoners, who would follow them. Paul was a good swimmer, and, though sixty years of age, may have aided some less fortunate prisoner.

The whole scene was one of desperate urgency. Men who had hesitated now plunged into the sea either to swim alone or to cling to planks or other objects from the ship. Slowly they gained the shore of the island of Malta or Melita—the island of bees and honey—and rose to their feet. Luke and Aristarchus counted them—two hundred and seventy-six souls—and Paul's dream had come true.

A cold rain was drifting in from the sea when the shivering multitude gathered upon the shore, but the islanders nearby who had witnessed the wreck hastened to the scene and built a fire and, later, opened their hospitable homes, showing great kindness to their exhausted guests. Paul, Luke, Aristarchus, and perhaps others were lodged graciously for three days at the home of Publius the "*protos*"[9] or chief man, of the island, whose estates were nearby.

Luke records two stories relating to Paul's experience on the island, showing how the credulity of the people worked to his advantage. According to the first, Paul took part with his comrades in the duties of their temporary camp and combed the beach in search of fuel. On his return, he was laying sticks on the fire when a snake that he had not noticed in his bundle bit and clung to his hand. When the islanders saw it, supposing it to be a poisonous viper, and seeing Paul under guard, whispered among themselves: "No doubt this man is a murderer. Though he has escaped from the sea, yet justice has not allowed him to live." But Paul shook the harmless snake loose and it fell into the fire.[10] He perhaps knew that vipers strike but do not cling to their victim. Wide-eyed, the superstitious islanders watched his hand expecting to see it puff up from poison or to see the supposed murderer drop dead. But when nothing untoward happened, they said, "He is a god!" Paul must have remembered his experience at Lystra, when Barnabas was taken for Jupiter and he for Mercury.

The second story presents Paul as a healer. While he was the guest of Publius, he learned that his host's father was sick with fever and dysentery and asked to see him. Luke adds that when Paul entered the room he "prayed, and putting his hands on him healed him."[11]

Shortly, the fame of Paul the prisoner spread throughout the island, and all who had diseases came to him "and were cured." Such rushing to healers is often paralleled at the present time, but it would be unjust to Paul to suppose that he posed as a wonderworker or a great healer. Luke's word for "cured" ranges widely in its meaning, allowing for the use of remedies, sufficient time for recovery, and even for treatment without success. Luke himself was probably the prescribing physician although he would subordinate his ministrations to Paul's act of faith in prayer and the laying on of hands.

For three winter months the centurion was delayed in Malta with his soldiers and prisoners. During that time Paul was doubtless permitted to teach his gospel. Since he and his companions received "many gifts" from the islanders, it may be supposed that they were honored not only as healers but also as messengers of the cross.

Somewhere on the island another ship of Alexandria had found shelter for the winter. On this, Julius the centurion engaged passage to Puteoli, the great emporium on the Bay of Naples for Egyptian wheat ships. On the day of the sailing, a number of the islanders, perhaps Publius and his father among them, came down to the ship to bid Paul and his companions farewell and to place on board for their use such things as might add to their comfort on their voyage.

It was a beautiful day in February when the great square sail took the breeze and led the ship slowly into the now peaceful blue waters. The ship had been cleaned of its foulness, the south winds were soft and sweet, and the sun with early spring gentleness bathed the decks in warmth and light— how unlike those fourteen days in Adria.

The shores of Malta now narrowed and faded and those of Sicily approached dimly as if ashamed of the loss of their ancient glory. The sun moved over from starboard to port. Under a failing wind, the ship made its way to Syracuse in Sicily, where it lay becalmed for three days. After this delay, the ship tacked its way to Rhegium, a small city on the "toe" of Italy, where it lay in port for another day. Finally, favorable winds began blowing from the south and the ship proceeded through the straits of Messina and made the passage safely between Scylla and Charybdis, the celebrated rock and whirlpool of both myth and history.

Now that the shores of Italy had been sighted, Rome seemed exceedingly near. Already a change was visible in Paul's manner. Already his thoughts were in Rome. Perhaps death awaited him there, but he would have time for a season of fellowship with the beloved brethren of that city. Had not Julius promised him all possible assistance?

It was a smooth sail of two hundred miles from the strait of Messina to Puteoli, the gateway to Rome, situated on a little gulf in the northern rim of the Sinus Puteolanus, or Bay of Naples. On the second day, the ship passed the little island of Capreae, the southern guardian of the bay, a bewitching spot in the soft light of the Italian spring, but putrid with the vices of the emperor Tiberius and his satellites. Then beyond the bay came into full view the broad imposing cone of Vesuvius, slumbering so peacefully that the shepherds, vine dressers, and agriculturists had taken possession of its fertile sides.

All vessels except the Alexandrian grain ships were required on entering the Bay of Naples to strike their topsails as a signal to one of the imperial fleets stationed under the guardian islands of Ischia and Procidia. As Paul's ship came into view, its character was quickly recognized and the idlers of Puteoli rushed to the harbor to see the first ship of the season that was supposed to have been daring enough to challenge the dangers of the winter sea.

When Julius and his soldiers came ashore with their prisoners, they went at once to the local barracks, leaving the other passengers to the mercy of the noisy jostling guides, innkeepers, and food vendors. As soon as Paul learned that Julius would be detained at the barracks for a week, he obtained permission from him to go with Luke and Aristarchus to a synagogue to inquire whether there were any followers of the Lord Jesus in the city. Soon a company of believers was discovered, who perhaps had brought the gospel to that place, or who may have received it from either Alexandria or Rome. These brethren at once begged their visitors to spend all their time with them; and it seems that Julius gave his permission.

REFERENCES
Chapter 16

1. Acts 27:1.
2. Ps. 19.
3. Cf. Acts 17:11; Col. 4:10.
4. Ps. 107:23-28.
5. Acts 27:23-24.

6. Acts 27:21.
7. Acts 27:25.
8. Acts 27:29.
9. Acts 28:7.
10. Acts 28:1-5.
11. Acts 28:7-8.

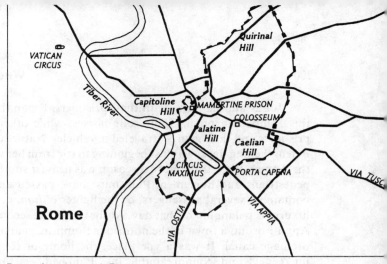

Rome, 1st century, A.D.

CHAPTER

17

Rome

A Triumphal Journey: Puteoli — Rome

SHORTLY AFTER PAUL'S ARRIVAL at Puteoli, word reached the church in Rome that he was on his way to that city. Nearly three years had elapsed since he had written about his proposed visit and in the meantime his imprisonment had made it extremely doubtful whether he would ever carry out his plans. But now that he was coming, even as a prisoner, the news caused a great wave of joy, and preparations were begun at once to welcome him by sending out a delegation to meet him on his way. It was an old custom to honor heroes, public idols, and other favorites in this manner.

A large company of brethren was organized to go as far as Three Taverns, thirty-three miles south of Rome, where some would wait and others would continue for about ten miles farther to Appii Forum, or the "Market of Appii." By this plan they aimed to avoid the overcrowding of inns, and at the same time to double the surprise and honor of their tribute to the "ambassador in bonds."

It was about one hundred and thirty miles from Puteoli to Rome, going by Capua over the Via Campania, and then turning to the left and following the Via Appia, the most celebrated of Roman roads.

199

Julius and his men, with their prisoners, began their journey across the Campanian plain. Some rode horses, while others, most likely the prisoners and their guards, traveled in vehicles. Nature under the influence of lengthening days, was just beginning to stir from her winter slumber. On the Appian Way, travel at that season was heavier southward, and besides pedestrians and horsemen, Paul must have passed an occasional *rheda* containing several passengers, or the lighter *cisium*, or even a *lectica*, the luxurious palanquin of that day. At the end of the second day they came to Appii Forum, a town in the notorious Pomptine marshes at the head of a drainage canal. It was a vile place, the home of rough bargemen, low innkeepers, and scoundrel publicans.[1] Paul had been thinking much about the church at Rome, wondering about the brethren there whom he had known in other cities. Just as his *rheda* came to a stop, he saw, as is safe to suppose, Aquila the tentmaker, his friend, who hastened to him with his greeting. And there were Epaenetus and Andronicus, Junius, others whom he knew, and strangers recently come into the Kingdom. It was a joyful surprise, and the apostle "thanked God and took courage."

After a night's rest, the centurion set out upon the last stage of his journey. Ten miles beyond Appii Forum, at Three Taverns, another group of brethren came out to welcome the apostle. If Paul had feared any disloyalty on the part of the church in Rome, this scene must have dissipated his last doubt and he could have exclaimed, "The firm foundation of God stands."

Far ahead could be seen that strange little group of isolated volcanic hills, the Alban Mountains, with their pine-clad heights and their waterfilled craters. It was an outfield of the Imperial city, a hive of wealthy Romans whose extensive villas and beautiful gardens covered its fertile foothills and made it an oasis of loveliness. The Via Appia touched the southern side of these hills, and at the point where it crossed the last summit, Paul got his first view of Rome—a great expanse of low buildings that had spread out beyond the remnants of the ancient walls and into which crept busy highways and massive dripping aqueducts. Paul must have thought of a score of other cities: Jerusalem, Damascus, Athens, Corinth, and even of his own Tarsus. Each had its own peculiar attraction but all were unlike the great metropolis before him. Rome, the mistress of the world, was proud, confident, powerful. Paul was glad that he had been born a Roman citizen. Thus far it had been his protection—but for how much longer?

After leaving the Alban Hills, the Via Appia became a street of tombs, the resting places of Rome's illustrious dead. Here the two streams of travel thickened: beasts, vehicles, and pedestrians contending for their shares of the overcrowded road. But Julius cleared the way for his men and for that strange mixed company that followed the chief prisoner.

Within the environs of the city they came in the evening to the old Porta Capena. The highway, after passing through this gate, led between two of Rome's famous hills directly toward the heart of the city. On the left, stood the Palatine Hill, where Nero the young emperor was chafing under the good advice of Seneca and Burrhus, planning secret murders, and dreaming of immoral revelries.

On the right, rose the Caelian Hill, a part of which was occupied by the camp of soldiers who traveled back and forth between Rome and her provincial colonies. These men were under the command of centurions, who were assigned to detached duty by the legionary commanders of the provincial armies to carry messages to and from the emperor and to perform various other duties. By them also, prisoners who appealed to Caesar's judgment seat were conveyed to Rome.

Julius was a centurion of this class, and therefore took his prisoners to the Caelian Hill and delivered them to the chief of the camp. At the Porta Capena the escort of brethren dispersed, though Luke and Aristarchus may have accompanied Paul as his attendants.

Julius must have given the chief of the camp a favorable report on Paul, for within three days the apostle had hired an apartment—possibly in the home of some Christian brother—and was in it with his guard and his two faithful companions prepared to resume the oversight of his vast evangelistic enterprise. The chief of the camp must have been a just man like Burrhus, the praetorian prefect over on the Palatine Hill, for he put the least possible restraint on Paul. It was necessary, however, that Paul be chained to a guard; but that precaution served as much for his own protection as for his restraint. He had full authority over his own apartment without interference.

Three days after Paul's arrival in Rome, he sent for the chief men of the Jews for an interview. When they came, Paul explained how he happened to be in bonds and asked whether the authorities in Jerusalem had made any report of his arrest. They told him that "We have received no letters from Judaea about you and none of the brethren coming here has reported or spoken any evil about you."[2]

A moment later, however, it became evident from their language that at least in a general way the apostle's reputation among the Jews elsewhere was well known to them. But Paul's dramatic statement, "because of the hope of Israel I am bound with this chain," touched a chord of sympathy and aroused such curiosity that the Jewish officials now offered him the very opportunity he had been seeking: "But we desire," they said, "to hear from you what your views are; for with regard to this sect we know that everywhere it is spoken against."[3] Thus the Jews themselves opened the way for Paul's first sermon in Rome, and even appointed the day on which it was to be preached.

It was a morning in April when "great numbers" of Jews assembled at the private prison of the "ambassador in bonds." From morning until evening the Jews listened to the most practical exposition of their scriptures that they had ever heard. Beginning with an interpretation of the Kingdom of God, Paul advanced to the messianic promise, picturing from the law and the prophets the nature of the Messiah's reign, and proving that the time of his advent had fully arrived.

Thus far his hearers were agreeably entertained. But when Paul attempted to prove that Jesus had fulfilled all the conditions of messiahship and had even demonstrated his claim to that office by rising from the dead, then the restlessness of dissent began to manifest itself. Some of those who had settled that question thirty years before, were ready to blaspheme the name as if Jesus had been but one of those numerous imposters who were making similar claims. There were some, however, who believed and when these made known their faith, the others became so vehement in their disbelief that Paul closed his discussion with the lashing words once used by Isaiah,[4] and which Jesus is said to have quoted:[5]

"The Holy Spirit was right in saying to your fathers through Isaiah the prophet:

'Go to this people, and say,
You shall indeed hear but never understand,
and you shall indeed see but never perceive.
For this people's heart has grown dull,
and their ears are heavy of hearing,
and their eyes they have closed;
lest they should perceive with their eyes,
and hear with their ears,
and understand with their heart
and turn to me to heal them.'"[6]

And then as if issuing a challenge, he exclaimed: "Let it be known to you then that this salvation of God has been sent to the Gentiles; they will listen."[7] Thus, as was his custom, Paul offered his gospel first to his own countrymen and, when they rejected it, turned to the Gentiles.[8]

With this incident Luke closed abruptly his story of the apostle's life, except to add a general statement of less than two score words in which he condensed the labors of two years: "And he lived there two whole years at his own expense, welcoming all who came to him, preaching the kingdom of God and teaching about the Lord Jesus Christ quite openly and unhindered."[9] Luke was not writing biography, except as it served his main purpose in giving a history of the spread of the gospel. Having traced that history as far as Rome, his purpose was accomplished and the biography closed. The modern reader is left to struggle with intriguing but unanswerable queries.

Since the lapse of two years would probably entitle Paul to his liberty if his accusers did not appear, and since Luke's closing words betray no note of impending misfortune, it is a fair presumption that the apostle was given his freedom. To Luke's brief summary, therefore, of two years of imprisonment may be added a few facts from Paul's own pen. Four letters almost certainly Pauline seem to belong to this period. Three of them were addressed to churches: Philippians, Colossians, and Ephesians; and one to an individual, Philemon.

It appears that Paul, besides preaching Jesus as the Christ to all inquirers, watched over his churches by sending out trained men to visit them with the authority to correct disorders and to teach. These men sometimes carried letters of encouragement, instruction, and admonition addressed to individual churches or to groups of churches. In the four letters just mentioned, the apostle speaks of himself as a prisoner, and in the letter to the Colossians calls Aristarchus his fellow prisoner. Epaphras is mentioned in the same way in the letter to Philemon. Timothy was with him as joint author when Philippians, Colossians, and Philemon were written. Mark, Luke, Demas, and Tychicus also were with him and were awaiting his orders.

It is evident that Paul was neither idle nor disconsolate as a prisoner. In fact he asserted that "what has happened to me has really served to advance the gospel."[10] Through the soldiers who guarded him, he had succeeded making Jesus known throughout the praetorian guard and had even reached the ears and some of the hearts of others who were in the household of the notorious Nero. Here, as everywhere, the apostle displayed a wide and penetrating knowledge of human nature and, though bound with chains, still exercised his genius for leadership.

Two of the prison letters, Colossians and Philemon, shed a momentary ray of light on the relations between Paul and Mark. Luke had dropped Barnabas and Mark from history after they had severed their connection with Paul and had departed for Cyprus. About fifteen years later Mark went to Rome where he was enjoying Paul's favor as a "fellow worker," to the credit of both men. Paul had even commended him by a special letter to the Colossians, and later requested that church to receive him. Though he had been a bitter disappointment at one time, Paul now said of Mark and two other Jews, Aristarchus and Jesus Justice: "they have been a comfort to me."[11]

Another ray of light upon Paul's life appears in his letters to Philemon and the Philippians, where he expressed a somewhat joyful expectation that he might soon be released from his bonds. In this hope, he promised a possible early visit to his friends, even requesting Philemon to prepare lodgings for him. At that very moment also he was detaining Timothy from a projected tour of the churches in order to make him the messenger of his fate, the alternatives of which were liberty or death.

Here the curtain falls never to rise nor to part again. Ecclesiastical tradition and conjecture now take the place of history. These may contain a modicum of truth, but the proof of it is always too elusive to show what is truth and what is error, or whether there is any truth at all. The earliest literature in which traditions have been preserved is too rhetorically vague, too patently false, and too doubtfully authentic to do much more than excite endless conjecture. If the three pastoral letters, First Timothy, Second Timothy, and Titus were written by Paul, they would add an authentic chapter to the apostle's biography, but they are so un-Pauline in language, and so greatly subject to suspicion for other reasons, that their authenticity is doubted, and their testimony therefore reduced in value to that of other traditions.

In all these sources, however, there is a general tendency in one direction that may be taken as evidence that they rest on three basic facts, namely, that Paul was liberated from his first Roman imprisonment, that he revisited some of his churches, and that he was again imprisoned and finally put to death.

When Paul swam ashore through the chill November sea at Malta, he knew that he should see Rome. As a youth he had been proud of his Roman citizenship, and he must have heard much from his father and others about Augustus who was then emperor—the man who had brought the world to quiet and order, who "found Rome built of brick and left it built of marble." Under his imperial favor literature had flourished, illumined by such familiar names as Virgil, Horace, Ovid, Livy, and others. Upon his death, Augustus was declared by the senate to be a god and his shrines must have appeared in Tarsus about the time that Paul was leaving for school in Jerusalem.

In Tiberius, that capable but cold occupant of the Palatine Hill, Paul must have detected some of the virtues of Augustus but only to see them perish in an avalanche of folly. And then, as he watched the course of history for signs of his Lord's return, he must have been convinced by the appalling depravity and insane conduct of Caligula and Claudius that the "man of lawlessness"[12] would soon be revealed as the precursor of the end of the world.

Nero, the last of the five Julian emperors, had been on the throne for about six years at the time of Paul's arrival in Rome, and was not yet twenty-three years of age. From the palace guards and others Paul soon became acquainted with the character and habits of the man to whom he had appealed—a man excessively vain, brazenly immoral, and murderously cruel. But the apostle had once written to the Roman Christians exhorting them to "be subject to the governing authorities,"[13] and by this rule he intended to govern himself so that no suspicion of disloyalty to the emperor could be laid against him or against the church of Jesus Christ.

If indeed Paul was released after two years of imprisonment in Rome, it would be almost certain that he had literally "stood at Caesar's judgment seat," under the celestial frescoes of the great marble halls of justice. His case was probably brought up at his own request, since his accusers had failed to appear within the legal time of eighteen months or two years.

And what picture, next to that of Christ before Pilate, could have presented such a striking contrast as that of Paul before Nero! Upon the judgment seat, a young man in extravagant judicial robes, a young man whose worst qualities were fast gaining the ascendency over his better, pathetically vain, insanely foolish, and abhorrently immoral. Seated near him, his twenty advisers waiting for evidence on which to render a verdict; at their stations, a detachment of trusted praetorian guards in threatening panoply; and near them the lictors, hoping for the excitement of using their blood-thirty rods.

Before the court stood an aged man in simple Jewish raiment, chained to a soldier in burnished armor; a cool self-mastered man, at ease in the wealth of his experience, serene in the righteousness of his life, and strong in the consciousness of his apostolic mission. He was an impressive personality, radiating the secret power of an ultimate victor.

There was but one course for Nero and his assessors to pursue. The Jews, knowing from their experience before the Judaean procurators that they could not prosecute their case with success before the supreme tribunal at Rome, had contented themselves with the fact that Paul by his own act in appealing to Caesar would have to remain a prisoner for a year and a half, or perhaps longer, if they should not appear against him. As the full time had now expired and no accusers had appeared, the case had to terminate in an acquittal in default. If it had come to a formal trial, however, the letter that Festus had sent to the emperor would, perhaps, have cleared Paul of any charge of disloyalty to the Roman government, and the case would have resolved itself into a purely Jewish dispute.

It is possible also that Burrhus, the praetorian prefect, and Seneca the stoic philosopher, though now fast losing their influence over Nero, would have interceded for Paul. Indeed, it is not wholly unlikely that the notorious Poppaea, mistress of the emperor, but a patroness of the Jews,[14] would have befriended the apostle had anyone made an appeal to her in his behalf. She was a half proselyte to Judaism, and at this very time, or near about, was persuaded by Josephus the historian to aid him in interceding with the emperor for the release of certain Jewish priests whom Felix had sent as prisoners to Rome.[15] Being much pleased with the brilliant young Jew, she would have espoused the cause of the priests with success, and then sent their intercessor home laden with gifts.

For four years or more, Paul had worn his chain. To him it had been a badge of loyalty to his Lord, and yet a restraint from which he rejoiced to be freed. He was soon in the arms of his fellow-workers—Timothy, Luke, Aristarchus, Mark, and the rest. And as the glad news of his freedom spread from Christian to Christian, the whole Roman Church vibrated with thanksgiving and praise. New hope and new courage sprang up among the believers.

Timothy had been awaiting orders and was now sent to Philippi and Colossae to spread the news of the apostle's freedom, and to prepare the way for his coming. But Paul would not have left Rome without first spending a season with the church in Christian fellowship and worship. He knew that the gospel from his own lips would have new weight, that his advice and encouragement were needed, and that the church would have to be fortified against heresies.

It had been Paul's original intention to visit Rome, and then to go from there directly to Spain; but more than four years had now elapsed since that plan had been formed and, in the interval, disturbing reports had been reaching him about conditions in the churches of Achaia, Macedonia, and Asia. He therefore hastened to go eastward instead of westward.

It is impossible to map these last journeys, or to fill them in with events that are more than guesses. It is certain, however, that his plans included visits to Philippi,[16] the home of Lydia, and Colossae, the home of Philemon, Onesimus, and Archippus.[17]

Besides the two regional terms, Macedonia[18] and Crete,[19] the pastoral letters mention the names of only three cities, Troas, Corinth, and Miletus[20] through which Paul may have passed, and two others, Ephesus,[21] and Nicopolia, where he had hoped to visit.

There is no clear evidence that Paul ever reached Spain. There is, however, an ambiguous statement made by Clement, one of the early Christian fathers,[22] that may be stretched in its application to include Spain, or be restricted to reach no farther than Rome. Unfortunately the rhetorical nature of the author's language makes his geography uncertain. He writes thus: "Paul also obtained the reward of patient endurance after being seven times thrown into captivity, compelled to flee, and stoned. After preaching both in the east and the west he gained the illustrious reputation due to his faith, having taught righteousness to the whole world, and come to the extreme limit of the west, and suffered martyrdom under the praefects."

About A.D. 170 the author of the Muratorian Fragment spoke of the visit to Spain,[23] but his language is not explicit enough to entirely exclude the annoyance of doubt.

Whether Paul's new freedom extended over one year or more, his labors and sufferings, his annoyances and abuses must have approached the limit of human endurance. During his long imprisonment the impenitent Jews and the Judaizing Christians had been doing their utmost to belittle him, to discredit his apostolic authority, and to prove that he was apostate. They reloaded the believers with the old burdens of legalism, superstition, and casuistry from which Paul had freed them, against which Jesus had hurled condemnation,[24] and about which even Peter had some doubts.[25]

Some of these disturbers were religious ultraists in masks of holiness, who insisted on ascetic practices by forbidding marriage and requiring abstinence from meats.[26] Some were parasites on the church, preaching for gain without regard to the true gospel.[27] Some were presumptuous theological critics, like Hymanaeus, Philetus, and perhaps Alexander[28] who argued mystically or allegorically that the resurrection had already taken place.[29] Or like certain Romans, who contended that Paul's doctrine of justification by faith, justified sin.[30] And some of the disturbers were syncretists, who contaminated the gospel with Gnostic philosophy, Oriental theosophy, and various absurd speculations from any source that caught their fancy.

But many of these troublers were Jews, of whom a great number were Nazorians or the Jerusalem type of Christian. Some Nazoreans accepted Paul as a true apostle, but did not agree with his advanced views about the ceremonial law, others rejected him entirely as an apostate and imposter. These, who in the course of time, were called Ebionites, or the "Poor," hated Paul with a malicious bitterness that expressed itself in constant efforts to worry him by stirring up strife in his churches and to bring him into disfavor with the authorities at Rome by misrepresenting him.[31] But while Paul was often angry with his tormentors, nevertheless he rejoiced in the fact that by their very opposition the name of Christ was being made known to all the world.[32] In the end it was Paul's Gentile church that survived, while the Jewish church, Nazorean and Ebionite slowly disintegrated.

While Paul the apostle was extending the outposts of the gospel, Nero the emperor, not yet twenty-seven years old, was heaping up the crimes that were eventually to make him one of the most heartless monsters of history. He was inordinately vain, tyranically selfish, and murderously savage. His fingers were already dripping with the blood of those who dared to stand in the way of his mad desires. His mother, who had secured the throne for him, was murdered at his behest; Britanicus, his half brother, was removed by poison; his young wife, Octavia, was first divorced, then banished, and later murdered. The noble Burrhus of the Praetorian Guard, one of the advisers of his youth, was made a victim of poison, and Seneca the philosopher, his faithful mentor, was already incurring the sentence of death.

The peak of crime was reached in A.D. 64. In July of that year a devastating fire broke out among the frame booths at the southeast end of the Circus Maximus, spread through the city, and raged for six days. As it abated, a second fire flamed up in another part of the city, and, like the first, was so timed and located that it was believed to have been the work of an arsonist. Nearly half the city was destroyed. Suspicion fell upon Nero, who, to clear himself and to divert public attention from other serious charges, put the blame on the Christians. In order to fit the charge of incendiarism upon the whole body of believers and to intensify popular feeling against them, Nero also accused them of introducing a new superstition in violation of Roman law[33]—and of "hating the human race."[34]

Upon these charges Nero and his companion in crime, Tigellinus, planned one of the most diabolical entertainments that ever emanated from the heart—a "hunt" and other horrible spectacles in which innocent and defenseless men and women were to be tortured for the amusement of a profligate court and a depraved populace. Calumnious stories about Christian practices were already in circulation and were believed by those who had ears for such evil reports. Nero's inhuman show was therefore assured of success. Before escapes could be made, those who confessed to being Christians were seized first, and then followed the arrest of others whose names were revealed by informers. Tacitus says that a "vast multitude was convicted."

Meanwhile Nero had turned over his gardens and the Vatican circus for his great spectacle. Then were brought forth men and women sewed up in the hides of wild beasts. Fierce hunting dogs, straining at their leashes were loosed upon them to chase and worry them, and to kill them with foaming fangs. Spectators applauded and Nero gloated.

Because the Messiah had been crucified, a forest of crosses soon rose in the Neroian gardens, every one bearing a blood-stained, praying, slowly dying saint who had been subjected like his Lord to cruel indignities.

As the maniacal spectacles continued through the day and into the night, other victims were brought forward from the pens and nailed to tall stakes or impaled upon them; and when wrapped in their own garments that had been soaked in pitch were set on fire for the illumination of the gardens.

When news of the horror reached Paul, he suffered the greatest agony of his life. Eagerly he sought news of the men and women who had been leaders in the church. Who of them had recanted, who had escaped, who had perished? What of Andronicus and Junianus, Ampliatus and Urbanus? Rufus and Epanetus? What of the households of Narcissus and Aristobulus? And what news of Tryphena and Tryphosa, of Mary and

Julia? Paul consoled himself in the belief that the saints would soon hear
the sound of the trumpet of God that would call them back to life from
their desecrated ashes to participate in the triumphal ascent into heavenly
glory.

Cristianity had made its great advance in the Roman world under the
shelter of Judaism as a licit religion, of which it was regarded as a sect. But
the Jewish opposition to Paul, the withdrawal of the Gentile church from
the synagogue, and the refusal of Christians to take part in pagan festivals
or to offer incense to the statues of emperors, gradually brought the church
under suspicion. When annoyance and persecution forced worshipers to
meet in secret, their enemies were the more ready to believe any calumny or
accusation that might be brought against them.

Paul did not know that his church was then facing two hundred and
fifty years of persecution. Every day he closed his devotions with the
hopeful words, "Come, Lord Jesus,"[35] believing that he should soon see the
heavens open for the mighty drama that would deliver the righteous and
send the unbelieving away to the doom that they had deliberately chosen.
He could not penetrate the centuries to see the flaming celestial cross that
was to show Constantine the way to victory and to open the portals of
Rome to Christianity. Nor could he see that his Lord would postpone the
consummation of history to harvest the earth for billions of souls yet
unborn. He could not stamp future events with their exact dates, and the
Church, therefore, in its long wait for the second advent, had to fall back
upon the words of the Psalmist, "For a thousand years in thy sight are but
as yesterday when it is past, or as a watch in the night."[36]

Assuming that the author of the pastoral letters, if not Paul himself,
knew some of the facts of the apostle's last days and being the earliest
writer to refer to the subject, it may be conjectured that a warrant for Paul's
arrest had been issued by the authorities in Rome. This may have come
from Nero and his co-monster Tigellinus, the praetorian prefect, or in their
absence, the second-in-command of the Praetorian Guard, or even the city
prefect. Perhaps Alexander, one of the Ephesian coppersmiths of that
name, and possibly the one whom Paul had excommunicated,[37] had
preferred charges against him,[38] hiring professional delators as witnesses.

The apostle's apprehension may have occurred at any time within four
years of the great fire, and perhaps, at Nicopolis in Epirus, where,
according to the letter to Titus, he had decided to pass the winter,[39] or even
in Rome itself. The charges against him may have been the introduction of
a new superstition, the instigation of his followers to the burning of Rome,
and the circulation of treasonable utterances against the Imperial
Government.

When the second letter to Timothy was written, Paul was in Rome, a
prisoner in chains, and possibly confined in some part of the horrible

Mamertine, or great state prison. His case had then passed its first or precognition stage, which appears to have been on the charge of teaching a new religion.

It had been a terrible ordeal in which the apostle was assailed as savagely as if he had been an arch-criminal, and in which he was forsaken by all his friends.[40] The trial occurred in one of the great basilicas of justice, which was crowded with spectators eager to get a glimpse of the man who had proclaimed the end of the world, preached a new god, and caused the Imperial City to be burned. So dangerous was it to be in any way associated with him, that no lawyer was willing to defend him and no influential friend dared to make the usual appeal for mercy. To his accusers and their witnesses and to the austere court he stood alone, but to the apostle there was an invisible presence, that of his Lord who stood by to support him in his last defense of the gospel.[41]

When at last he was called upon to speak in his own behalf, he felt a great spiritual elation that gave him full command of all his powers and enabled him to hold all his hearers in silence. With convincing argument he proved his gospel to be the natural development and true fulfillment of Judaism, and in no way a new religion outside the protection of Roman law. He ignored his own uncomfortable lot, made no appeal for mercy, hurled no bitterness at his enemies, but turned his whole defense into a mighty proclamation of his gospel. It was his last sermon. An unfriendly audience became sympathetic, and the court sustained his defense.

This, however, was only the first hearing of his case, and he was remanded to prison to await further trial. Paul knew that his enemies would now redouble their efforts for his destruction and that he could no longer escape their machinations nor look for justice.

Soon after the unexpectedly favorable outcome of the first trial, four members of Paul's evangelistic force were permitted to visit him in his prison. One of these was Luke, the "beloved physician." The others were Crescenus, whom he sent to Galatia, Titus to Dalmatia, and Tychicus to Ephesus. There had been a fifth man with him, but Paul wrote disappointedly of him, "Demas, in love with this present world, has deserted me and gone to Thessalonica."[42]

Knowing that his case would be delayed, Paul wrote Timothy somewhere in Asia Minor, sending the letter by Tychicus, who was going to Ephesus, telling him of the progress of his trial and its probable outcome. The letter contained much advice as if the apostle meant it to serve as a last message in the event that he and Timothy should never meet again. He urged Timothy to go to Rome before winter storms should close the seas to travel or make the long land route slow and difficult. On his way he was to find Mark and bring him along. At Troas he was to stop at the house of Carpus and get a cloak and some books and parchments that had been left there.

Much kindness appears to have been shown the apostle during the first stage of his imprisonment, for he was permitted to receive and instruct workers, to write letters, and to have fellowship with several Roman Christians. Perhaps he had won the secret friendship or at least the respect of the city prefect.

But Timothy and Mark may have arrived early in November, greatly to the joy and comfort of the apostle. If so, the oversight of the Gentile work was doubtless committed at once to Timothy as the man best fitted by vigor, training, long experience, and disposition for the Herculean task, an office that seems to have been contemplated in the two letters previously addressed to him.[43]

But if his case was taken up again without delay, Paul may have received his sentence and been committed again to the state prison before his friends could reach him, there to await the expiration of the ten days' grace before the penalty of his supposed crime could be inflicted. Perhaps, however, the whole scene may have closed before the men arrived. A trial in which the apostle had been pictured as a monster more evil than Nero himself may have taken place, followed by an incarceration that may have carried with it confinement in the stocks, or even submersion in the horrible *tullianum*—the unutterably foul underground dungeon. And finally there may have been the execution, one in which the only sign of respect was that Paul was executed as a Roman citizen. There remains a possibility, however, that Timothy and Mark may have arrived several months before the final hearing of the apostle's case.

While it is almost certain that Paul suffered martyrdom at some time within the period from A.D. 64 to 68, the exact year, month, and day have been lost to history. Epiphanius places his death in the twelfth year of Nero's reign, A.D. 65-66; Eusebius, in the thirteenth year, or 66-67; and Jerome, in the fourteenth, or 67-68.[44] Dionysius of Corinth seems to make the martyrdom of Peter and Paul occur at Rome at the same time.[45] At an early period, the Roman Church began celebrating the twenty-ninth day of June as the anniversary of their deaths, though that date originally may have commemorated nothing more than the translation of their supposed relics. Also the language of Dionysius is too weak for the burden placed upon it.

But these dates did not find their way into history until three to five hundred years after the event. Assuming the very doubtful pastoral epistles to be Pauline, however, or at least to be based upon a knowledge of Paul's last days, and adding such evidence as tradition seems to afford, it may be concluded that the apostle's martyrdom probably occurred in the year A.D. 67.

Perhaps it was at an early hour on a sultry morning in June when Paul was brought forth from prison, where he had spent his last night on earth in prayer for the Church. He was then led by a detachment of the praetorian guard under the command of a centurion towards a selected site beyond the walls of the city. An increasing rabble followed at a safe distance, wondering who the prisoner was and what crime he had committed, and morbidly eager to witness a bloody death. Perhaps a few friends risked their safety and followed near to catch some parting word and to claim the lifeless body of their Lord's most devoted apostle. Perhaps Mark, Timothy, and Luke—Jew, half Jew, and Gentile—pale from long fasting, anxiety, and pleading were the leaders of his company and kept as close to the prisoner as the tolerance of the centurion would permit.

But Paul had fulfilled his mission: He had "fought the good fight," had "finished the course," and had "kept the faith."[46] He was now on his way to receive the "crown of righteousness," which no headsman's sword could intercept. His poise and step were those of a victor, for death that had shadowed him for years would now defeat itself by a last desperate stroke; and Paul could exclaim exultantly—"O death, where is thy victory? O death, where is thy sting?"[47]

From the Ostian Gate, past the white pyramid of Castius, the executioners marched with their prisoner out of the Ostian Way and shortly turned into an amphitheater of hillocks. The place of execution, whatever its name at the time, became known later as *Aquae Salviae*, "healing waters," and still later, as *Tre Fontane*, the "three fountains."

There was no delay. But to the apostle, the few moments that elapsed were like a dark and crushing weight. Sounds and scenes were strangely magnified and unnatural, and both were laden with a loneliness such as the Christ had suffered before he expired upon the cross. There was no yielding of faith, no faltering of courage, no surging of emotion.

At the command of the centurion, Paul was placed in position. The headsman proudly trimmed himself for a master stroke. The soldiers stepped back, the rabble became silent, and Timothy placed a hand over his eyes. Paul's eyes were bound and his face was turned downward; he did not see the heavenly vision that had thrilled Stephen in his last moments, but his spiritual eyes were opened an instant later when the sword of Rome that had long been his protection was turned against him.

Friends gathered up his body for burial, and went back to proclaim the glory of martyrdom.

Thus terminated the life of the man who saved Christianity from an oblivion so dark that the very name of Christ might otherwise have been lost forever, who organized the Christian church as separate from the synagogue, furnished it with its credal material, and committed it to the care of the Gentiles until the Jew should be brought to repentance. And this, as if his Lord at the last moment had chosen him for that very task.

In Paul's death was the ultimate, though negative, triumph of those who for a quarter of a century had cruelly maligned, murderously hated, and relentlessly persecuted him. But while the Sanhedrin was gloating, the Judaizers exulting, and the scribblers adding defamation to death, Paul's blood surged through the arteries of the church to ultimate triumph.

REFERENCES

Chapter 17

1. Horace, *Satires.* I. 5. Lines 1-4.
2. Acts 28:21.
3. Acts 28:22.
4. Isa. 6:9-10.
5. Matt. 13:14-15.
6. Acts 28:26-28.
7. Acts 28:28.
8. Acts 13:45; 18:6.
9. Acts 28:30-31.
10. Phil. 1:12.
11. Col. 4:11.
12. II Thes. 2:3.
13. Rom. 13:1-5.
14. Josephus. *Antiquities.* XX. 8. 11.
15. Josephus. *The Life of Flavius Josephus.* Chap. 3.
16. Phil. 2:24.
17. Philem. 22 with Col. 4:9, 17.
18. I Tim. 1:3.
19. Tit. 1:5.
20. II Tim. 4:13, 20.
21. I Tim. 3:14; 4:13; but see Acts 20:38.
22. Clement of Alexandria.
23. For the Latin text of this see A.C. McGiffert, *A History of Christianity in the Apostolic Age.* (New York: Charles Scriber's Sons, 1906), p. 416.
24. Matt. 23:4.
25. Acts 15:10.
26. I Tim. 4:1-3.
27. Tit. 1:10-14.
28. I Tim. 1:19-20; II Tim. 2:16-18.
29. II Tim. 2:18.
30. Rom. 3:8.
31. Phil. 1:16-17.
32. Phil. 1:18.
33. Suetonius. *The Lives of the Caesars.* VI. "Nero." Chap. 16.
34. Tacitus, *The Annals.* XV. Chap. 44.
35. Rev. 22:20.
36. Ps. 90:4; II Pet. 3:8-10.
37. I Tim. 1:20.
38. II Tim. 4:14.
39. Tit. 3:12.
40. II Tim. 4:16.
41. II Tim. 4:17.
42. II Tim. 4:10.
43. I Tim. 6:20; II Tim. 1:12-14.
44. "Paul," *Cyclopaedia of Biblical, Theological, and Ecclesiastical Literature,* ed., J.M. McClintock and J. Strong (New York: Harper & Brothers, 1894) VII, p. 816.
45. Eusebius. *The Ecclesiastical History.* II. 25.
46. II Tim. 4:7.
47. I Cor. 15:55.

CHAPTER
18

Paul in Perspective:
Tarsus — Rome

LIKE SOME DISFIGURING PARASITE, legend is ever ready to attach itself to the lives of religious heroes. Paul lived at a time when men who made unusual claims to sanctity or wisdom were expected to authenticate themselves by performing wonders or miracles.[1] It was also a time in which the deeds of all popular heroes quickly took on legendary enlargements. Paul did not escape this. Legends that credited him with miraculous powers found their way into Luke's Acts of the Apostles[2] and into the apocryphal literature of the early church.

Some years after the deaths of Paul and the other apostles, the church became conscious of its need for an approved literature. Nothing authoritative existed, except for a few letters, the most important of which had been written by Paul. These were collected and to them were added four propagandistic biographies of Jesus that were built from the current teachings in the churches as they had taken form towards the close of the first century,[3] a propagandistic history of the Church, and the Apocalypse of John. These formed the canon of the New Testament—much of it, originating in the Pauline branch of the church and having the Pauline outlook.

215

This recognized need of biographical and theological literature led to the production of a great quantity of apocryphal writings containing stories of Mary, Joseph, Jesus, Pilate, the apostles, and others, written by overcredulous men, or men who wished to propagate questionable doctrines, encourage ascetic practices, or make heroes of persons who had been associated with the founders of the church. Such stories, however, are now without appeal, except to childish credulity and morbid piety. In this apocryphal literature a place was found for Paul; notably in the Apocalypse of Paul, the Acts of Peter and Paul, the Story of Perpetua, the Acts of Paul and Thecla, the Acts of Barnabas, and the Teachings of Simon Cephas.

It is still told in Rome that when Paul was on his way to martyrdom, he was met by a woman named Perpetua, who was weeping for him. Seeing that she was blind in one eye, he asked her for her handkerchief, promising to return it. She insisted that the soldiers use it for binding his eyes. After the execution, the blood-stained handkerchief was returned and Perpetua's sight was restored. Such a legend would seem to link itself with Paul's experience at Corinth when his touch was supposed to have given healing virtue to handkerchiefs and aprons.[4] The legend of Perpetua, together with the story of Jesus' agony in the Garden of Gethsemane,[5] perhaps suggested the latter and similar legend of Saint Veronica who gave her handkerchief to Jesus when he was on his way to Calvary and received it again with the imprint of his face upon it.

The legend of three fountains at the supposed site of Paul's execution says that when Paul's head was cut off, it bounded away striking the ground three times, and that from these blood-stained spots three fountains of healing waters gushed forth.

Another legend says that a woman named Lucina had Paul's body buried on her property. This supposed burial place later became the site of the present basilica of San Paolo Fuori le Mura.

The splendor of Paul's life, however, needs no supporting legend, the wisdom of his words no miraculous verification, and the honesty of his convictions no supernatural testimony. Paul was without a peer as a religious leader. Although it would seem that the inherent merits of Christianity should have made the gospel self perpetuating, it was Paul who gave it the impetus that sent it down the centuries and the penetration that made it fill the world.

To know Paul is to have the experience of being under the sway of the same Spirit that ruled his life; have the same reactions towards the social, moral, and religious customs of his time; and aim at the same compelling objective that was always uppermost in his thought and deepest in his heart. Paul had nothing to conceal. Thus his conduct, unlike that of lesser men, was logical and consistent. In his letters he may be seen face to face, though across a vast chasm of time and at moments when he was under severe emotional strain or was occupied with special problems. In the Acts of the Apostles he is seen as others incidentally interpreted him in their story of the beginning and progress of the gospel. But when the background of his age is set in place, Paul's figure stands out in beautiful proportions. All that at first seems strange in his words and deeds is quickly explained, and he is seen to be a normal man of penetrating mind and delicately balanced judgment.

As "a Pharisee, a son of a Pharisee," Paul obeyed the letter of the law from his youth up. He was a literalist, but with a normal amount of mysticism. Nature had endowed him liberally with latent gifts that were early unfolded by his careful training. His faith in the scriptures of his fathers was implicit and tenacious. In him all belief expressed itself in immediate action. There was no place in his mind for an idle creed: to believe was to act.

The Jewish Scriptures had promised a Messiah, and the Jews everywhere were discussing the person and the time and the manner of his approach. Pretenders to that exalted office had already appeared and even Jesus had been rejected with them. To Saul the Pharisee, the claims of Jesus and of his followers had soared to the point of blasphemy; a crime that, according to Jewish law was punishable by death. Constrained by an unquestioning devotion to the law,[6] and driven by youthful impetuosity, Saul sprang at once to the defense of his Jewish faith—to the synagogue, a protector; but to the church, a persecutor.

He shared with his age, in a belief in dreams and visions, the natural product of his severe manner of life and the depth of his convictions. Out of a profound faith sprang an unquenchable zeal which, in turn, yielded a fountain of revelation ever ready to pour forth when stimulated by fastings and prayer, or when rudely opened by shock, weariness, anxiety, or other physical or mental disturbances. Paul dreamed and saw and heard so realistically that he could not doubt the apparent evidence of his senses. Thus he saw Jesus of Nazareth, confessed him as Lord, and received from him the commission of apostleship.

That vision, however induced, marked one of the most important epochs in all religious history: it changed the direction of a great life that was projecting itself with fierce momentum, captured the whole endowment of a mighty personality for the extension of spiritual righteousness, and released a masterful mind from the bondage of rabbinic traditions to give it the task of interpreting the messianic theology.

By that inexorable word "why," Paul's pre-Christian career was suddenly halted. "Saul, Saul, why do you persecute me?" His supreme faith now rested upon the fact of the resurrection of Jesus as proved to him in the heavenly vision,[7] his master motive was now the constraining love of

Christ,[8] and his daily inspiration the hope of the second coming of his Lord.[9] As an ambassador of the Christ[10] he now rose to the full height of his stature, molding his life anew after the ideals of his sacred office.[11]

It is not necessary to think of Paul as a philosopher, especially of the type common to his day, in order to ascribe greatness to him. He certainly would have resented any plaudits coming to him from that source. The Greek tried to reason his way into truth, but Paul the Jew grasped truth intuitively and used his dialectic to defend it. To him intuition or revelation, as certainly as logic, had its proper sphere and, within its domain, lay some of the greatest mysteries and values of life. With his alert mentality, however, he could have got the general drift of the philosophies of his day, if not in the schools, certainly from the lecturers who frequented the agoras. While certain extremists among the Jews could say, "Cursed is he that shall teach Greek science to his son,"[12] nevertheless there were other men who discussed philosophy in their schools; and Philo, about the time when Paul was perfecting his theology, was attempting to harmonize Plato and Aristotle with Moses.

Paul was a prophet, and eschatology was his great theme. As soon as he was convinced that Jesus was the promised Messiah, he believed that the Kingdom of Heaven was at hand and that the Roman age was about to close. Accordingly he cast his whole life without reservation into the greatest and most thrilling prospect that ever engaged the mind and heart of man.

The profundity of the apostle's faith manifested itself at once in all his actions, and made of him a most effective religious leader. He not only preached his gospel, but he proved by his own life that it was a livable religion and an inexhaustible fountain of hope, peace, and joy. His unquenchable enthusiasm, inexhaustible energy, and unerring capacity for understanding all kinds of men made him an inspiring leader and a prolific father of leaders.

His faith stimulated in him all the human virtues, and he strove continually for the goal of perfection. His virtues were not one-sided, inept suppressions, but mighty surges of soul. In him, love, compassion, and tenderness were delicately coordinated with vigorous leadership and stern discipline. His sensibilities were living, delicate, and keen; his emotions, oscillating between wide extremes, were like the soft response of the lyre or the deep swelling of the sea; his affections, like the tender caresses of maternal love, or the healthful overflowings of a great masculine heart.

Among his sterner virtues, Paul displayed a remarkable degree of independence, such as springs from wide human contacts, penetrating judgment, and fixed convictions. The trait was inborn, but it fitted consistently into his great faith, giving him a genius for command that was refined and directed by his own complete submission to the leadership of the Holy Spirit. He was never disconcerted in the presence of men who held official positions, or men who for any reason thought themselves his superiors. Proconsuls and procurators, praetorian prefects and philosophers, common soldiers and sailors, weavers and tentmakers, dyers and tanners were all simply prospects to him for the Kingdom of Heaven. He adapted himself to them according to their various stations: as refined as the courtier, and as unconventional as the lowly.

He made no compromises with any, where principle of liberty of the gospel was involved, yet was never fanatical about the observance or nonobservance of those religious practices that were only signs, but not essentials, of the inner life. For prudential reasons he could take the vow of a Nazarite, or circumcise a convert, or refuse to eat meat slaughtered by a non-Jewish butcher, but he would perform none of these acts if they bore adversely upon the liberty of the gospel. Thus, circumcision being neither good nor evil, he circumcised Timothy that he might have inoffensive access to the Jews; but when the Jews demanded the circumcision of Titus on the ground that this rite was necessary to faith, he refused with angry vehemence.

Paul was too broadly intelligent to deny a place to rational rites and ceremonies in the outward expression of religious life, but he warned against the substitution of the form for the fact. He practiced the laying-on of hands, administered baptism and the Lord's Supper, fasted and spoke with tongues; but rebuked the Corinthians for making too much of the instrumental side of baptism, and warned them against the danger of over-estimating the value of glossalalia.

Another of the apostle's sterner virtues was his disciplinary firmness, the characteristic that had once made him relentless as a persecutor. Under the control of grace, this firmness had made him an extraordinary executive. With compelling appeal he gathered multitudes of men and women and organized them for citizenship in the Kingdom of God. Enemies of the apostle who objected to his liberalism appeared everywhere and not only sought his life, but by both open and insidious opposition also labored incessantly to destroy his work. This interference made stern discipline within the church a constant necessity for its protection.

Then, too, many of the members of the primitive church came from the lowest levels of paganism, and were prone to relapse into their former immorality. Others fell into selfish rivalries with consequent jealousies and contentions,[13] and some who had a speculative turn of mind strayed dangerously far from the purity of the apostle's theology. Always these conditions were treated with firmness;[14] but it was the discipline of mercy to salvation,[15] administered with a compassionate rod, and a judgment flexible enough to insure both justice and mercy.

Paul never played the role of a holy man. He did not try to draw attention to himself by peculiarities of dress, eccentric mannerisms, holy aloofness, or insipid unworldliness. The coming conquering Christ, not self, was his theme and he moved among his fellow men as one of them.[16] From his own day to the present, however, there have been men who tried to clothe him with their own eccentricities, to force his thoughts into their own molds, and to compress his breadth and depth into their narrowness and shallowness.

Nor did Paul pose as a reformer. He did not try to change the social customs of his day. His one great task was that of proclaiming the Kingdom of Heaven and the immediate necessity of man's reconciliation to God. He could not pause to attempt the reformation of existing institutions that he believed would soon perish with the earth. His duty was to call men out of the world[17] and to put them in readiness for the Messiah's advent. The slave should remain faithful to his master and the soldier to the emperor.

While there were inherent elements of the gospel that would ultimately deliver believers from all kinds of burdensome customs, Paul advised men and women to avoid suspicion and scandal by behaving according to the best accepted standards of their day and place. He did not liberate woman from subserviency to her husband, nor remove the restriction placed upon her in the house of worship.[18] These conditions, like slavery, would disappear with the approach of the Messiah.

Paul did not attempt to win applause by making a display of learning. "For I decided to know nothing among you except Jesus Christ and him crucified,"[19] he once said to the philosophers of Corinth, who, perhaps, had not learned that the boasted knowledge of one age is but ignorance to the next. He did not divert the attention of men from his one great theme by discussing the form and laws of the material universe. The popular view of the earth and heavens was no obstacle to the truth in righteousness, and the best science of that day would have been of little or no service to his cause.

Paul did not even seek a special revelation concerning the existence of good and evil spirits—he accepted a universal belief which in his age gave the only explanation for many strange phenomena. What matter whether a disease was caused by the presence of an evil spirit or an evil bacterium. The hypothesis of a spirit was but a first step in science.

Nor did Paul imitate the Attic scholars of his day by speaking and writing in the formal or classical Greek. He spoke a type of Greek normally spoken by Jews in the Greco-Roman world. It was a "yiddish" Greek mingled with semitisms and Hebrew sentence structure. Today it is called "Koine" Greek.

But Paul used that language with amazing skill, recasting old words for new meanings, enlisting the aid of familiar Hebraisms, crowding phrases and sentences to their utmost capacity with surging thought. Nowhere else do words become so nearly animate agents as in Paul's letters. There they quiver with life, filled with the spirit of the author, and energized by his unparalleled theme of the crucified Christ. There are wooing words, weeping words, commanding words, and, when exigencies require, there are words that flash like burnished swords.

The dialect that Paul employs casts no reproach upon his scholarship. In his eulogium of love[20] he is both a philosopher and a literary genius, and in his letter to Philemon he is a master of epistolary style and the art of persuasion.

It was Paul's apocalyptic outlook that lifted him above other men and determined his attitude toward the world. The outlook of Rome was purely mundane and that of Jerusalem was a kind of heavenized earth. Paul's outlook swept beyond terrestrial life to a celestial kingdom where the mystical and spiritual became eternal realities. With the cross, he marched far out beyond the exasperating confines of rationalism into the vast unknown and brought back light and hope for the human soul.

Great as his heavenly urge may have been, Paul owed something to the spirit of his age—an age of surging activity on land and sea, of individual and public enterprise. It was an age of flourishing cities, imposing architecture, crowded schools, exciting sports, and unprecedented travel. The times were still feeling the impress of great men and glowed under the presence of others who were rapidly rising to fame. It was the age of such familiar names as Cicero, Sallust, Virgil, Horace, Strabo, Philo, and Augustus on the one part, and Seneca, Pliny, Josephus, Quintillian, Plutarch, Tacitus, and others of greater or less fame on the other part. No man of superior genius could have slumbered in such an age.

Paul faced his age with deep-seated racial characteristics, with intellectual hunger, and with a knowledge of the world that had been gained from Gentile contacts in a great commercial and university city. The great strength of his natural bent determined the general direction of his self-projection, and the hope of Messianic advent gave him a definite field of action.

In making known the Christ, Paul wrote his own name across the world. Ignatius called him the "Christ Bearer," and Chrysostom pronounced him the "Heart of the World." He may well be called the father of Christian theology, for it is to his letters and the writings of men who walked in his footsteps and later produced the other portions of the New Testament that theologians turn for authority.

Judging from the New Testament and from the ultimate world-conquering achievements of his apostleship, it is clear that Paul far surpassed all of the Twelve, not only in labor, but also in the clearness of his conception of the messianic character and mission. Although the Twelve were convinced that the Kingdom of Heaven was at hand, they were slow in reaching the conclusion that Jesus was the Christ. According to the author of the first Gospel, who wrote nearly three-quarters of a century after the event, it was the impulsive Peter who, in a burst of faith, first exclaimed, "You are the Christ, the son of the living God."[21]

Jesus had been acting as the herald of a heavenly kingdom but without openly claiming the Messiahship for himself. When he decided to further enlighten his disciples, he put two questions to them to determine their innermost thoughts of him: "Who do men say that the Son of man is?" "But who do you say that I am?" Peter's reply showed that his conception was not the result of a process of reasoning with material evidence, but a direct spiritual apprehension. Therefore, because in his confession Peter had enunciated the very truth that constituted the keys of the Kingdom of Heaven for use by the church, Jesus pronounced him qualified for the apostleship, and then complimented him with two words that showed him to be spiritually related to the spiritual Christ: "You are Peter and upon this rock I will build my church."[22]

After the other disciples had assented to Peter's pronouncement, and perhaps with emphasis as great as his, Jesus charged them that they should tell no one that he was the Christ[23] until his sacrificial death should occur and his resurrection could be adduced as proof.[24] But Peter's faith could not grasp the purpose of a sacrificial death, and his blindness soon brought him a stinging rebuke from his Master that must have smarted worse than the "thorn in the flesh"[25] by which Paul was restrained from boasting "Get behind me Satan! You are a hindrance to me."[26]

Then a little later Peter prepared himself for an even greater humiliation by declaring that he would never deny his Lord.[27] First he slept while Jesus prayed in Gethsemane,[28] and later, in a most cowardly manner denied him three times.[29] Then after fifteen years of apostolic service, when even death should have lost its terrors, he went to Antioch to inspect the work among the Gentiles. There, his weakness again overcame his faith, and Paul had to rebuke him openly.[30]

Peter was never wholly defeated by his besetting weakness. Always if cast down he rose again to follow his Lord; and in this respect as well in his other moral qualities he was sufficiently rock-like to justify his Aramaic and Greek names: Cephas and Petros.[31]

There were differences between Paul and Peter that made Peter the better subject for fanciful traditions and the more natural object of superstitious reverence. Paul's faith gripped like steel; Peter's wavered in the presence of danger. Paul's love was like a steady glow; Peter's impulsive warmth was like a leaping flame. Paul hewed to the line with a steady exactness that produced permanent results; Peter hewed without a line and would have been forgotten had it not been for Paul. Paul commanded respect because of his unfailing self-mastery; Peter won sympathy because his failures were pathetically human. Certain Aramaic Christians, as those of Corinth, preferred "Cephas" to Paul, perhaps because he was one of the original Twelve; while Ebionites everywhere went still further and rejected Paul altogether, condemning him as a heretic.

The custom, before the Gospels had been written, of relating stories in religious meetings about Jesus and his apostles gave Peter a leading position before Paul had received his call. And when the traditions that had grown up in the churches were collected and given permanent form in the Gospels and the Acts, they gave Peter the leading place among the Twelve.

Tradition tinged with jealousies then attempted to add to Peter's fame by thrusting him into territory, like Corinth and Rome, where Paul was known to have been the chief actor. It is possible that Peter could have visited both cities, but the proofs adduced that he did so tend rather to strengthen the proofs that he did not. And if he did visit them, his stay must have been short and unimportant. Any attempt to give him a stationary position, as bishop or pope, ignores not only his questionable fitness for such positions in a great Gentile city, but the very important fact that his apostolic duty was itinerant.

Long after the deaths of Paul and Peter, while jealousies and Ebionite hatred were still discrediting the former in favor of the latter, there appeared a quantity of apocryphal literature that purported to be sketches of certain New Testament and other characters. Incredible as these stories were, they nevertheless aided in perpetuating the unfavorable comparison between the two men, a comparison that still lingers vaguely in the popular mind. Although Paul spoke of himself with commendable humility, saying to the Corinthians, "I am the least of the apostles, unfit to be called an apostle, because I persecuted the church of God;"[32] yet he also defended his apostolic rank, saying "For I am not inferior to these superlative apostles, though I am nothing."[33]

Legend gave to Peter the bishopric at Rome, but it was legend based upon the pseudo-epigraphic Clementines and Recognitions, heretical fiction that appeared long after the apostle's death. After the story of episcopacy had gained credence, it was further expanded by making Peter hold office for twenty-five years until his death; a conjecture that runs contrary to the New Testament records and is without trustworthy support from any other source.

There never had been rivalry between Paul and Peter for the bishopric in Rome. Neither apostle would have taken such a stationary office. Both knew that the foundation and bond of the church was the everlasting Christ.

As a theologian, Paul carved out new channels of religious thought, extending them far into the realms of hope. Judaism, by bewildering exegesis, had dimmed the light of its sacred writings and had made righteousness to consist largely in the observance of countless rules and ceremonies. The higher, finer aspects of faith were lost in the miasmic bog of "Jewish fables,"[34] "cunningly devised fables,"[35] and "profane and old wives' fables."[36] The Jew was not insincere, he had a zeal for God, "but it is not enlightened."[37] Preferring ostentatious works to simple faith, he "walked in the darkness."[38] Yet through him came the light that sent the hordes of pagan gods into oblivion.

Paganism, too, was excessively religious but it weltered hopelessly in the midnight of ignorance, crying unto a multitude of gods whose ears were of brass and whose hearts were of stone. When Paul made his famous speech before the philosophers of Mars Hill, he began by saying, "Men of Athens, I perceive that in every way you are very religious."[39] He, of course, knew that every man by nature carried in his consciousness a sense of subordinance, a feeling that in the darkness of ignorance led men to supplicate imaginary deities and to placate malevolent spirits. The heathen had failed to find the God whom Paul was declaring:[40] philosophy, with knowledge so scant that it was full of contradictions, had failed to reveal him.[41]

But nowhere was religion lacking; the world was "very religious." It was, however, the misdirection of the religious faculty, then as now, that kept mankind in spiritual darkness. In Paul's theology, God puts himself within reach of all men, and conditions them for finding him: "that they should seek God, in the hope that they might feel after him and find him."[42] In the lawlessness of imagination, man makes for himself gods who can be persuaded to do his bidding; and sometimes, in the vanity of limited knowledge and the pride of rudimentary intellect, loses sight of all gods.

Paul makes the first step in the exercise of the religious faculty to be a humble act, as that of a deaf and blind man who finds a living presence by feeling after it. The intellectual apprehension of God then follows upon the elemental desires—spiritual hunger and thirst—that open the way for it.[43] Paul's conception of God was that of the Hebrew Scriptures—a conception exalted and beautiful, though of necessity very anthropomorphic.

Believing that the Messiah had appeared, Paul was forced to revise his theological thinking to harmonize it with the character of a God who would provide salvation for the world through the suffering of his Son. It was very good theology to ascribe holiness, wisdom, justice, truth, and might to God as his father had done, though these attributes were rather cold, distant, even forbidding. So when Paul decided that love and grace had actuated God in sending the Messiah, his whole theology began to vibrate with a new vocabulary, and his thought became saturated with such magnetic words as grace, faith, hope, joy, peace, love, and glory; "God" became "Father" in the tenderest sense of that term. Thus was enlarged the answer to the religious faculty.

Paul, however, did not attempt to construct a system of theology that would be a complete revelation of God. Such a task would have required equality with God. But recent events had enabled him to see a little further than the older prophets could see, and in great leaps of faith he touched the high points in the divine character that indicated to him the way of truth. Paul did not waste time and effort in attempting to show the exact sequence of all theological ideals, or to explain the interaction of the divine attributes. He was not concerned with the number and arrangement of stones in the pavement of the heavenly highway; it was enough for him that a highway was there. In his spiritual urge, he dashed over apparent inconsistencies; in his flight of faith, he soared into the entrancing heights of mysticism; and in his desire for light, he materialized his dreams and victories.

His theology was thus a theology of experience, fundamentally Jewish, but rebuilt, expanded, and adjusted to worldwide needs; subject, of course, to the errors of human experience, but nevertheless the greatest beacon of light ever erected for religious guidance. The Christ, the light of the world, is its flame; the unalterable truth of God, its foundation.

Paul's theology was a search for eternal unchangeable truth; the truth that is independent of man's speculation about it; the truth that binds together all things both spiritual and physical under one divine law. His method was unlike that of the scientist because he had to reach a conclusion in one mighty effort. The scientist by slow steps and many errors labors to discover the fixed laws of the physical universe as the sure footing of all progress. He uses the accumulated knowledge of the past, whether true or defective, upon which to build hypotheses for his next step. Paul was not an astronomer, nor a physicist, nor a chemist. He was, however, a specialist in the field of religion, a field in which the Jews had made amazing advances until their progress stagnated in the swamps of tradition.

Paul was a seer and a prophet; he looked far beyond, seized upon great thoughts and then threw them into a workable system that has given to the world more light, hope, peace, joy, and comfort than has ever been offered in any other system of religious practice. He caught clear sight of the fundamentals, and revealed them in the language and customs and incidents of his own times. He believed the utmost that faith could grasp, and refused to dwarf the splendor of life or mar its beauty by cultivating petty doubts.

Sift from Paul's theology the primitive beliefs of his age that he accepted or permitted to stand, adjust it to the light and language of today, cleanse it from the incrustations of superstition that have accumulated through the centuries, and there will be left, not a mere residuum, but rather an augmentum—a great practical theology of beauty and power that, whether taken literally, hypothetically, symbolically, or mystically will demand of man his highest allegiance to the unalterable laws of life.

Paul's theology abounds in great words and phrases that glow and gleam like pure gems cut and polished by master hands; words that liquify for the apostle's pen and flow in living streams to waiting hearts. But they are words that men have often devitalized by withdrawing from them their intended use, or they have divested them of their richness and degraded them to such ordinary uses that they no longer strike fire when uttered or heard. It is so with "love," which has lost the aura it must have displayed when Paul exclaimed, "The love of Christ constrains us," or when John wrote, "For God so loved the world."

Likewise, the regal word "Grace," that most astounding word of all scripture, that reveals the benevolent character of God—"By grace have you been saved through faith; and that not of yourselves, it is the gift of God."[44] In fact it was Paul who retrieved and rehabilitated most of the scintillating and dynamic words and phrases that appear in the New Testament, for that literature is fundamentally his theology. He contributed its oldest parts, and the remainder appeared long after his death, largely or wholly the work of his followers.

Paul's language was quickly seized by extremists, schismatics, and superstitionists who did not note its flexibility, nor realize the fact that no language is sufficiently accurate to exclude all possibility of misunderstanding. Some of his words, therefore, were made receptacles for strange thoughts, some were deliberately poisoned with error, some were overladen with meaning in order to obtain support for some questionable assumption. If Paul were living today he would certainly rebuke those theologians who bewilder and divide the church by disputing about words and ways until the very Christ himself becomes secondary to a sacrament and brotherly love shrivels to bitterness and ends in hate.

While Paul's theology reveals his Christ, it also reveals the man Paul. No artist with brush has ever portrayed his features except by conjecture, and that, too often based upon apocryphal story. With his own pen, however, Paul has unconsciously given a picture of himself far excelling the skill of any artist: a man of culture, courage, energy, and power; a man of penetrating understanding, common sense, superior judgment, inflexible purpose, unwavering faith, and spiritual grasp; a man master of himself, rich in personal and social graces, distinct and commanding in personality, and filled with the fruit of the indwelling Spirit of God.

Paul was a truly great man who probed the heart of the world to its vital depths, who commanded the greatest and the most vitalizing religious appeal that ever stirred the consciousness of mankind; whose words of spriritual wisdom outshine the soulless glory of all speculative philosophy, and whose achievements are still in progress as his gospel of a world Messiah brings hope and peace to worried millions.

Like many others of the world's most useful servants, and like his Lord, Paul had to suffer for daring to offer a better light to stumbling, straying humanity; for when the enemies of light discovered that they could not extinguish it by their raging denunciations, they became impatient to destroy its disseminator. The cross has been invoked against the Christ, and now the sword of Rome against His apostle. Deliberately the world plunged back into the darkness of blindness. But the Light still shines: Jesus and Paul died triumphant.

REFERENCES
Chapter 18

1. Cf. Mark 8:11.
2. Acts 14:3, 10; 16:18; 19:11-12; 20:9-10; 28:3-5, 8.
3. Cf. Luke 1:1-4.
4. Acts 19:11-12.
5. Luke 22:24.
6. Gal. 1:14; Phil. 3:6.
7. Acts 26:19.
8. II Cor. 5:14.
9. I Cor. 11:26.
10. Eph. 6:20; II Cor. 5:20.
11. Cf. Rom. 6:6; Eph. 4:22; Col. 3:9.
12. *Talmud, Babylonian Talmud. Baba Qana.* 82b. see also Mishna *Sotah* 9:14.
13. Cf. II Cor. 12:20-21.
14. Cf. II Cor. 13:2.
15. Cf. I Cor. 5:5.
16. Cf. Acts 14:15.
17. II Cor. 6:17.
18. I Cor. 11:2-16; 14:34-35; I Tim. 2:9-15.
19. I Cor. 2:2.
20. I Cor. 13.
21. Matt. 16:16.
22. Matt. 16:18.
23. Matt. 16:20.
24. Matt. 16:21; Cf. I Cor. 15:13-17.
25. II Cor. 12:7.
26. Matt. 16:23.
27. Matt. 26:31-35.
28. Matt. 26:40.
29. Matt. 26:69-75.
30. Gal. 2:11-21.
31. John 1:42.
32. I Cor. 15:9.
33. II Cor. 12:11.
34. Tit. 1:14.
35. II Pet. 1:16.
36. I Tim. 4:1-7.
37. Rom. 10:2.
38. John 12:35.
39. Acts 17:22.
40. Acts 17:23-28.
41. I Cor. 1:21.
42. Acts 17:27.
43. Ps. 42:2; 63:1; 143:6; Matt. 5:6; John 7:37.
44. Eph. 2:8.

GENERAL REFERENCES

Acts of Paul and Thecla. See *Apocrypha,* New Testament, and Good-speed, Edgar J.

Aeschylus. *Agamemnon.* See Oates, Whitney J.

Apocrypha of the Old Testament. Translated out of the Greek and Latin tongues. Oxford World Classics. Oxford, 1926.

Apocrypha of the New Testament.

Apollonius of Tyana. See Philostratus.

Aristophanes. *The Birds.* See Oates, Whitney J.

Arnobius of Sicca. *The Case against Pagans.* 2 vols. 7 books. Newly Translated and Annotated by George E. McCracken. Westminster, Maryland, 1949.

Baba Mezia, see *Talmud.*

Book of Jubilees. See *Apocrypha.* Old Testament.

Chrysostom, St. John. *Orationes.* ed. T. Hemsterhusi. Lugdini Batavorum, 1784. See Holton, Thomas, and Migne, Jacques Paul.

Clement of Alexandria. *The Rich Man's Salvation.* trans. G.W. Butterworth. London, 1919.

Clement of Rome (St. Clemens Romanus). *Recognitions.* trans. Thomas Smith. Edinburgh, 1868.

Dio Chrysostomos. *Discourses.* 5 vols. Loeb Classical Library. London, 1939.

Dictionary of the Talmud, Midrash, and Targum. B. Krupnik and A.M. Silberman. 2 vols. London, 1927.

Encyclopedic Dictionary of the Bible. See Hartman.

Ethics of the Talmud. See *Sayings of the Fathers.*

Eusebius. *The Ecclesiastical History.* 2 vols. trans. Kirsopp Lake. Loeb Classical Library. London, 1928.

Goodspeed, Edgar J. *The Book of Thekla.* Chicago, 1901.

Euripides. See Oates, Whitney J.

Hartman, Louis F. "Son of God," *Encyclopedic Dictionary of the Bible.* New York, 1963.

Holton, Thomas. *In Praise of Paul.* Boston, 1968.

Horace. *Satires, Epistles, and Ars Poetica.* trans. H. Rushton Fairclough. Loeb Classical Library. London, 1932.

Herodotus. *History of the Greeks.* 4 vols. trans. A.D. Godley. Loeb Classical Library. London, 1931.

Jerome. *Select Letters of Jerome.* trans. F.W. Wright. Loeb Classical Library. London, 1933. See also Migne Jacques Paul.

Josephus, Flavius. *The History of the Jewish Wars against the Romans.* 2 vols, 7 books, trans. H. St. J. Thackeray. Loeb Classical Library. London, 1927-28.

——————— . *The Jewish Antiquities.* 6 vols, 20 books, trans. H. St. J. Thackeray. Loeb Classical Library. London, 1930 and Ralph Marcus and L.H. Feldman. Loeb Classical Library. London, 1934-65.

——————— . *The Life of Flavius Josephus.* H. St. J. Thackeray. Loeb Classical Library. London, 1926.

Juvenal, Decimus Junius. *The Satires of Juvenal Literally Translated into English* by Lewis Evans. New York, 1931.

Kidduschin. See *Talmud.*

Langlois, V. *Le Denuk-Dasch, Tombeau de Sardanapalus Tarsous.* Paris, 1853.

Lucian. *Dialogues.* 8 vols. Loeb Classical Library. London, 1927-67. Vol. 8, "The Patriot," trans. by M.D. McLeod.

Maccabee. See *Apocrypha*, Old Testament.

Mellink, M.J. "Tarsus," *Interpreters' Dictionary.*

Midrash. Old rabbinical commentaries on the Old Testament between the 6th and 12th centuries. Two types: Haggadah (homilies) and Halaka (discussions of the law).

Migne, Jacques Paul. *Patrologiae Cursus Completus.* 221 vols. of the *Patrology* (Greek) and *Patrology* (Latin). Paris, 1844-64.

Milton, John. *Paradise Lost* in *Milton's Complete Poems,* ed. F.A. Pattersen. New York, 1933.

Mishna. Collection of Rabbinical discussions (learning, repetitions, instruction) on the law of Moses, orally transmitted until the end of the 2nd century A.D. when the patriarch Judah I collected, arranged and codified the accumulated material in its present shape, according to six orders, 63 tracts, and various chapters. These with their commentaries (the *Gemara*) constitute the *Talmud.*

——————— . Text with Commentary of R. Obadiah of Bertinore. trans. with Introduction and New Commentary by Jacob Herzog. Jerusalem, 1947.

——————— . Mishna *Sotah.* trans. from the Hebrew by Herbert Danby. Oxford, 1933.

Oates, Whitney J. and Eugene O'Neill, Jr., eds. *The Complete Greek Drama.* 2 vols. New York, 1938.

Aeschylus, *Agamermnon,* I, 167; Euripides, *Bacchae*, II, 227; Aristophanes, *Birds*, II, 733.

Petronius, Titua (Petronius Arbiter). *Satyricon* ed. Adapted from translation of W.C. Firebaugh. Liveright, 1927.

Philo. *Works.* 10 vols. Loeb Classical Library, London, 1929-62. Vol. 10, *The Embassy to Gaius.* trans. by F.H. Colson (1962).

Philostratus. *The Life of Apollonius of Tyana.* 2 vols, trans. by F.C. Conybeare. Loeb Classical Library. London, 1912.

Pinchas. See *Midrash.*

Pindar. *The Odes of Pindar*. trans. by Sir John Sandys. Loeb Classical Library. Cambridge, 1937.

Sanhedrin. See *Talmud*.

Sayings of the Fathers and the Ethics of the Talmud. ed. with Introduction, translation and commentary by R. Travers Herford. New York, 1962.

Seneca, Lucius Annaeus. *Works*. 11 vols, including Moral Epistles and Moral Essays. trans. by R.M. Gummere, et al. Loeb Classical Library. London, 1917-22.

_____ . *Epistolae Senecae ad Paulum et Pauli ad Senecam*. (doubtful work) ed. Claude W. Barlow. Rome, 1938.

Strabo. *The Geography*. 8 vols, 17 books, trans. by H.L. Jones. Loeb Classical Library. London, 1917.

Suetonius. *The Lives of the Caesars*. 2 vols, 8 books, trans. by J.C. Rolfe. Loeb Classical Library, London, 1935.

Tacitus, Cornelius. *The Annals*. 2 vols, 16 books, trans. by Clifford H. Moore. Loeb Classical Library. London, 1931.

Talmud, Babylonian Talmud. ed. I. Epstein et al. London, 1935-55.

_____ . *Baba Mezia*. trans. Hebrew Teachers College. Boston, 1938; *Kidduschin*, New York, 1941-47; *Sanhedrin*, M. Rawicz. Frankfurt, 1892; *Yebamoth*. Solomon Dremer. Brooklyn, 1945.

_____ . See also *A Talmudic Miscellany. . . or a Thousand and one extracts from the Talmud*. F.W. Farrar. Boston, 1890.

Tanhuma. See *Midrash* and edition by Solomon Buber, 1913.

Tertullian, Quintus Septimus Florens. *De Baptismo Liber* (Homily on Baptism). ed. with Introduction, translation, and commentary by Ernest Evans. London, 1964.

_____ . *Adversos Marcionem*. ed. and trans. by Ernest Evans. Oxford, 1972.

Thucydides. *A History of the Peloponnesian War*. 4 vols, 8 books, trans. by C. Foster Smith. Loeb Classical Library. London, 1923-25.

Xenophon. *Anabasis*. 2 vols, 7 books by O.J. Todd. Loeb Classical Library. London, 1932.

Yabemoth. See *Talmud*.

APPENDIX

Pauline Chronology

The most solid bases for beginning a chronology of Paul are the terms of office for Aretas, king of Arabia, and Pontius Pilate, prefect of Judaea. Pilate was prefect from A.D. 26-36, during which time Jesus was crucified. If we assume that the crucifixion cannot have occurred before A.D. 26/27, we should think of A.D. 27/28 as the earliest possible date for Paul's conversion. Aretas ruled Arabia from 9 B.C. until A.D. 40, during which time Paul escaped from Damascus (II Cor. 11:32-33). Since Paul left Damascus three years after his conversion (Gal. 1:18), his conversion can have taken place *no later* than three years before the death of Aretas, or A.D. 37. First attention will be given to the latest possible date for Paul's activities.

After leaving Damascus, Paul spent fifteen days in Jerusalem (Gal 1:18), after which he left for his missionary activity in the regions of Syria and Cilicia (Gal 1:21).[1] He returned to Jerusalem fourteen years later (Gal 1:24). From Galatians alone, it is not clear whether the fourteen-year period was counted from Paul's conversion or from his visit to Jerusalem, three years later, and there is not enough evidence anywhere to be sure which event is the correct one. There is, however, some tantalizing evidence to suggest that Paul was counting from his conversion. To the Corinthians Paul also mentioned a fourteen-year period. This was a reference to the time that had elapsed since his revelation of the Lord (II Cor 12:1-4). Since both the Corinthian and Galatian account tell of Paul's departure from Damascus, his conversion, and fourteen years that had elapsed, unless this is sheer coincidence, both fourteen-year periods refer to the same time that had elapsed, and both refer to the same event, Paul's revelation of the Lord which was also his conversion. If this is true, Paul wrote his letter to the Galatians the same year he wrote to the Corinthians, fourteen years after his conversion. This seems reasonable.

Galatians seems to have been written after the council which Paul described (Gal 2:1-10) and before the collection had actually begun, because Paul told there of his promise to take up a collection for the poor, but he gave no report of its progress (Gal 2:10). Although Paul said he was glad to do that and seemed optimistic of his success, the "harsh letter" of Paul to the Corinthians (II Cor 10-13) seems to reflect a different immediate reaction of the church at Corinth to Paul's suggestion that it contribute to the poor in Jerusalem. All Jews in the Roman empire were expected to pay a poll tax to Jerusalem once every year.[2] The fact that the apostles in Jerusalem only agreed to leave the territory in the diaspora to Paul, confining themselves to the "circumcised" in Palestine, on the condition that Paul remember the poor (Gal 2:7-10), implies that he had *not* been requiring diaspora churches to pay the normal apportionments to the community at Jerusalem which called itself the "poor." It makes good sense, then, to assume that Paul wrote II Cor 10-13 during the same year that he wrote to the Galatians and mentioned the same fourteen-year period in both letters in similar contexts (Gal 1:24; II Cor 12:2). The Galatian letter did not indicate any of the difficulty Paul reflected in his Corinthian letter, so this probably means that it was written just before Paul began the collection that caused the trouble. The "letter of reconciliation" (II Cor 1:1-9:4 minus 6:14-7:1) renewed the discussion about the collection, once peace had been restored. Extensive plans were made to complete as soon as possible this project which had been started a year earlier (II Cor 8:10; 9:2). This indicates that at least a year was involved in taking up this collection, but at the end of that year Paul expected the work to be completed soon. Collections were evidently being taken in all the Asia Minor churches simultaneously, since a certain brother had already been assigned to the churches to assist in this task (II Cor 8:18-19). He seems to have been at work in other churches earlier and was free to go to Corinth as soon as the Corinthians were prepared to receive him. The extensive correspondence with Corinth on the subject suggests that Corinth may have resisted the collection more than other churches and therefore may have been one of the last to complete the collection. At least Macedonia had finished sooner (II Cor 8:1-4). Allowing two, or even three, years to complete a collection which took a little more than one year at Corinth seems to be more than a generous length of time for a collection from churches that were organized and established in less than eleven years. But if that much time were allowed, the collection would still have been completed by A.D. 53 or 54 at the very latest. Paul wrote to the people at Rome near the completion of the collection before going back to Jerusalem with the money (Rom 15:25-33).

If Paul left Damascus during the very last year of Aretas' reign, spent eleven years organizing the churches of Asia Minor, and an additional three full years canvassing the same churches for funds, it is remotely possible that he finished the collection and wrote to Romans as late as A.D. 54, the year Claudius died. If anyone refused to accept Paul's conversion as the time from which Paul calculated the fourteen years, he/she could still add only three years to this, making A.D. 57 as the very latest possible date for Paul's composition of Romans, written just before he returned to Jerusalem with the collection to the poor (Rom 15:24-31). It is not reasonable to suppose, as many have done, that Paul made this journey back to Jerusalem some time in the sixties. From his own letters,

Paul is not pictured as one who made many "missionary journeys" to Asia Minor from Jerusalem. He went from Jerusalem to Asia Minor, returned once for the council with the apostles, and planned to return again to Jerusalem with the collection before going on to Rome and Spain.

It is even more reasonable to believe that Paul wrote to the Romans *before* the edict of Claudius in A.D. 49 than that he wrote it after A.D. 54. To accept A.D. 48, for example, as a date for Paul's letter to Rome, it would only be necessary to assume that Paul was converted as early as A.D. 32, spent three years in Damascus (A.D. 35) before going to Jerusalem, returned to Jerusalem fourteen years after his conversion (A.D. 46), and spent a maximum of two years taking the collection (A.D. 48) before he wrote the letter to Rome. This would mean that Galatians and Corinthians would have been written about one or two years earlier (A.D. 46-47). Considerations of any date for the collection letters (Galatians, I and II Corinthians, and Romans) after A.D. 54 seems unlikely, and after A.D. 57, impossible. Dates between A.D. 48 and 54 seem reasonable.

These are all the reliable bases on which scholars may confidently fix points of Paul's career. In The Acts of the Apostles there are other historical figures mentioned on the basis of which some historians attempt to be more precise in their dating. Herod Agrippa was ruler over Judaea from A.D. 41-44 (Acts 12:1-23). Claudius was emperor of Rome from A.D. 41 to 54 (Acts 11:27-30; 12:25; 18:2). Junius Annaeus Gallio was proconsul of Achaia from A.D. 51 to 58. Felix was procurator of Judaea from A.D. 52 to 59 (Acts 23:24-24:27), and was succeeded by Festus (A.D. 60-62; Acts 24:27-26:32). The tendency on the part of the author of Acts, however, was to relate events of the church to well-known historical figures and large, prominent, geographical sites. This raises suspicions about the reliability of his historical data, and warns the historian not to accept as certain those dates which conflict with dates given in Paul's own letters.

GEORGE WESLEY BUCHANAN

---

[1] See further J. Knox. *Chapters in a Life of Paul* (New York, c1950) and "Romans 15:14-33 and Paul's Conception of his Apostolic Mission," *JBL* 83 (1964), pp. 1-11.
[2] Tacitus, *Fragments*.

INDEX

ABOUT THE AUTHOR

Hubert Rex Johnson was a man of broad scholarship, with extraordinary qualities of mind and spirit. He was born near Steubenville, Jefferson County, Ohio, on July 1, 1858. He graduated from Richmond College, Richmond, Va., in 1879; received an S.T.B. degree (Bachelor of Theology) from the Western Theological Seminary, Pittsburg, Pa., in 1885; and an M.A. degree from Washington and Jefferson College, Washington, Pa., in 1896. He served as Pastor of

Hubert Rex Johnson

several Presbyterian churches in Pennsylvania: Natrona, 1886-93; Reynoldsville, 1893-96; President of Blairsville College for Women, Blairsville, Pa., 1896-98; Pastor at Neshannock, New Wilmington, Pa., 1899-1901; Vandergrift, Pa., 1901-08; and Chevy Chase, Washington, D.C., 1909-24.

A man of broad interests, Dr. Johnson published a history of the Neshannock Presbyterian Church, New Wilmington, Pa., together with an account of the settlement of that part of northwestern Pennsylvania in which the church was organized. He also published a botanical manual describing the plants of the area. He wrote numerous articles, was a lecturer of note, and a frequent speaker before teachers groups.

He enjoyed the perfection of geometry, and copyrighted two works on mathematics, "The Pythagorean Theorem: A Collection of Original and Copied Proofs," and "Recreational Exercises in Mathematics."

An admirer of the intrepid Paul, Dr. Johnson spent the last twenty years of his life writing an account of the life and work of that apostle. His object was to promote an understanding of Paul, to make him "come alive," and to enable the reader to know the great apostle rather than to know only about him. He titled his work "Who Then Is Paul?," from I Corinthians 3:5, of the King James version of the Bible.

Hubert Rex Johnson died on April 14, 1945, before the manuscript could be published.

DATE DUE		
DEC 18 '85		
DEC 18 '85		
MR 09 88		

DEMCO 38-297